ROBERT BARCLAY

ROBERT BARCLAY

D. ELTON TRUEBLOOD

Professor at Large

Earlham College

HARPER & ROW, PUBLISHERS

NEW YORK, EVANSTON, AND LONDON

For

VIRGINIA

in partnership and affection

FIRST EDITION

LIBRARY OF CONGRESS CATALOG CARD NUMBER: 68-11731

M-R

CONTENTS

APPENDIX

Picture section follows page 82

PREFACE

BECAUSE BARCLAY had been a household word from my earliest memories, it came to me as a surprise, when I reached maturity, to realize that a full-length treatment of this famous Quaker thinker had never been produced. I knew that his *Apology* was the most widely read and distributed of all the many volumes of Quaker literature in three hundred years; I knew, likewise, that Barclay stood at the very pinnacle of the Quaker leadership of the seventeenth century, usually being mentioned along with Fox and Penn. But whereas there have been numerous books interpreting Fox and Penn, the careful treatment of Barclay has been curiously neglected. Many other Quaker worthies have been honored by studies in depth, among them being Margaret Fell, John Woolman, William Savery, Elizabeth Fry, Joseph John Gurney, and Rufus M. Jones. Hundreds of other Quaker leaders are known because of the meticulous journals published after their deaths. But there is no published journal of Robert Barclay.

Though I was much involved in other duties when the oddity of this situation struck me, I decided that, though it might not be possible to account for the strange neglect, it *was* possible for me to do something about it. My first opportunity came in 1939 when, on leave from Stanford University, I became a Fellow of Woodbrooke and enjoyed several months of uninterrupted study in England. Soon the decision to study Barclay was reached. Very early I began to note references to a "pocket book." I first noted this in the *Genealogical*

Account attributed to the second Robert Barclay, the son of the Apologist and himself the Laird of Ury, who mentioned this pocket book, or diary, "all wrote with his own hand and preserved in the family; wherein he gives a very exact and particular account of many transactions of his life until some weeks of his death, which hath been much assistance to me in writing this account." It is evident that this source was available in 1833 when John Barclay edited the manuscripts he had found at Ury, because he quoted from it. When Joseph Smith published in 1867 *A Descriptive Catalogue of Friends' Books,* he listed, apropos Robert Barclay, "A Journal or Account of his Life written by himself? in manuscript only, never having been published" (Vol. I, p. 187).

The most important feature of my research in the spring of 1939 was the discovery of a manuscript book, said on its cover to be "Robert Barclay's Notebook." This was a small volume bound in leather, much of it in the known handwriting of the Apologist. I approached the little treasure with excitement, surmising that it might be the diary which had been mentioned in both the eighteenth and nineteenth centuries. To my chagrin I found that a substantial part of the Notebook was written in a shorthand which I could not translate. Colonel Barclay kindly provided me with photostatic copies of the pages, which I took home to America. Because my own efforts to decipher this material were fruitless, I sought the help of others who were reputed to have skill in solving puzzles of this kind, but there was for some time no success at all.

Soon after my return home the war broke out, and most lives were drastically changed for several years. At least this particular work could wait. When the war was over I again gave what time I could spare from my duties, first at Stanford University and later at Earlham College, to Barclay studies. I was able to visit Ury and the Aberdeen Tolbooth, the scene of Barclay's longest imprisonment, and to give the Barclay Tercentenary Lecture in Edinburgh, in August, 1948. The beginning of publication came with an article, "The Vocation of Barclay," which appeared in the *Friends Quarterly* for October, 1948. This I then thought might be a chapter in my book, which was confidently announced. Still, however, no one could help me in translating the shorthand part of the Notebook. I realized that the material in the unfamiliar script might prove to be worthless, but I also realized that no one could reasonably attempt to produce a thorough treatment of Barclay's life and thought without at least knowing what the Notebook contained. Thus the final writing of my book was necessarily postponed.

The big surprise came one day in 1959 when I received a letter from Muriel Hicks of the Friends House Library, London, saying that an Englishman living in Ethiopia, by the name of Douglas G. Lister, was ready to help me. Mr. Lister had learned during a visit to England that I needed assistance in deciphering some seventeenth-century shorthand, and because this was his hobby he was glad to try. It is really a fascinating story, connecting Ethiopia, America, and England. As soon as possible I secured more photographs from London, because mine were with another potential translator. To my astonishment, Mr. Lister managed, almost at once, to identify the code which Robert Barclay had used nearly three hundred years earlier. He decided, however, to postpone the careful translation of this difficult material until my retirement, which came in 1966. The Listers meantime settled in England, and now every page, though not every word, has been translated. Partly because of the faded ink there are a few words which cannot be made out, but the meaning is nearly always clear. The Notebook is described in detail in Appendix C, and numerous references to its contents are found in the text of this book.

One of the rewards of working in England has been the free access to the collection of manuscripts and other treasures at Bury Hill, which began in 1854 with the breakup of the Ury mansion. The friendship of the various members of the Barclay family, during twenty-eight years, has been both delightful and rewarding. My first contact was with the late Colonel Robert Wyville Barclay. The second was with his son, the late Major Robert E. Barclay, who provided photostats for me to send to Ethiopia. Mrs. Robert Barclay, widow of Major Barclay, in whose home the Bury Hill Collection has recently been housed, and John S. Barclay, the present head of the family, have been uniformly helpful.

The major advance in Barclay research in 1967 has been the discovery of Robert Barclay's diaries, written by his own hand. These are described in Appendix D. Many, including myself, had come to the sad conclusion that the diaries mentioned so confidently by the

Apologist's son and grandson in the *Genealogical Account* of 1740 had been lost, and that further search was hopeless. Benjamin Rhodes came to this conclusion when *Three Apostles of Quakerism* was published in 1884. Of Robert Barclay, Rhodes wrote, "He kept a diary, but it seems to have been lost." In spite of this judgment, I could never put out of my mind a letter which had first come to my attention at Woodbrooke in 1939, written July 28, 1884 by J. G. Barclay (1816–1898). In it he said, "R. B. of Bury Hill has the Apologist's pocket diary, I know." This encouraged perseverance. While the contemporary members of the Barclay family could not identify such a manuscript, they generously gave unlimited opportunity to search among their treasures. The search was rewarded in April, 1967. We were reminded how Benjamin Rhodes had added in a footnote the query, "Is this amongst the Bury Hill MSS?" It is now possible to answer his question in the affirmative.

Even the cursory reader of the various brief accounts of Robert Barclay's life which have been published during three centuries can hardly fail to note considerable disagreement on matters of historical fact. Several false statements which have been perpetuated, in succeeding generations, by copying from secondary accounts can now be corrected. Since the known way in which a reasonable degree of accuracy can be achieved is by the mutual confirmation of several documents, the necessary task is that of bringing together all available sources until they reveal a pattern of objective fact. The chief sources are the Notebook, the diaries, letters, contemporary accounts of others, public documents, and hints in the author's own published or unpublished writings. We cannot be sufficiently grateful for the salvaging work of Hudson Gurney, who rescued and preserved valuable documents when the big house at Ury was demolished. It is a pleasure to say that I have found the London Friends Library, with its excellent facilities, the ideal place in which to do the major research and writing. Not least of the advantages has been the gracious cooperation of the Librarian, Edward Milligan.

Thus, after intermittent study of Barclay for twenty-eight years, I have been able to complete my task and do something to correct a long-standing injustice. I am really glad that the work was not completed earlier, because the added years have permitted me to engage in unhurried research and to see the entire subject in better perspective. My purpose has been, whenever possible, to let the author speak for himself in terms understandable to the last third of the twentieth century. It is particularly gratifying to be able to complete this work on the three hundredth anniversary of Barclay's public commitment to the Quaker way of life and thought.

D. ELTON TRUEBLOOD

London, 1967

ROBERT BARCLAY

CHAPTER I

BARCLAY IN HISTORY

> *At last Robert Barclay, a native of Scotland, Presented to the King in 1675 His apology for the Quakers, a work as well drawn up as the subject could possibly admit.*
>
> —*Voltaire*

ROBERT BARCLAY (1648–1690) was a great man. His name is not as familiar as that of his close friend, William Penn, but because of his work and that of his numerous descendants it has been known by great numbers during the last three hundred years. Though he died when he was a little less than forty-two years of age, he left an enduring mark, particularly on the Quaker Movement. This movement, now known in most parts of the world, might, apart from Barclay, be remembered only as a minor historical episode of a remote period.

When the Quaker Movement began in the middle of the seventeenth century it appeared, to the outside observer, to be merely one of the many crude and fanatical sects which arose in the decade following the execution of Charles I. One indication of how Quakers appeared in the eyes of their neighbors is indicated by the laconic entry in the *Diary* of Samuel Pepys to the effect that Penn's son "is a Quaker again, or some very melancholy thing."

George Fox, a man of energy and courage, had grasped a great idea, the idea that Christian experience could be couched in the present tense. He was able to arouse men and women in a remarkable way by the direct question: "What canst *thou* say?" He discovered the power which always emerges when men move over from speculation to experience, and when they provide a verification of the reality of what they experience by the only evidence which is convincing, the evidence of changed lives.

The strangest feature of the career of George Fox is not that he could arouse listeners. Other men of his type could do the same, yet be forgotten in a short time. What is strange is that the message of Fox endured, evolving a distinctive culture which has remained, with some developments, to this day. Why did Quakerism continue and thrive, becoming a powerful force in the English colonization of North America, when other and apparently similar religious movements died so quickly that they are remembered only as historical oddities? Why, historians have asked repeatedly, did the influence of Fox differ so radically from that of Lodowick Muggleton?

The answer to this question, which is reasonably clear, was given expression by Lord Macaulay when he said that "Fox made some converts to whom he was immeasurably inferior in everything except the energy of his convictions. By these converts his rude doctrines were polished into a form somewhat less shocking to good sense and good taste." Though Macaulay was manifestly unfair to George Fox, his answer was essentially correct. Men of the character of Muggleton never drew really able followers, but Fox did. Indeed, he attracted a veritable galaxy of them. The most eminent of these were three: Isaac Penington, son of the onetime Lord Mayor of London; William Penn, son of Admiral Penn; and Robert Barclay of Scotland, Laird of Ury and distant relative of the reigning Stuart kings. That Fox could attract the admiration and loyalty of men of this stamp was no accident, and the very fact that he could do so tells us something about both his character and his message. We understand something of this when we read the moving Preface which Penn wrote for the grand edition of George Fox's *Journal.* "He was an original," said Penn, "and no man's copy." The fact that a man of no education could attract so many persons of learning and brilliance honors both him and them.

There was a time when it was generally said that the privileged followers of Fox were relatively few, the vast majority being those of the rude eloquence of Edward Burrough, but now we are tending to alter our judgment. We are impressed, for example, with the fact that not only Penn, but nearly all of the men of financial power who purchased both West and East Jersey were Quakers. Of the twenty-four proprietors who took over East Jersey in 1682, twenty were Quakers. Only the wealthy and influential had an opportunity to participate in a venture of this magnitude. Early Quakerism did, it is true, attract the rabble and even part of the lunatic fringe, but a remarkable number of Quakers were marked by literary ability and public position.

The message of Fox, which shines through his *Journal*, had its own inner validity. William James was telling part of the truth when he said, "In a day of shams, it was a religion of veracity." But if Fox had not had the support of men like Penn and Barclay, succeeding generations would have been wholly ignorant of this message. Fox could still, it is true, have dictated his *Journal,* but without the fastidious work of Thomas Ellwood it would not have been publishable, and without Penn's Preface it would not have had such wide acceptance.

No spoken message, however vivid, can endure unless it is provided with a written and intelligible form. A movement, if it is to survive the first generation of vitality, must be able to attract some of the best minds and thus be given an intellectual structure which can appeal to other good minds. The potent leader needs the intellectual follower to turn his vivid and aphoristic expressions into something which is logically defensible. It was this need which was met by Robert Barclay when the infant Quaker Movement was only about twenty-five years old. Without Fox, Barclay would have had very little to say, but without Barclay, what Fox said would have been forgotten. By the genius of Barclay the basic Quaker ideas were translated into the language of thoughtful men, who in the end are the ones who establish the climate of opinion.

The central paradox of Barclay's work was that he sought to reach learned men with something which unlearned men had discovered. The *Theses* were addressed "To the Clergy of what sort soever, unto whose hands these may come; but more particularly to the Doctors, Professors and Students of Divinity." He was, indeed, seeking to win the respect and assent of the intellectuals. But what he said to them was the surprising news, "Therefore hath God laid aside the Wise and Learned, and the Disputers of this World; and hath chosen a few despicable and Unlearned Instruments (as to Letter-learning) as he did Fisher-men of old." Barclay was in the strong position of a scholar who could, when necessary, minimize the importance of scholarship.

In spite of Barclay's disclaimers about worldly honor, it must be admitted that a great deal of it finally came his way. The appreciation of his fellow Quakers was vividly demonstrated by the fact that his collected works were brought out in 1692, in a really noble volume. The appealing title was *Truth Triumphant Through the Spiritual Warfare, Christian Labours and Writings of that Able and Faithful Servant of Jesus Christ, Robert Barclay*. In addition to a long Preface, Barclay's works are preceded by testimonies to his character on the part of George Fox, William Penn, Patrick Livingstone, and Andrew Jaffray, the latter two writing as fellow Scots. The entire work is magnificently printed in more than 900 folio pages. Equal honor was done to Fox two years later, in the production of the Ellwood edition of Fox's *Journal*.

The loss to the Quaker Movement in the deaths of both Barclay and Fox, as well as others, within the space of a few weeks, was a very great blow and marked vividly the end of one chapter. Penn called it "the overcasting of so many bright stars, almost together." The sad truth was that the period of greatest Quaker creativity, both spiritually and intellectually, was over. The two ambitious publications, however pleasing they were, represented the waning of the vitality which they glorified. The issuing of Barclay's collected works preceded that of Fox by fully two years, largely because Barclay's work required practically no editorial labor, while the *Journal* of Fox required a great deal. One of the happiest features of the twin publications was that William Penn was alive and, as the best-known living Quaker, wrote introductions to both. Though the long "preface to the Reader" is not signed, John Barclay attributed it to Penn. More important than this, however, is the two-page "Testimony to the Memory of Robert Barclay by his faithful friend, William Penn," which includes some of Penn's finest eloquence. The heart of his witness was the following:

We sometimes travelled together both in this Kingdom, and in Holland, and some parts of Germany, and were Inward in divers Services from first to last: and the Apprehension and Sense I had of him, was this, He loved the Truth and Way of God, as Revealed among us, above all the World, and was not ashamed of it before Men; but Bold and Able in Maintaining it: Sound in Judgment, Strong in Argument, Chearful in Travails and Suffering; of a Pleasant Disposition, yet Solid, Plain and Exemplary in his Conversation. He was a Learned Man, a good Christian, an Able Minister, a Dutiful Son, a Loving Husband, a Tender and Careful Father, an Easie Master, and a good and kind Neighbour and Friend.

Our best contemporary evidence of the pride which Quakers felt in the publication of Barclay's collected works comes, not from Quaker sources, but from outside. John Norris, Rector of Bemerton near Sarum and onetime Fellow of All Souls College, Oxford, wrote in 1692 of "the general exultation and Triumph that is among the Quakers upon the late Publication of Mr. Barclay's Works in Folio." The exultation seemed to this learned author to be no occasion for surprise. "I know," he wrote, "of no Church or Society of Christians that is already so rich in Reputation for Great men, but might well be proud of the Accession of so considerable a writer." Norris's general opinion of Quaker writers was that most of them were not even *intelligible,* let alone being *intelligent*. For this reason he was wholly willing for "the Quakers to swell and plume a little." With this as a gracious beginning, Norris went on to express one of the clearest judgments of Barclay's superiority: "Mr. Barclay is a very great Man, and were it not for that common Prejudice that lies against him, as being a *Quaker*, would be as sure not to fail of that character in the World, as any of the finest Wits this age has produced."

John Norris set out to confute the Quaker system, but admitted in the end that Barclay had made his task extremely difficult. Referring to the principles of Quakerism he said, "That Great and General Contempt they lie under, does not hinder me from thinking the Sect of Quakers to be by far the most considerable of any that divide from us, in case the Quakerism that is generally held be the same with that which Mr. Barclay has delivered to the world for such; whom I take to be so great a Man, that I profess to you freely, I had rather engage a Hundred Bellarmins, Hardings, or Stapyltons, than with one Barclay."[1]

The admiration of Voltaire for Barclay's achievements is well known. In his *Letters Concerning the English Nation,* he expressed especial admiration for Barclay's address to King Charles II, with which the famous book began, and said, "A more surprising circumstance is, that this epistle, written by a private man of no figure, was so happy in its effects as to put a stop to the persecution."[2] Gracious as this well-known remark may be, we are forced to say that Voltaire exaggerated. Barclay's efforts to stop persecution, though they were considerable, were supplemented by the efforts of many others, and cannot be given the sole or even the major credit for the victorious outcome. In the second place, it is hardly accurate to say that Barclay was a "private man of no figure." His connections were many and powerful, including those which came through his friendship and correspondence with Princess Elizabeth of the Rhine and with the reigning Stuarts.

Inaccurate as Voltaire's conclusion may have been, his reported experience in England provides one more significant item of evidence concerning the wide acceptance of Barclay's intellectual leadership on the part of Quakers in the early eighteenth century, when the *Apology* was a source of both pride and comfort. After the English edition of the *Apology* had been available for exactly fifty years, a Quaker said to Voltaire,

> I have not employ'd a hundredth part of the arguments which might be brought, to prove the truth of our religion, but these thou thyself mayest peruse in the Exposition of our Faith written by Robert Barclay. 'Tis one of the best pieces that ever was penn'd by man; and as our adversaries confess it to be of dangerous tendency, the arguments in it must necessarily be very convincing.[3]

With a recommendation of such a character, it is not surprising that Voltaire promised to read the book. Voltaire's high praise is matched by the statement in the French *Encyclopédie,* "though it was first published at a time when religious controversy ran very high in

[1] John Norris, *Two Treatises, Concerning the Divine Light* (London, 1692), Part II, pp. 1, 32.

[2] London, 1733, Letter III, p. 23.

[3] *Ibid.,* Letter I, p. 7.

Europe, it was never answered in a manner to weaken the force of any of its arguments."

The reference works of Boyle in France and Collier in England gave Barclay very high marks. In short, Barclay probably more than any other individual made Quakers respectable, even though some looked upon his major work as "an ingenious and learned attempt to defend a bad cause."[4] The famous ecclesiastical historian, J. L. von Mosheim, could not ignore Barclay, though he claimed that the Apologist was more advocate than teacher and expounder. Gough says that Mosheim, in his hatred of Quakers, wrote "as if he was mortified to find that any amongst them could defend their cause so well."[5] John Gough's own estimate of Barclay's intention and subsequent success is carefully stated.

> That Robert Barclay did really appear as an expounder, and an honest expounder of this people's doctrines, I believe very few who have read his *Apology* can entertain a doubt; that he modified the opinions of his sect after a manner inconsistent with truth, is implied; but not admitted or proved; but admitting he was an advocate of his own cause, and that of his fellow members of a society (not *odious,* unless innocence and rigid virtue deserve that epithet) he is still as defensible in standing forth for a champion in the defense of the injured, as those who unprovoked appear as champions against them, to render them on groundless accusations odious to the world.[6]

Leslie Stephen may be taken as representative of a host of friendly outsiders, being neither Quakers themselves nor antagonistic to Quaker ideas, who have seen that Barclay's work is something that cannot be lightly dismissed. Writing in the *Dictionary of National Biography,* Stephen said, "Barclay's great book 'The Apology' is remarkable as the standard exposition of the principles of his sect, and is not only the first defense of those principles by a man of trained intelligence, but in many respects one of the most impressive theological writings of the century." As a professional critic Leslie Stephen added, concerning the *Apology*, "it is impressive in style; grave,

[4] The words are those of Samuel Newton of Norwich, who wrote *Leading Sentiments* (1771).

[5] John Gough, *A History of the People Called Quakers,* Vol. II (Dublin, 1789), p. 402.

[6] *Ibid.,* p. 402*n*.

logical, and often marked by the eloquence of lofty moral convictions."

The most ecstatic estimate of Barclay's achievement came from a fellow Scot, Alexander Gordon, who wrote as a non-Quaker theologian.

> Here indeed [he said] is a genuine outcome of the inner depth of the nation's worship; something characteristic and her own; a gift to her religious life akin to her profoundest requirements; and, if she did but know it, far worthier the thankful acceptance of her people than any religious aid which she has ever welcomed from the other side of the border. . . . One great original theologian and only one, has Scotland produced.[7]

In the years succeeding the publication of *Truth Triumphant*, Barclay's *Apology* came rapidly to be looked upon as the standard exposition of Quaker thinking. Quakers had no creed then, as they have none now, but Barclay was often the final court of appeal. Some said the *Apology* was a sort of Quaker Bible. However that may be, the editions were numerous and the number of copies which were distributed by Friends prodigious. Over and over the Quaker journals record the distribution of the *Apology* as a means of evangelism, particularly among thinking people. For example, William Savery, the traveling minister who was largely responsible for the conversion of Elizabeth Fry, records how he met a man in Germany who seemed interested. Almost as a matter of course Savery reports, "We gave him Barclay's *Apology* in Latin, and are in hopes that our observations will not be lost upon him."[8] The Latin *Apology* was especially valuable in making contact with those who could not read English.

Most of the traveling ministers seem to have taken copies of the *Apology* as standard equipment. Thus Thomas Shillitoe says, in 1803, "Having provided ourselves with Barclay's *Apology*. . . . " Even John Woolman, who did not quote much from other men, quoted Barclay when he wrote an epistle in 1772, just prior to his famous final journey. A contemporary, Samuel Scott, wrote in his diary under date of 1782, "I spoke only the words of truth and soberness, as they are set forth in the Holy Scriptures, Robert Barclay's *Apology,* and the

[7] *Theological Review,* Vol. XI (1874), p. 528.
[8] "Friends Library," Vol. I, p. 393.

writings of other faithful men." Sarah Grubb indicates that giving away the *Apology* often in Dutch, German, or Latin was a matter of Quaker routine. That conversion sometimes followed confrontation with Barclay's thought is illustrated in the following account from about 1702, of Samuel Crisp:

> I had occasion to be one day at a bookseller's shop, I happened to cast my eye on Barclay's works; and having heard in the country, that he was a man of great account amongst the Quakers, I had a mind to see what their principles were, and what defence they could make for themselves. . . . I took Barclay home with me and read him through in a week's time . . . I soon read enough to convince me of my own blindness and ignorance in the things of God.[9]

Of all the reprints of the English *Apology* during the last two hundred and eighty-nine years, the most distinguished was the eighth edition, printed at Birmingham by Baskerville in 1765. This is now a prized collector's item, chiefly because of the beauty of the printing. Copies of it are extremely rare. This edition is the one which was brought to Dr. Samuel Johnson's attention in a Quaker home in Birmingham in 1776. The relevant passage in Boswell's account is as follows:

> As Dr. Johnson had said to me in the morning, while we walked together, that he liked individuals among the Quakers but not the sect; when we were at Mr. Lloyd's I kept clear of introducing any questions concerning the peculiarities of their faith. But I having asked to look at Baskerville's edition of Barclay's *Apology,* Johnson laid hold of it.

That the reputation of Barclay's thinking has fluctuated during three hundred years of Quaker history is not really surprising. In spite of the enormous respect usually accorded the *Apology* in Quaker circles, Barclay has had Quaker critics, some of whom have been disturbed by the vigor of his attacks on his opponents in debate. This led George Harrison in the "Prefatory Address" to his abridged edition of the *Apology*,[10] published at London in 1815, to explain to readers what the earlier style of controversy was, so that they would not be shocked. Explaining that Barclay was really a man "of a re-

[9] *Letters of Samuel Crisp,* "Friends Library," Vol. XIII, p. 154 (c. 1702).
[10] There have been several shortened versions of the *Apology*. Harrison's version included all fifteen propositions.

markably mild disposition and great suavity of manners," he went on to warn that "if, therefore, the reader should feel his mind disturbed, or unpleasantly affected, by the severity of any strictures which remain in the following work, upon the opinions or conduct of any description of Christian professors, it is hoped that he will ascribe it, less to the habit of the writer than to the temper of the times, when theological controversy was conducted with too much asperity, even on the side of truth."

Most serious among Quaker criticisms of Barclay in the nineteenth century were those from the evangelical wing. A good example is provided by Samuel Tuke of York (1784–1857), who was clerk of London Yearly Meeting in 1832. Tuke, believing that Barclay's style was too scholastic, wrote, "It is known that some of the right minded members of the body in early times did not thoroughly approve of it, and that others of great weight considered it as written with a particular reference or condescension to the learned."[11] The strongest opponents came from both the extreme left and the extreme right, the attacks coming for opposite reasons.[12]

It is important to recognize the fact that both sides, in each of the major Quaker divisions, could always quote Barclay, precisely because he had such a comprehensive view. Thus Hannah Barnard (1754?–1829), when questioned, claimed to be in complete unity with Barclay, even though she was suspected of Unitarianism. She held, she said, as Barclay did, that a religious experience was something very different from "a belief in historical facts." Indeed, it has frequently been observed that the sorrowful Quaker divisions of the nineteenth century arose, in each case, because each party stressed one side of an issue already handled by Barclay, but without equal reference to another side which Barclay also stressed. Many Quaker errors may thus be seen as truths out of context. The most tragic of

[11] This extract is quoted from "Unpublished Letters," *The Friend* (London), Vol. XIII, p. 34.

[12] In America, those of the extreme theological left were dubbed "Hicksites" by their opponents, while those of the extreme theological right in England were termed "Beaconites." The Beaconites pushed to the logical limit the views held by the dominant party in a more balanced and moderate way. Their criticism of Barclay had already been expressed by John Wesley, who in 1738 issued "A Letter to a Person lately joined to the People Called Quakers." He wrote twenty pages in which he attacked Barclay and claimed that there were ten points "in which Quakerism differs from Christianity."

all Quaker separations, that of 1827–28, may be best understood as a division between reliance on the "Christ of experience" and reliance on the "Christ of history," both of which are integral to Barclay's synthesis. By failing to hold the two positions in tension, each was right in what he stressed, while each was wrong in what he omitted.

By 1870 the evangelical attack on Barclay had become sufficiently strong to check publication of the *Apology* in a cheap edition. Writers in *The Friend* (London) represented themselves as disturbed by Barclay's strict rationality, and asserted that people are not brought to God by rational argument. That Barclay had defenders as well as critics is shown by the following from Edward Alexander (1788–1836):

> Were he now writing he would probably adopt a very different form; but which the same spiritual truths would shine through. For it is one of the remarkable characteristics of Barclay, that while his great work is addressed to the learned and competent, its power and virtue are perceived as well by the plain and simple understanding, beneath the scholastic form, if once the spiritual sense is awakened in the inquirer.[13]

Much more fundamental than the nineteenth-century criticisms were those of the early twentieth century, on radically different grounds. Largely through the influence of Rufus M. Jones, many Quaker writers and speakers came to the conclusion that Barclay's presentation had ceased to have contemporary value because his thought was couched, they said, in outworn and discredited forms. A vivid expression of this change was shown with the institution of the annual Swarthmore Lectures in 1908. The first three volumes included select bibliographies on the thought and history of Friends, but in these there was not one reference to Barclay, though there were many to Fox and some to Isaac Penington and Thomas Ellwood.

In 1917 the intellectual tide against Barclay was running strongly. A. Barratt Brown wrote boldly that the Barclay analysis of the relationship betwen God and man was impossible for modern minds.[14] Edward Grubb had already pointed out the two major aspects of

[13] Edward Alexander, *Barclay and His Assailants*, p. 9.

[14] *The Universal Light, A Statement of the Quaker Faith* (London, 1917), p. 6.

Barclay's thought about human life and held that they were mutually inconsistent. "Out of this inconsistency," he said, "has come division within the Society of Friends itself, and to it we may probably look for one of the chief though hidden causes of its failure to move the world. . . . [Their truth] needs to be restated in modern language and in the light of modern knowledge."[15] In 1919, when an important volume in the Rowntree series, *The Second Period of Quakerism,* was published, its author, William C. Braithwaite, said flatly, "The old dualistic conception of the universe is dead or moribund."[16] Barclay's trouble, it was said, was his inevitable failure to understand ideas which have only become current in our modern times. "With our fuller conception of personality, our wider historical outlook, and our philosophic sense of an ultimate Reality which includes and explains the whole of life, we formulate the central experience of Friends differently from Barclay."[17] In the Introduction to the same volume Rufus M. Jones added his voice to the prevailing criticism.

> Robert Barclay [he wrote] is not to be blamed for the historical tragedy. The formulations of truth in any field are bound to use the psychology and metaphysics of their age. They must think, if they think at all, through the terminology of their time and in the concepts that prevail around them, and they invariably determine the line of march of human thought and even fix in advance the kind of intellectual questions that will be asked in succeeding periods.[18]

What Rufus Jones lamented most was the fact that Barclay was so much influenced by the central stream of Christian thought through Augustine and Calvin, and so little influenced by the mystics and spiritual reformers to the study of whom Rufus Jones' own life was chiefly devoted. "The formulation of Quaker doctrine was, in my judgment," he said, "not performed in a manner as accordant with the genius of the movement as was the form of the organization of the Society."[19] It was confidently asserted by many that there was a clear contrast between Fox and Barclay.

[15] Edward Grubb, *Authority and the Light Within* (London, 1908), Preface.

[16] William C. Braithwaite, *The Second Period of Quakerism* (London: Macmillan and Co., 1919), p. 395. (References are to this edition unless otherwise specified.)

[17] *Ibid.,* p. 396.

[18] *Ibid.,* p. xiv.

[19] *Ibid.,* p. xxx.

The general attack on the adequacy of Barclay's presentation of Quaker thought centered on two points, quietism and dualism. The writers of the Rowntree series of histories, since they deplored the quietistic period of Quaker history, spanning as it did the greater part of the eighteenth century as well as much of the nineteenth, sought the cause or causes of decline from the earlier vitality. They thought that they had found this in the dominant influence of Barclay. Rufus Jones' accusation is vigorously unqualified. "The *Apology*," he wrote, "is beyond question the primary influence which made Friends quietistic."[20] This is a stronger assertion than the following one, made earlier, in the Introduction which Professor Jones wrote for the book written by his friend William Charles Braithwaite:

> It will not do, of course, to attribute the appearance of Quietism in the Quaker movement to one sole influence. Group-attitudes and habits are subtle things and can seldom be traced to one isolated cause. But it is a plain and patent fact that Barclay's formulation is charged and loaded with the essential conditions and tendencies of Quietism. The entire basis and framework of Quietism are already there.
>
> All forms of Quietism start with a despair of the natural man. They begin with a recognition of the spiritual bankruptcy of mere man. Every spiritual step, every act that has to do with religion and salvation, Quietism maintains, must be done in man by some Divine power beyond him. *His* only part in the transaction is a passive part. He ceases to resist the operations of God, and waits in quiet for 'visitations,' and for the coming of supernatural assistance.[21]

The Faith of a Quaker, by John William Graham, was devoted to the ambitious purpose of doing for the twentieth century what Barclay had done for the seventeenth. Of the *Apology* Graham said, "It is fair to remember that the very atmosphere which renders it philosophically useless to us was what rendered it useful to the Friends who welcomed it. It was the voice of their age."[22]

Graham's essential criticism was that Barclay did not hold human nature in sufficiently high esteem. The point of difference was vividly portrayed by the title of one of Graham's books, *The Divinity in*

[20] Rufus M. Jones, *The Later Periods of Quakerism* (London: Macmillan and Co., 1921), Vol. I, p. 60.

[21] William Braithwaite, *Second Period of Quakerism, op. cit.*, pp. xii, xiii.

[22] *The Faith of a Quaker* (Cambridge, Eng.: The University Press, 1920), p. 159. The whole of Book II, Chap. IV is devoted to the *Apology*.

Man.[23] Since in this book the author went all the way in divinizing man, it is not surprising that he rejected Barclay's balanced view, with its emphasis on both the sinfulness of man and the universality of the divine effort to reach him. Barclay was criticized because he opposed the doctrine of natural human goodness as much as he opposed the doctrine of absolute reprobation. Thus we find Graham saying that the Apologist "was baffled by his unfortunate belief in human helplessness and emptiness of any good thing."[24] Of the "Man of Sin" he asserted flatly, "Certainly there was never such a creature."[25] That the contrast with Barclay is total is indicated by the use of a phrase with revealing capitalization, "the godward organ of Man." What Graham did not see was that Barclay, by his clear distinction between the human and the divine, was protecting Quaker doctrine from any tendency to deify man. "Such protection," writes Francis B. Hall, "is important because it keeps man from being sentimental, superficial and idealistic about his own nature."[26]

It is important to remember that Graham, in spite of his serious opposition, especially in regard to the nature of man, did not hesitate to call the *Apology* "one of the great and memorable books of the world, the single and authoritative textbook of Quaker divinity, a book still honored, though it has ceased to be read; but which was, for two centuries, a living book, read by serious-minded Friends, and the armory of texts for thousands of sermons."[27] Nevertheless, Graham's final judgment was that the usefulness of Barclay's book, however great at one time, was irretrievably gone. "No one except a historical scholar will now read it, but that is not because its conclusions are unsound, but because our whole thought of God has moved, and the processes of the divine life are working in other parts of the field."[28]

These confident conclusions of a generation ago have been belied by the event. It is now widely recognized that the estimate of the goodness of man, so popular forty years ago, is more obviously dated than is Barclay's more sober appraisal. After two world wars, with

[23] London: George Allen and Unwin, 1927.
[24] *Ibid.*, p. 274.
[25] *Ibid.*, p. 275.
[26] "The Thought of Robert Barclay: An Evaluation," *Quaker Religious Thought,* Vol. VII, No. 1 (Spring, 1965), p. 17.
[27] *The Faith of a Quaker, op. cit.*, p. 134
[28] *Ibid.*, p. 148.

abundant evidence that our highest aspirations are tainted, modern thinkers tend to reassert a view of human nature essentially like that which Barclay delineated. Once it was possible to discount a man by showing evidence of "Calvinist" leanings, but this is true no longer. The climate of opinion has changed since the early part of the twentieth century, and it has changed in a manner distinctly favorable to a better reception of Barclay's conclusions. Howard Brinton has pointed this out by saying that "Barclay's conception of the nature and function of the Christian religion is again coming to the fore. His interpretation is in closer accord with religious thinking today than with that of a generation ago."[29] Dr. Brinton was even more explicit when, ten years later, he wrote his book of Quaker history to mark the beginning of the fourth Quaker century. The important passage is:

> The position of Robert Barclay, who set the pattern for early Quaker thought, was intermediate between the two poles of Hegelian idealism and Neo-Calvinism. Barclay was pessimistic regarding what he called "natural" man's present condition, but optimistic in respect to man's capacity for regeneration and union with God even in this life. He thought that, with divine help, man might, as God's creation, become perfected here and now. The present writer sympathizes with Barclay's position, while rejecting much of his terminology.[30]

With startling unanimity students of the history of ideas on both sides of the Atlantic now conclude that the earlier estimate of Puritanism was unjust and inaccurate, and that at the heart of the Puritan ethic there was a profound sense of the direct experience of the Holy Spirit. Quakerism is consequently seen today, not primarily as the product of mystical influences from the European continent, but as "a natural, almost a predictable outgrowth of Puritanism."[31] One result of this remarkable change has been a new readiness to listen to Barclay, since he was certainly closer to the Puritan thinkers than to the Continental mystics or even to the Cambridge Platonists, with

[29] *Barclay in Brief*, Eleanor Price Mather, ed. (Wallingford, Pa.: Pendle Hill, 1942), Preface by Howard Brinton.

[30] *Friends for 300 Years* (London: George Allen and Unwin, 1953), p. ix.

[31] William C. Braithwaite, *Second Period of Quakerism, op. cit.* (2d ed.; Cambridge, Eng.: The University Press, 1961), Introduction by Frederick B. Tolles, p. xxvii.

some of whom he was familiar. Accordingly, when Henry J. Cadbury undertook in 1957 the editorial revision of *The Second Period of Quakerism*, it was decided to omit the Introduction originally written by Rufus Jones, which represented an estimate of Barclay no longer relevant. It would not be fair to the memory of Rufus Jones, however, to leave the impression that his criticism of Barclay's intellectual system blinded him to the beauty of Barclay's life and character. In the midst of the discussion which is now omitted from the contemporary edition, he wrote,

> Barclay possessed a beautiful inner spirit. His character was one peculiarly marked by sweetness, though at the same time not lacking in firmness and strength. His religion went all through him. His soul was reached by a real experience, and all the springs of his life were fed by his experimental discovery of God.[32]

One of the first evidences of a swing of the pendulum, in respect to the Quaker acceptance of Barclay, came in the work of H. G. Wood when his was an essentially lonely voice.[33] Even in his Swarthmore Lecture of 1920, Professor Wood deplored the Quaker "tendency to distrust the intellect, to suspect the outward, and to neglect the historical."[34] Soon voices from outside the Quaker fold were raised in an effort to do justice to Barclay. Thus R. N. Flew wrote, "It may be questioned whether the distinction between the teachings of George Fox and the formulation of Robert Barclay is as sharp as Dr. Rufus Jones maintains."[35]

Though some aspects of Barclay's published thinking undoubtedly gave support to eighteenth-century Quaker quietism, as it gave support to so many other Quaker tendencies, his total impact was of another character. We remember that Rufus Jones once defined

[32] *Ibid.* (1st ed.), p. xxxi.

[33] The changes which have occurred in the twentieth century estimates of early Quakerism and its historical roots are outlined in an essay by Frederick C. Tolles, "1652 in History: Changing Perspectives on the Founding of Quakerism," *Then and Now*, Anna Brinton, ed. (Philadelphia: University of Pennsylvania Press, 1960), pp. 73–94. An important factor in the change of intellectual climate has been the work of Geoffrey Nuttall.

[34] H. G. Wood, *Quakerism and the Future of the Church* (London: Swarthmore Press, 1920), p. 70.

[35] R. N. Flew, *The Idea of Perfection in Christian Theology* (London: Oxford University Press, 1934), p. 290.

PART I

LIFE

CHAPTER II

FAMILY MAN

There is a good deal to be said for choosing parents descended from Robert Barclay.

—Paul Bloomfield

ROBERT BARCLAY differed in one important way from the other notable aristocrats of the early Quaker Movement. Though William Penn, Isaac Penington, and Thomas Ellwood all had to face harsh opposition from their fathers, Barclay did not. Far from opposing his son's choice, the elder Barclay preceded him in the faith which he came to prize so highly.

When John Greenleaf Whittier sought subjects for his poetic efforts he naturally included, as W. M. Rossetti said, "the preachings and persecutions of the Quakers." Ideal therefore for his purpose was the scene, admired by Quakers in various generations, in which the Apologist's father, the previously honored veteran of the wars, including those of Gustavus Adolphus, was publicly insulted in the streets of Aberdeen because he had become a Quaker and was being taken as a prisoner to the Tolbooth. Whittier pictures the "Laird of Urie" as unperturbed by the violence of the mob.

> Yet with calm and stately mien,
> Up the streets of Aberdeen
> Came he slowly riding;
> And, to all he saw and heard,

Answering not with bitter word,
Turning not for chiding.

One of his relatives lamented, on an occasion of uncommon rudeness, that the Colonel should be situated so differently from what he had formerly been. To this the old soldier replied "that he found more satisfaction, as well as honour, in being thus insulted for his religious principles, than, when some years ago it was usual as he passed this city, for the magistrates to meet him several miles out, and conduct him to a public entertainment in their town-house, and then convey him so far out again, in order to gain his favour."[1]

This man, David Barclay (1610–1686), son of David Barclay of Mathers, was a professional soldier. In 1648 he married Katharine Gordon, daughter of Sir Robert Gordon of Gordonstoun, second son of the Earl of Sutherland and also second cousin to King James I of England. In the same year that he married, Colonel Barclay purchased the estate of Ury,[2] near Stonehaven. Robert, the first child of David and Katherine Barclay, was born at Gordonstoun, December 23, 1648. There were four other children, two sons, John and David, and two daughters, Lucy and Jean. The mother died in 1663. When Robert, later the Apologist, was married in 1670, the father presented him with the estate, though the elder Barclay continued to reside there until his death in 1686.

Colonel David Barclay fought on the royal side in the Civil War, with a commission in the Scotch army, but left active service when Cromwell entered Scotland. Since he was on the losing side, his estate was forfeited, but he obtained a seat in the Scotch Parliament and regained possession. Later he became a commissioner for the forfeited estates of the loyalists. We get some indication of the confused situation of this very perplexing time when we realize that, in spite of his loyalty to his Stuart kinsmen, he was arrested a few years after the Restoration and committed to Edinburgh Castle. This, his first imprisonment, was crucial for his own career and for that of his descendants, because it was the occasion of his meeting a highly

[1] *A Genealogical Account of the Barclays of Urie* (Aberdeen, 1740), pp. 27–28.

[2] The name of the estate was sometimes spelled Ury and sometimes Urie, even by the owners. In this book the spelling Ury is used, except in documents which employ the alternative spelling.

persuasive fellow prisoner, John Swinton (1621?–1679), who had become a Quaker.[3] Hearing much of the Quakers, the elder Barclay made the important decision, "I'll examine and see." He noticed that the Quakers "never shunned sufferings or persecution for their testimony; that they gave up their all for the sake of their religion; that they had beat their swords into plow shares, and their spears into pruning-hooks, and neither taught nor exercised war any more." The professional soldier was deeply impressed, especially by the fact that these people loved one another, which was the mark of veracity stressed by Christ in John 13:35. The sincere seeker "therefore came to a certain conclusion within himself, if Jesus Christ hath followers, disciples, or a visible church on earth, these must be they."[4]

Once having arrived at this conclusion, David Barclay in 1666 publicly acknowledged himself a Quaker. He did not think of himself as joining a sect, but only of announcing his humble intention of becoming a Christian in the clearest and purest manner that he knew or could imagine. Though the Colonel suffered several subsequent imprisonments, especially in the Aberdeen Tolbooth, he never wavered in his testimony. It is fortunate for posterity that we have an authentic account of Colonel Barclay's life and Christian experience from his grandson, Robert, who helped to produce the *Genealogical Account* and to whom the older man communicated both the story of his inquiry and "his private thoughts." In short, what is preserved for us today is this man's record of his own convincement. Part of the authority arises from the fact that the chronicler was sixteen when his grandfather died in October, 1686.

While still imprisoned at Edinburgh in 1667, the elder Barclay sent his son Robert, then eighteen years old, to live at Ury, and when he was set free in 1670 he built the mansion which stood for one hundred and eighty-five years. After joining the Quakers Colonel Barclay was the leading Friend of the area, noted for his quiet reverence and patience. "It was observable," said his grandson, "that he always knelt in time of public prayer."[5]

[3] One of Swinton's descendants was Sir Walter Scott, who took a deep interest in his colorful and persuasive ancestor. Fuller information about Swinton is available in *The Diary of Alexander Jaffray*, John Barclay, ed. (Aberdeen, 1856), pp. 185–87. See Appendix B, p. 253.

[4] *Genealogical Account*, *op. cit.*, p. 26.

[5] *Ibid.*, p. 28.

There is something deeply appropriate about the fact that Robert Barclay's literary executors, of whom William Penn appears to have been the chief, decided to conclude the magnificent *Truth Triumphant* with Barclay's "Testimony" about his revered father. We are especially moved by his account of his father's death. We are told that the old soldier spoke to the people in his room on the afternoon before he died, saying, "How precious is the love of God among his children, and their love one to another! Thereby shall all men know, that ye are Christ's disciples, if you love one another. How precious a thing it is to see brethren to dwell together in love! My love is with you: I leave it among you." The son's narrative goes on:

> About eight at night standing about the bed, he perceiving some of them to weep, he said, 'Dear friends, all mind the inward man, heed not the outward; there is one that doth regard, the Lord of hosts is his name.' After he heard the clock strike three in the morning he said, 'Now the time comes:' and a little after he was heard to say, 'Praises, praises, praises to the Lord! Let now thy servant depart in peace: unto thy hands, O Father, I commit my soul, spirit and body; thy will, O Lord, be done in earth, as it is in heaven!' These sentences he spoke by little intervals one after another. And so a little after five in the morning, the twelfth day of the eighth month, 1686, he fell asleep like a lamb, in remarkable quietness and calmness.[6]

It is not surprising, in the light of such an account, that following the death of the Apologist only four years later, George Fox said, "And his father was a noble man for the Lord and his truth."

About four years of Robert Barclay's boyhood were spent in France, where he was sent while only ten years old to study under his uncle, for whom he was named and who was the Rector of the Scot's College of Paris. This institution, which is still in existence, had as its primary purpose after the Reformation the training of missionary priests prepared to return to Scotland, in the effort to win that country back to the Roman Catholic fold. The uncle, who was both an ardent Roman Catholic and personally wealthy, was so fond of the boy that he offered to make him his sole heir, providing he would remain in France. This might have occurred, and the whole course of his life been consequently different, had it not been that in 1663 his

[6] *Truth Triumphant,* p. 908.

mother made it her dying wish that he be brought back to Scotland. Her fear was that her son might, if he remained in Paris, become a Roman Catholic. Accordingly Colonel Barclay, after his wife's death, obeyed her last wish by traveling to Paris and bringing his son home, much to his brother's chagrin.

Considerable discrepancy has appeared in the judgments about the length of Robert's stay in Paris, the accounts varying as much as two years. The *Genealogical Account* says that the Colonel "went over for him, about the seventeenth year of his age," while in *Quakerism Confirmed* we are told that he came home "in his 15 year."[7] In *Some Account of the Life and Writings of Robert Barclay,* published by Friends in 1801, there is a third variation to the effect that the father went for his son "when he was not much more than sixteen years of age."[8] Though we cannot now be certain about the dates, we are able to reach a highly probable solution of the problem by bringing together all the available resources, including personal letters. By such means we conclude that the education in Paris has often been exaggerated both in content and duration. His own statement was that he learned only "a little grammar." The chief advantages which he gained from this formal education were that he learned to write Latin with ease and that he also learned how to debate. Apropos the latter, others noticed "his quickness at their public disputations."[9]

We are helped in ascertaining the date of the departure for Paris by a letter from the Earl of Marischal, who wrote to David Barclay on March 12, 1759, and asked to be remembered "both to your Lady and little Robin."[10] Since Robin was the boy's nickname, we conclude that he had not yet departed for Paris in the spring of 1659. The likelihood is that he went there the following summer, when he was ten years old.

It is reasonably sure that Robert's return to Scotland occurred in the late summer of 1663, about five months after his mother's death in March. The best evidence of the time when Colonel Barclay went

[7] *Truth Triumphant,* p. 612.

[8] Page 14. The phrase used is evidently copied from John Barclay, *Memoirs of the Rise, Progress, and Persecutions of the People Called Quakers in the North of Scotland* (Aberdeen, 1856), p. 222.

[9] *Genealogical Account,* p. 32.

[10] This letter is reproduced in the *Genealogical Account,* pp. 22, 23, and in *Reliquiae Barclaianae* I.

to get his gifted son is provided by a letter preserved in the Bury Hill manuscripts and written by Robert's Grandmother Gordon. Since the date of the letter is July 17, 1663, we know that he was not at home at that time, but the letter indicates plans for his return shortly afterward. We conclude, then, that the return was in August, 1663, making the entire time in France about four years. The relevant portion of Lady Gordon's letter is that in which she says, "I bless God for the resolution to fetch your son, although your brother would not send him to you to the Rhine, yet I cannot believe that he will keep him against your will. You shall do well to walk wisely to get your son with the consent of his uncle, but if he will not, then you were better want his kindness than buy it with the loss of your son. Let not therefore the hope of worldly gain persuade you." The result was that the Colonel rejected the temptation to appeasement or the acceptance of virtual bribery, and went to Paris forthwith. Since Lady Gordon's letter to her son-in-law was addressed to him at London, he was apparently on his way to France already. The decision to return to Scotland was clinched when young Robert said to his uncle, "He is my father and must be obeyed."

Once home, young Barclay settled down to practice the life of a scholar, first at Gordonstoun and then at Ury. The pages of the now available Notebook reflect something of the studies in which he was self-guided. From his earliest years at Gordonstoun, the studious boy had had access to an excellent library collected by his maternal grandfather, Sir Robert Gordon. With no hint of immodesty, but in simple honesty, he said of himself, "From my childhood I was very ambitious of knowledge and by a certain felicity of understanding I was successful beyond my equals in age." What is remarkable is that the boy was able to guide his own education and that he worked so diligently to prepare himself for a life of scholarship. A few books from his Ury library are extant. One of these, a bound volume of Quaker pamphlets bearing Robert Barclay's signature, is in the Haverford College Library. In the Notebook we find evidence of his efforts to perfect his use of the Greek language, one example being the fact that he copied the first five chapters of Matthew's Gospel. He also taught himself Hebrew and, reading voraciously among the Church Fathers, sought to become thoroughly acquainted with ecclesiastical history.

In the account which he later wrote while imprisoned in the Aberdeen Tolbooth in the winter of 1676–1677, he stressed the degree to which, like his father, he was determined to be a careful seeker and thus to canvass as many live options as possible. "The time that intervened," he wrote, "between my forsaking of the Church of Rome, and joining with those with whom I now stand engaged, I kept myself free from joining with any sort of people, though I took liberty to hear several." Because we do not have the advantage of reading a journal of Barclay's earlier years, we are wise to pay more attention to the autobiographical passages which appear in his printed books, and these by good fortune refer sometimes to the period of his youth about which we should otherwise be largely in the dark. Herein lies the value of the following passage:

> I had scarce got out of my childhood, when I was by the permission of divine providence cast among the company of papists, and my tender years and immature capacity not being able to withstand and resist the insinuations, that were used to proselite me to that way, I became quickly defiled with the pollutions thereof; and continued therein for a time, until it pleased God through his rich love and mercy to deliver me out of these snares, and to give me a clear understanding of the evil of that way.[11]

The shorthand part of the Notebook indicates that the seeking period, with visits to various groups, took the young man as far as the English border country, where he heard Quakers mentioned. The people whom he met, when they spoke of Quakers, "did applaud them highly for the reasonableness of their principles, the chastity of their lives, the meekness of their spirit." This made the serious youth want to learn more about such people. The outcome was that in 1667 Robert Barclay, aged eighteen, took the same step which his father had already taken and publicly joined the despised Quaker Movement. "Although, during his father's imprisonment in Edinburgh Castle, the governor denied him all access to him for the space of several months; yet he had had sufficient occasion to observe the circumspect example and genuine piety of his worthy parent, as well as that of other servants of the Lord, who entertained similar views."[12] At the first Ury meeting, held in June, 1667, the younger Barclay was deeply moved by the cryptic words, uttered by an attender, "In still-

[11] *Truth Triumphant,* p. 678.
[12] John Barclay, *Memoirs* of Scottish Quakers, *op. cit.,* p. 223.

ness there is fulness, in fulness there is nothingness, in nothingness there are all things." David Barclay was delighted with his son's convincement, though he had been careful to bring no pressure to bear, because he wanted his son's religion to come from conviction and not from imitation or inheritance.

By Robert Barclay's own testimony he was "reached" not merely or chiefly in his understanding, but in the very center of his life.

For not a few have come to be convinced of the truth after this manner, of which I myself, in part, am a true witness, who not by strength of arguments, or by a particular disquisition of each doctrine, and convincement of my understanding thereby, came to receive and bear witness of the truth, but by being secretly reached by this life; for when I came into the silent assemblies of God's people, I felt a secret power among them, which touched my heart, and as I gave way unto it, I found the evil weakening in me, and the good raised up, and so I became thus knit and united unto them, hungering more and more after the increase of this power and life, whereby I might feel myself perfectly redeemed. And indeed this is the surest way to become a Christian, to whom afterwards the knowledge and understanding of principles will not be wanting, but will grow up so much as is needful, as the natural fruit of this good root.[13]

The words just quoted are undoubtedly the best known and best loved which Robert Barclay ever wrote. They are autobiographical, though they are the result of later reflection and were written several years after the experience so eloquently described. Now we have the added advantage, because of the shorthand Notebook, of observing his development near the time of his convincement. The unknown men whom he met just south of the border appear to have been very influential. One significant passage is as follows: "In my journey I met in the road with two as reasonable men as ever I have spoken with in this British Isle, with whom I had a large discourse."[14]

Even before his father's release from prison, Robert Barclay established residence at Ury, where much of the burden of managing the estate was carried by David Falconer, a Friend who had already suffered for his faith. Ury lacked some things, but it provided, especially in the new house with its study, after 1670, a splendid setting

[13] *Apology,* Proposition XI, vii.
[14] Shorthand Notebook, p. 3.

for a life devoted to intellectual labor. The buildings, including barns and stables, were a full mile from the gatehouse, and near the stream which traverses the estate. There was no long view from the main house site, which seems to have been chosen for shelter from the wind, but there were excellent short views across open low fields and the stream, with woodland beyond. The estate now abounds in beech with some pine, larch, and elm, the different greens making excellent color contrasts. There are alternating areas of wood, pasture, and wheatland. The "Howff," where both David and Robert Barclay are buried, is located on the top of a high, wooded hill, about a mile from the house. From the top of this hill there is an excellent view eastward to the village of Stonehaven, the harbor, and a stretch of the North Sea, while the view to the west is of distant peaks, including those near Balmoral. The meetinghouse, according to the standard picture, was a separate small structure standing close to the main house. That the conventional representation is reasonably accurate is shown by a photograph long in the possession of the late M. Christabel Cadbury. Captain Robert Barclay-Allardice, the last of the family to live at Ury, became increasingly embarrassed financially, so that in 1844 he made a transfer of his property in trust to his creditors. On November 8, 1854, after his death, his trustees sold the entire estate to Alexander Baird, who took down the house the following year.

Five years before the death of the last occupant of the old mansion, the house was the scene of an interesting ghost story. The Captain's affairs were then in great disorder, so great indeed that when he proposed to sell the property to satisfy his creditors, the deeds could not be found. While he was in this quandary he was visited by Lindley Murray Hoag, an American Quaker who was traveling in the ministry in Scotland in 1849. As told by John Wigham Richardson, the story was that the visiting Friend, being chilled by a raw October day, went straight to bed upon arrival. The next morning at breakfast he looked at a portrait of Colonel David Barclay, the Apologist's father, and said, "Ah, there is my friend of last night." He went on to say that, just as he was dropping off to sleep, there was a knock at the door and a sweet old gentleman came, apologizing for the intrusion. Hoag, according to this account, watched the old man as he opened a cupboard in the wall "taking out some old papers which looked like parchments."

Captain Barclay-Allardice and his sister both exclaimed, "Why, there is no cupboard there." But when they went upstairs, they noticed a hollow sound in the wall where there was no visible cupboard. Tearing off paper and wood, they found an iron door, which a blacksmith was able to open. This was the door of a safe, and inside were the missing deeds. The story now depends on Richardson's account,[15] with no substantiating evidence. So far as contemporary members of the Barclay family are aware, there is no portrait of Colonel Barclay.

On the death of Captain Barclay-Allardice in 1854, the representation of the family passed to the Barclays of Bury Hill. Thus Barclays have been gone from Ury for more than a hundred years, while the Quakers have been gone still longer. In the neighboring village of Stonehaven there is now a street named Barclay and another, parallel to it, named Robert, but these are mere reminders of something from the past.

It was to this beautiful place that Robert Barclay brought his bride in 1670, and it was here that he died and was buried in 1690. In all of his travels and difficulties Ury was always a place of refuge. The first extant writing from Barclay's pen is his letter which he wrote to Christian Molleson of Aberdeen when he was twenty years of age. She was the daughter of Gilbert Molleson, a merchant and magistrate of Aberdeen, and his wife, Margaret, who had become a Friend earlier than other members of the family. She was, indeed, one of the pioneer Quakers of Scotland. The style of the young suitor is likely to amuse the modern reader.

28th of 1st month, 1669.

DEAR FRIEND;

Having for some time past had it several times upon my mind to have saluted thee in this manner of writing, and to enter into a literal correspondence with thee, so far as thy freedom could allow; I am glad that this small occasion hath made way for the beginning of it.

The love of thy converse, the desire of thy friendship, thy sympathy of thy way, and meekness of thy spirit, has often, as thou mayest have

[15] *Memoirs of John Wigham Richardson* (privately printed, Hugh Hopkins, Glasgow, 1911), pp. 37, 38. See also *Journal of the Friends Historical Society,* Vol. X, No. 3 (1913), p. 187; and *A History of the Barclay Family* (London, 1934), Vol. III, pp. 232, 233. See p. 255 of this volume.

observed, occasioned me to take frequent benefit of thy company; in which, I can truly say, I have often been refreshed, and the life in me touched with a sweet unity, which flowed from the same in thee,—tender flames of pure love have sprung up in me to the God of our salvation, for what he hath done for thee! Many things in the natural will concur to strengthen and encourage my affection towards thee, and make thee acceptable unto me; but that which is *before all and beyond all,* is, that I can say in the fear of the Lord, that I have received a charge from him to love thee, and for that I know that his love is much towards thee; and his blessing and goodness is and shall be unto thee, so long as thou abidest in a true sense of it.

ROBERT BARCLAY[16]

The marriage of Robert Barclay and Christian Molleson, which took place at the home of Gilbert Molleson in Aberdeen, was a reverent affair, but it infuriated the neighbors. Since it was solemnized without the words of a priest, the Friends present witnessing to the vows of Robert and Christian, members of the clergy thought that their authority was being slighted. The consequent stir was great because of the novelty of the situation, this being the first marriage after this manner in Aberdeen. Barclay's own position was already clear, but the most precise statement of it came seven and a half years later, in Holland, when he said at the Dutch General Meeting, "We marry none; it is the Lord's work and we are but witnesses."[17] Though letters designed to summon Barclay before the Privy Council for an unlawful marriage were procured, the threat was never executed. The date of the marriage was February 1670, about eleven months after the letter quoted above.

Christian Barclay was a devoted and intelligent companion to Robert Barclay, and the mother of his nine children. Of the seven who reached maturity there were three sons, Robert, David, and John, and four daughters, Patience, Catharine, Christian, and Jean. The record in the family Bible indicates that another David, the first-born, died at the age of ten weeks, while Margaret, the third child, died in 1685 when she was eleven. Christian Barclay was a widow for thirty-three years, dying on February 14, 1724. She was accounted a "pub-

[16] John Barclay, *Memoirs* of Scottish Quakers, *op. cit.*, p. 241.

[17] *William Penn's Journal of his Travels in Holland and Germany* (London, 1835), p. 9.

lic Friend," that is, one who shared in one form or another in the public ministry. There is a joint tablet in the mausoleum at Ury commemorating both her and her husband. Her son wrote of her, "And as she lived an exemplary life, so she made an happy end, whereof I, among many others, was a witness; dying in great peace and serenity of mind, upon the 14th of February, 1724, and was buried in her husband's grave."

There is evidence that Barclay's theological self-education was continued after his marriage. John Barclay (1797–1838) who visited Ury in 1826 when the Apologist's study was still little disturbed, discovered "a thick quarto volume in manuscript, of between 300 and 400 closely written pages, bound in leather and entitled, 'Questions Proposed by Mr. Charles Gordon, concerning the Quakers' principles, to Robert Barclay; with his answers thereunto.'" John Barclay concluded the date of this correspondence to have been as early as 1670, the year of his ancestor's marriage. He also believed that Barclay had other pursuits than those we know about from his published works. "From some memoranda in his own hand-writing, it would seem far from improbable, that he had some design and plan of a History of the Church."[18] This helps to explain the abundant historical allusions used later in the *Apology*.

The young author's first known publication was ready within two months after his marriage. Calling it *Truth Cleared of Calumnies* he devoted himself solely to answering an attack on Friends which William Mitchell, a "preacher" near Aberdeen, had made in a form of a *Dialogue between a Quaker and a Stable Christian*. By reference to an appendix to his work, which Barclay added in January, 1670–71, we learn that the clergy of Aberdeen had urged the magistrates to search Barclay's book, had forbidden their parishioners to read it, and had compared it to poison. Since William Mitchell answered Barclay's answer, Barclay felt bound to write a second book, dated December 24, 1671, and entitled in a more colorful way than the former volume. This one was called *William Mitchell Unmasked; or the Staggering Instability of the Pretended Stable Christian Discovered, His Omissions Observed, and Weakness Unveiled.*

This controversy has no present interest except that it helped to

[18] John Barclay, *Memoirs* of Scottish Quakers, *op. cit.*, p. 434.

sharpen the intellectual tools of the young thinker, whose second book was finished when he was barely twenty-three years of age. William Mitchell helped not only to develop Barclay's skill, but also pointed out numerous important objections to the Friends' position which Barclay considered later in the *Apology*. One of the strongest features of the *Apology* consists in the effort to remove specific objections, but we are not surprised at this when we study the early controversial writings.

The year 1672 was for Barclay and his fellow Quakers in Scotland a year of crisis. On March 5, the Friends of Aberdeen, having bought a record book, made a solemn occasion of signing their names. Those who signed were ten men, including Keith and the two Barclays, and fourteen women. Exactly a week later the keyed-up young scholar wrote, at Ury, a "Warning" to the people of Aberdeen calling them to repentance. The epistle was intended both to reinforce and to explain a curious act in which he had engaged only a few days before, when he had felt divinely led to walk through the streets of Aberdeen, covered with sackcloth and with ashes on his head. Like George Fox, Robert Barclay had one, and only one, such experience. That of Fox came when he was impelled to take off his shoes and walk barefoot through Lichfield crying, "Woe to the bloody city of Lichfield." These acts seem more strange to us than they seemed to our ancestors three hundred years ago, when fanatical exhibitions were common. Some of these included actual nakedness, on the part of both men and women. Barclay was not the only Scottish Quaker to walk the streets of Aberdeen as a sign. Andrew Jaffray, having become "deeply affected and laden in his mind, under an unusual sense of the corrupt and ungodly condition of many of his fellow citizens," walked on a market day in June 1677, much as Barclay had walked five years earlier.[19] William James made the careful judgment that Fox was, at the time of his Lichfield episode, skirting the line which separates what we call sanity from pathological behavior. Had he not moved into integrating experiences, he would have had a breakdown. The same conclusion seems reasonable in reference to Barclay, who passed his danger point in 1672, after which the sense that he was led to make a spectacle never returned. The explanation of his act is obvious, and is understandable

[19] *Ibid.*, pp. 314, 315.

in the light of the strain under which he and his fellow Quakers were living. Being keenly aware of the precedent set by Hebrew prophets in giving their messages by signs rather than by words, he did what he thought was inwardly commanded. He denied explicitly that his message came to him "from any Light or Illumination, in him as a man." The only source, he affirmed, was "the Immediate Testimony of the Spirit of God in his heart." He did not, however, claim that he had heard an audible voice.[20] Fearful that his act might be misunderstood, or that he might appear as one seeking publicity, he was quick to explain his purpose, showing that his deed was done without either premeditation or joy.

> And the command of the Lord concerning this thing came unto me that very morning as I awakened, and the burden thereof was very great; yea almost seemed insupportable unto me (for such a thing, until that very moment, had never entered me before, not in the most remote consideration). And some whom I called to declare this thing, can bear witness, how great was the agony of my spirit, how I besought the Lord with tears that this cup might pass away from me.[21]

Before we sit in judgment on Barclay for his one fanatical exhibition, with its evident lack of balance, we need to remember the vivid warning of Charles Morgan when he wrote in *The Fountain*, "the hopelessly sane men are the bores."

By the good fortune of now having available young Barclay's Notebook, we have a better insight than was possible before into the crucial decisions of his life in 1672. The Notebook gives us Barclay's record of a dream or vision which came only a little more than three months after the sackcloth episode. Part of the account is as follows:

> Presently I was standing by a marsh side in which I beheld a rich yellow matter which lay like clogs of wood in it, which matter as conceiving it to be very useful and beneficial unto me, I went about eagerly to gather, but while I went into the bog to get them out, I was like to sink, falling in to the ankles and sometimes further. Methought also there stood one by, nearly related unto me, who took me by the hand upon such occasions to relieve me and who also went in to gather the matter with me and passed upon the marsh more lightly than I.

[20] *Truth Triumphant,* p. 107.
[21] *Ibid.,* p. 105.

It is obvious that the yellow matter is gold and that the companion is his wife, Christian. The dream is important because it makes us know that part of the strain which Barclay was under was the strain of decision. He knew that he could easily and naturally go into a life of business and thereby gain wealth, as some of his descendants later did. He knew also that he could give himself, with a deep sense of commitment, to the work of scholarship, perhaps providing the world with an intellectual formulation of Christianity which had not previously existed. The dream marked the end of uncertainty. "This appearing to me," says the account, "at a Juncture of time when I was beginning more eagerly and carefully than before to concern myself in my outward affairs I thought it worthy of observation." It appears, then, that after the summer solstice of 1672 the die was cast, so far as Barclay's major vocation was concerned.

Though we cannot know with precision what went on in Barclay's consciousness, we can note that there came, following the crucial experiences in 1672, a striking change in his entire style. After his first imprisonment late in the year 1672, Robert Barclay was ready for intellectual production, the first evidence being *A Catechism and Confession of Faith,* completed August 11, 1673. When this work appeared, it was clear that he had left behind his apprenticeship and had become a serious theologian rather than a sincere but overwrought youth, as the earlier productions suggested. The point to understand is the rapidity with which Barclay outgrew both the mood of overexcitement and the jargon in which his first prophetic utterances were couched. *A Catechism and Confession of Faith,* which occupied most of his time in 1673, gave evidence that Barclay had found the major pattern of his life by the time he was twenty-four years old.

A good case can be made for the proposition that, in spite of his writings, Robert Barclay's most valuable production was his family. The pattern which the Apologist established continued long after his untimely death. Part of the evidence for this is provided by accounts of contemporary visitors to Ury. For example, a traveling Quaker minister, John Gratton, reported in his journal his impressions on the occasion of a visit to Ury three and a half years after the Apologist's death.

We came to Ury, where the Widow of Robert Barclay dwelt, there we staid several Days, in which time I observed, that when her children were up in the Morning and drest, she sat down with them before breakfast, and in a religious Manner waited upon the Lord, which pious Care, and Motherly Instruction of her Children, when young, doubtless had its desired Effect upon them; for as they grew in Years, they also grew in the Knowledge of the blessed Truth, and since that Time some of them are become publick Preachers thereof.[22]

We know from the accounts left by other reporters of the family life at Ury that the children followed faithfully the examples of their two parents. When Robert, the eldest, was only twenty-two years of age he is said to have "reached and melted our hearts in a wonderful manner," by his testimony. His sister Christian, named for her mother, engaged in public prayer at the age of fourteen, and Catharine shared her experience at the age of sixteen. A few days later the elder sister Patience, who had been so reticent to speak earlier, followed the example of the others.[23]

All seven of the children who reached maturity were vigorous, both intellectually and physically, and all seven were alive in 1740, fifty years after their father's death. Their descendants have not only multiplied prodigiously, but have left a mark on public life which few families can match. This has been true, not only of those who have carried the Barclay name, but also of those in the Gurney and Buxton lines, as well as many more. The famous Gurneys of Earlham, of whom Elizabeth Fry was the brightest star, were descendants of Barclay through their mother, Catherine Bell, Robert Barclay's great granddaughter.

While the Apologist's eldest living son, Robert, succeeded his father as Laird of Ury, the second son, David, became a prosperous London merchant engaged in the American trade. His home in Cheapside, opposite the Church of St. Mary-le-Bow, was a place of gracious entertainment. He was honored on more than one occasion by royal visits, when the reigning monarchs used the balcony of his house as a convenient place from which to view the annual Lord Mayor's Procession. The story of the impromptu entertainment of royal guests,

[22] *A Journal of the Life of that Ancient Servant of Christ, John Gratton* (London, 1720), p. 125.

[23] Frances Anne Budge, *The Barclays of Ury* (London, 1881), pp. 28, 29.

whom David Barclay addressed simply as "George" and "Charlotte," has often been told.

Still more eminent was David's son David, usually designated as David Barclay of Walthamstow (1728–1809), in his day the last surviving grandson of the Apologist. He was a man of large affairs and broad sympathies, who took his religion so seriously that he liberated the slaves of his estate in Jamaica at a cost of £10,000. Realizing full well that mere emancipation might prove to be a doubtful blessing, he further hired a vessel to transport the liberated slaves to North America, where they were assisted in establishing themselves in handicraft trades.[24] He shared with his close friend, Benjamin Franklin, a deep desire to avoid war between the English colonies and the mother country. Along with Dr. John Fothergill, these remarkable men made, in the winter of 1774–75, a written proposal for conciliation, but unfortunately it was not taken seriously by the government and the War of Independence began. On another side of his life, David Barclay was one of the founders of Ackworth School.

Perhaps the best-known aspect of this David Barclay's life is that of his part in the purchase of the famous brewery which had formerly been owned by Dr. Samuel Johnson's friend and erstwhile host, Henry Thrale. As all careful readers of Boswell's *Life* are aware, the Barclays bought the brewery in conjunction with Mr. Perkins, Thrale's superintendent, paying a then fantastic sum of money. Because Dr. Johnson, who was residing in the Thrale mansion at the time of Henry Thrale's death, acted as an administrator of his friend's estate, it was the famous lexicographer who insisted on a price so high. When the purchasers resisted, Dr. Johnson enunciated the economic principle of the capitalization of prospective income by his famous rejoinder, "We are not here to sell a parcel of boilers and vats, but the potentiality of growing rich beyond the dreams of avarice." This prediction on the part of the great man was wonderfully accurate. If any modern reader is surprised to learn that eighteenth-century Quakers would purchase and manage a brewery, he should understand that the Quakers of the period had almost no objection to the use of alcoholic beverages. The objection is modern! When Rachel Wilson of Kendal undertook a long ministerial visit to the English colonies of America, in 1768, she

24 Richard Pike, *Quaker Anecdotes* (London, 1881), p. 206.

made a record of her supplies. Among those taken by the saintly woman were the following:

2 doz. Madeira Wine
2 bottles Jam^{ca} Spirit
Keg W I Rum
4 bottles Brandy[25]

What began as a business operation between David Barclay and Doctor Johnson went on to become a happy personal relationship. Barclay saw Johnson in his last illness, when he received the old man's blessing as he knelt beside him. Boswell said of Barclay that he was "remarkable for maintaining the principles of his venerable progenitor with as much of the elegance of modern manners as is consistent with primitive simplicity."[26]

The interest in Barclay's descendants has been stimulated by a book by Paul Bloomfield, with the title *Uncommon People*.[27] The subtitle is "A Study of England's Elite." The author lays great stress upon what he calls the "Quaker elite," with especial reference to those descended from the Apologist. Naturally he mentions the Colonel, but goes on to say, "Robert Barclay looks to me like a genuine *New Variation* in the family. He not only had moral and physical courage, and brains, but was what he was from the start."[28] Bloomfield's mention of the great names of Britain descended from the Barclays of Ury is extremely convincing. The significant fact about the Apologist, he claims, is that he became "the revered ancestor of his vast and talented progeny." The author has taken careful note of the standardized practice of marrying cousins, most remarkable in the Gurney line. "The intermarriage of Robert Barclay's descendants," writes Bloomfield, "have given us men and women about whom there is pedigree almost in the canine sense of the word."[29] In similar vein he says, "The earlier Barclays, by cousin inter-marriage, practically created a class of their own to go on marrying into." By

[25] *Isaac and Rachel Wilson, Quakers of Kendal* (London: Swarthmore Press, 1924), p. 50.
[26] Boswell's *Life of Johnson,* Augustine Birrell, ed. (London, 1912), Vol. V., p. 252.
[27] London: Hamish Hamilton, 1955.
[28] *Ibid.,* p. 53*n*.
[29] *Ibid.,* p. 187.

intelligent choice of mates they accomplished "the standardizing in their families of healthy, intelligent, and good-looking types of manhood and womanhood." If the enduring effect of the Quaker Movement is more in people than in books, or even in ideas, Robert Barclay undoubtedly deserves the prize. His descendants include leaders in business, in government, in letters, in philanthropy, and in the ministry. The Archbishop of Melbourne is among the latter.

The fertility of Robert Barclay's descendants has been astounding. When his eldest son wrote about him in 1740, he reported that the Apologist already had between fifty and sixty descendants. In 1801 David Barclay, the Apologist's grandson, wrote that there were nearly two hundred and fifty people who called him uncle. A highly entertaining account of some of the numerous and closely linked progeny is provided by the pictorial notebook of E. Ellen Buxton, which has been printed in our time.[30] The descendants and their servants who gathered regularly at Northrepps Hall, Cromer, sometimes numbered as many as fifty-six in the house.

Katharine Fry, granddaughter of John Gurney of Earlham Hall and, through her grandmother, Catherine Bell, a descendant of Robert and Christian Barclay, referred in 1873 to "one hundred and sixty grandchildren and great grandchildren living now."[31] When we realize that this, the Gurney branch, was only one of many illustrious branches, we get some idea of the magnitude of Barclay's contribution as an ancestor. His influence in this regard was in striking contrast to that of the other leading Quakers of his time. George Fox was childless, and most of the descendants of William Penn had no interest in the Quaker faith, but among the descendants of Barclay were exponents of that faith for fully two centuries.

It is our misfortune that we do not have any likeness of the man who was both a famous thinker and a famous ancestor, though there is reason to believe that a portrait once existed. Indeed, the *Edinburgh Magazine* for May, 1787 reported (p. 332) "His portrait is preserved in the family of Urie."[32] The probability is that the por-

[30] E. Ellen Buxton, *Family Sketchbook a Hundred Years Ago,* arranged by her granddaughter, Ellen R. C. Creighton (London: Geoffrey Bles, 1964).

[31] *Katharine Fry's Book*, Jane Vansittart, ed. (London: Hodder and Stoughton, 1966), p. 22.

[32] See Joseph Smith's Catalogue, *op. cit.* (Preface of this book p. iv), Vol. I., p. 189.

trait was lost, along with many other valuables, during the confused last years before the old mansion was destroyed. We do have a lock of the Apologist's hair, apparently removed at the time of his wife's interment in his grave, a third of a century after his death. The hair is light brown, without a trace of gray.

Though we do not know exactly how Barclay looked, we do know something of his dress and his manner of life. For example we have today more than one sample of the Apologist's waistcoat, made of green brocade.[33] This indicates that he did not adopt a Quaker uniform of gray, and probably had the same opinion of the foolishness of such a stereotype as that of his good friend, Margaret Fell. The color of the scholar's coat gives appropriateness to the famous remark of Dr. Johnson, to the effect that a man who cannot get into heaven in a green coat will not get there any sooner in a gray one. Something of Barclay's love of beauty and even elegance is indicated by his walking stick, which has an ivory handle. Several pieces of silver from his home have been preserved. We do not know enough about him, but at least we know that he did not make a virtue of ugliness.

One signal advantage of the present availabilty of Barclay's diary is that it shows something of the purely personal side of his life, especially with reference to home and family. One insertion is called "Concerning the ordering of clover seed," while in another place the scholarly writer reminds himself to inquire about licorice plants and indicates their probable price. A shopping list includes

A barrel of green ginger
A comb for my wife
3 ell of small satin ribbons[34]
To my father a satin cap
2 neck night cloths
A pair of rib stockings
A green mohair petticoat

[33] One piece is in the Bury Hill Collection, while another is part of the collection of Edward Backhouse, Jr., of Ashburn, Sunderland. The latter is now in the possession of Amy E. Wallis, "Moreland," 26 Abbey Road, Darlington.

[34] An ell was 45 inches in England and 37.2 inches in Scotland. The ribbons were presumably for his daughters.

Such items help us to know that Barclay was a man and not merely a book. We are glad to be told that, in September, 1679, he paid Leonard Fell £36 *Os. Od.,* Scots' money for a horse "for Arent Sonmans to come home on." Barclay was a thinker, but this did not prevent his deep involvement in the common life about him. He cared for his family and his family cared for him. One of our valued treasures is his wife's book of recipes, dealing with both food and health.

CHAPTER III

SCHOLAR

We shall never thrive upon ignorance.

—*Joseph John Gurney*

BARCLAY'S MOST creative writing was done, not only at an early age, but in a surprisingly short time. As we reconstruct his life, we can see that the major writing was done between his twenty-fourth and twenty-seventh birthdays. By the time he was twenty-seven, in December, 1675, the Latin *Apology* was complete, with actual publication coming in 1676. There was, of course, more literary work after that, including the translation of the *Apology* into English and the production of remarkable short works while the author was incarcerated in the Aberdeen prison, but the *opus* itself was done while Barclay was only twenty-six. In this regard his career was parallel to that of John Calvin, with whose *Institutes* the young Scot was familiar. The flame of authorship burned brightly in the twenties and then, partly because of other responsibilities, it burned no more. Barclay wrote nothing of importance in the last twelve years of his short life. Indeed, it can be truly said that he lived his life in chapters, the chapter devoted to Christian scholarship being the first major one and incomparably the greatest. Noble ideas, especially when expressed in eloquent words, are remembered longer than even noble deeds.

Three creative years, devoted chiefly to writing in the new study in the new house, enabled Barclay to produce three major works, all of which are beyond the juvenile stage, though progress can be noted within them. These three are *A Catechism and Confession of Faith,* 1673, *The Anarchy of the Ranters,* 1674, and *An Apology for the True Christian Divinity,* in Latin, 1675.

Though we are perplexed when we first contemplate the amount of writing, including thousands of Biblical and other references, which Barclay was able to accomplish in a few years, we finally have a partial answer to our perplexity when we recognize his method. Nearly everything which he searched out was used more than once, because his literary career was strikingly cumulative. This is easier to see once Professor Hayes has pointed it out.

> At first sight it seems very remarkable how much writing he was able to do, in view of the scholarship which his pamphlets implied and the many other calls upon his time. But if it is carefully noted how he used the same theological material again and again, how he built each work on those that preceded, not starting afresh each time, but enlarging the design upon the earlier foundations, it becomes plain that though Barclay did work rapidly, posting through the affairs of life as if he were aware of the early end that awaited him, his facility in writing is not difficult to explain.[1]

The first of Barclay's serious works, *A Catechism and Confession of Faith,* was really a foretaste of much that was to appear two years later in a more finished form. His main intention was to show that the principles upheld by those "who are reproachfully called by the name of Quakers" are not those of some new and strange sect, but of a people who are trying to be faithful to the basic and universal faith represented by the primitive Church and resulting directly from the teaching of Christ Himself as the "Chief Speaker." The preface was dated at Ury, August 11, 1673 and signed, not by Robert Barclay, Quaker, but by "Robert Barclay, a Servant of the Church of Christ." At about the same time, he was writing in his Notebook of the groups he knew and loved as "Churches of Christ." He reveals the background of the work when he says, "Not long after I had received and believed the Testimony I now bear, I had in my view both the possibility and facility of such a Work;

[1] George P. Hayes, Barclay Dissertation, p. 116 (see Appendix B, p. 256).

and now after a more large and perfect acquaintance with the Holy Scripture, I have found access to allow some time to set about it; and have also been helped to accomplish the same."

This reference to "help" is very important for the present study. It was essential to Barclay's genuine humility, as well as honesty, to avoid claiming absolute originality or independence in all of his scholarly work. We know from other sources that the chief helper was the famous George Keith. Keith's friendship goes back to the very beginning of Barclay's public acknowledgment of himself as a Quaker. On his first ministerial visit, at the age of eighteen, both John Swinton and George Keith were his companions.[2] The opportunities of the younger man to get help and advice from a seasoned scholar were many. There are two references to George Keith in the Notebook, which evidently refer with gratitude to both the oral and written work of Keith in answering William Mitchell, the Aberdeen clergyman mentioned in Chapter II.

George Keith (1639?–1716) became a Quaker in Edinburgh, about four years prior to Robert Barclay's convincement. He is mentioned favorably in the *Diary of Alexander Jaffray* and was apparently one of the authors of the "Historic Account of Quakers in Scotland" which John Barclay discovered in manuscript in the Apologist's study in 1826. In the year 1673, while Barclay was writing his first mature book, Keith was working in the vicinity of Aberdeen as a surveyor. There is every reason to think that there was abundant opportunity for the two men, both devoted Quakers and intelligent men, to make joint plans. In any case we know that it was Keith who, late in 1674, took the Latin *Theses* to Amsterdam for publication.

The closest cooperation between Keith and Barclay occurred on April 14, 1675, when they conducted a formal debate with certain theological students of Aberdeen. The debate was carefully organized, with two moderators, one representing each side. This was an important chance for Barclay, then deeply involved in the actual writing of the *Apology,* to clear his ideas on many points, and Keith's sharp answers to difficulties were eminently helpful. That the debate was far from fruitless is shown by the fact that four of the students were, as a consequence, convinced of the truth of the Quaker position. One of these, Alexander Seaton, later preached to the public through

[2] *Record Book of Friends of Urie,* printed in *Journal of Friends Historical Society,* Vol. VII (1910), p. 92.

the windows of the Aberdeen prison and became a prominent traveling minister.

When the account of the debate with the students was published, George Keith signed the Postscript. Furthermore, *Quakerism Confirmed* (1676) is listed on the title page as written by Robert Barclay and George Keith. Keith signed, along with Barclay, the analysis of the argument of the Dutch correspondent Adrian Paets, who was at one time ambassador to Spain from the states of the United Provinces. Keith's life in America, whither he went through Barclay's influence, will be mentioned in Chapter VI of this volume. Suffice it now to say that he grew more bitter and controversial as he grew older, while Barclay became more mellow and tender. Keith ultimately became so critical of his former associates that he started a new society, which he called "Christian Quakers." In 1692 Philadelphia Yearly Meeting formally testified against him, and his appeal to London Yearly Meeting in 1694 was turbulently unsuccessful. In 1702 Keith joined the Church of England and was sent to America as a missionary to the supposedly misguided Quakers. It is probable that, in spite of his censoriousness, he was an asset to the Quaker Movement in helping to save Quakers from underemphasis upon the historic Christ. In spite of his early fondness for Barclay, Keith made the only known moral criticism of the Apologist, in saying that Barclay used quotations at second hand and that some of these had been provided by himself.[3]

The best available evidence leads to the conclusion that Keith helped Barclay, but not as much as he supposed when he looked back after a quarter of a century. His own claim of precedence was made when he wrote, "For to say the truth, most or rather all the arguments that seemed most rational to me which are in my books in vindication of the Quakers, I find them in the *Apology* of the said author, many of which I had used before him."[4] What Keith did not recognize with a graciousness equal to that of Barclay was the help which the younger man had evidently given him, thus making the

[3] The best study of the relationship between the ideas of the two men is that of J. Philip Wragge, *The Faith of Robert Barclay* (London: Friends Home Service Committee, 1948). See further reference in Appendix B.

[4] George Keith, *The Standard of the Quakers Examined* (London, 1902), Preface. For Keith's life see Ethyn Williams Kirby, *George Keith* (New York: D. Appleton-Century Co., 1942).

assistance mutual. Barclay wrote parts of Keith's book *Quakerism No Popery,* published in 1675, at the time of the closest collaboration between the two men. These were the "Epistle to the Reader" and the final two sections of the book.

The *Catechism* may be looked upon, in every way, as an earlier attempt to do what was done more ambitiously in the *Apology*. The ecstatic manner is gone, as well as the excessive sectarianism, for the work is addressed not to Quakers, but to "all other Professors." The book attempts to deal rationally, and from the point of view of the Scriptures, with the entire ground of religious truth. This work includes fourteen chapters of general questions and answers, a confession of faith with twenty-three articles, and two concluding chapters devoted, first, to an appeal to all other Christians, and second, to an examination of the alleged Scripture proofs used in the Westminster Catechism and Confession of Faith.

The *Confession of Faith,* with its twenty-three articles, is intended as the Quaker opposite number to the Westminster Confession, which was presented to Parliament December 3, 1646 and adopted by the Scottish General Assembly, August 27, 1647. This famous document, coming out just prior to Barclay's birth, had been part of his conscious background from his earliest memories. His own statement is, "My first education from my infancy up fell amongst the strictest sort of Calvinists."[5] A comparison of the articles in Barclay's Confession of Faith with the articles in the Westminster Confession is instructive in that it shows both his dependence upon the established pattern and the ways in which he had departed from it. One revealing difference was that, whereas the Westminster divines began with an article on the Scriptures, Barclay began with one on the knowledge of God. His mature philosophy started with epistemology.

Throughout much of 1674, Barclay was able to concentrate on a new step in his intellectual development and one of great importance for the Quaker Movement, as he produced his book *The Anarchy of the Ranters.* In this he was bringing his keen young mind to bear upon the question of order in the religious life. Earlier he had been so full of enthusiasm for the old-new message that he was not greatly disturbed by the possibility of extravagance in thought or action, but

[5] *Truth Triumphant,* p. 678.

at the age of twenty-five he felt this problem with intensity. The Ranters were those who held that the freedom of the gospel is so great that there must be full expression of every leading of the Spirit, and furthermore, that no act is wrong if done by the saved person.

There is no doubt that some people with Ranter leanings early found their way into the Quaker Movement. Many were troublesome, not only to other people but to Quakers themselves, since they went to absurd lengths in trespassing against the rules of decorum. The way in which a few broke into solemn services of worship, and even Holy Communion, to disturb the worshipers and denounce their reverent acts, makes us tend to sympathize more with those who suffered the intrusion than with those who perpetrated it.

As the young scholar of Ury began to consider Christian life in its entirety, he saw that it must involve order as well as liberty, and that there must be some right way in the matter of discipline. While he was increasingly conscious of the dangers of libertinism and fanaticism, he continued, fortunately, to be equally conscious of the opposite dangers of authoritarianism. The Ranter, Barclay thought, represented one of these extremes, while the Papist represented the other, and he was sure that the truth lay equidistant from both. Heresy, he held, is always the extreme position, and it is heresy precisely because it lacks some of the wholeness of life. Complete predestination is a heresy, but complete Pelagianism is likewise a heresy. Like the judicious Richard Hooker almost a century before him, Barclay sought a mean of comprehension rather than a mean of exclusion. Man, as we know him in his present state, is always "inclinable to lean either to the right hand or to the left," but this inclination must be consciously and thoughtfully resisted.

Barclay was convinced that the good life, especially when lived in societies, must include both *freedom and order*. His book, therefore, became what he called "a two-fold apology." The practical reason for the wielding of this two-edged sword was the fact that the new Quaker Movement had been criticized by some as being Papist, while by others it was criticized as being Ranter. Barclay was eager to reveal the erroneous character of both allegations and to show, furthermore, that the truth lay in the avoidance of these very positions. The Quaker position was such that "we have laboured to walk amidst these extremities." The dangers of Roman authoritarianism were easily presented and needed little elucidation at the time, because a pretended succession from the Apostles was made "to cloak and cover all manner of abuses, even the height of idolatry and superstition." But the problem could not be solved by merely letting the winds of freedom blow.

Why was Robert Barclay so conscious of this problem in 1674, whereas his earlier writings do not show a like recognition of it? We have part of our answer when we note the highly relevant fact that in 1673 he made his first trip to London, attended Yearly Meeting, and became conversant with some of the major problems beginning to arise in a movement which included incompatible elements. He signed the important epistle issued by the Yearly Meeting of 1673.[6] Then in 1674 he visited London again and, in company with several other Friends, had an interview with the celebrated fanatic Lodowick Muggleton. By this and other experiences Barclay, before he started to write the *Apology,* had already adopted a consciously mediating position.

Though Barclay's new topic was highly relevant to what was called the Wilkinson-Story controversy, which raged in 1674, he wrote without prior knowledge of this unhappy development. The essence of the conflict was that a few were arguing for a degree of freedom which would have been inconsistent with order, and which would undoubtedly have destroyed the Quaker Movement had it continued unchecked. Barclay's book on Church order, while not as mature as the *Apology* which followed immediately, was one of the valuable weapons used by George Fox and others in avoiding the danger of religious anarchy. Ranterism was something against which a man with his clear mind was bound to react. He saw that the appeal to freedom can, in any generation, be a specious gesture, leading to the libertinism which tolerates abuses against other people and encourages harsh judgments. Barclay had grown much since he walked the streets of Aberdeen in sackcloth. His astute observation was that

> some are so great pretenders to inward motions and revelations of the spirit, that there are no extravagances so wild, which they will not cloak

[6] This epistle is printed in A. R. Barclay, *Letters, etc. of Early Friends* (London, 1841), pp. 336–42. It is not in London Yearly Meeting manuscript Minutes. George Fox was not a signer, being in America that year.

with it; and so much are they for every one's following their own mind, as can admit of no Christian Fellowship and Community, nor of that good Order and Discipline, which the Church of Christ never was nor can be without.[7]

After the writing of this book, and its hearty acceptance by Fox and other Quaker leaders, there was no more excuse for any literate person to think of Quakerism as rampant individualism.

This is not to say that all controversy in the Quaker Movement came to an end. The most articulate of Barclay's adversaries, a Bristol merchant named William Rogers, wrote a work which was long circulated in manuscript and which attacked Barclay's thesis. Rogers so emphasized the individualistic side of religion that he saw Barclay, with his insistence on the authority of group experience, as a serious threat. Even after an official confrontation between the two men, with the result that the critic declared himself satisfied, Rogers renewed the attack. His book was answered by Barclay under date of March 6, 1679, from Aberdeen prison.

The encounter with the celebrated fanatic Lodowick Muggleton in 1674 is well reported to us by one of the participants in the conference, John Gratton. "On seventh day," he says, "I met with three Friends who were going to see Lodowick Muggleton, viz. Robert Barclay, Patrick Livingstone and William Hague, and I went along with them." Muggleton, whose followers were also called Friends and who had some superficial resemblance to Quakers, was not only unconciliatory, but positively rude. After some conversation, Muggleton suddenly stopped and said, "You are Scotchmen, and I will have nothing to do with you."[8] The encounter did not lead to a reconciliation, but it makes us know incidentally that Barclay's accent was a bit different from that of Englishmen! Furthermore, it had the effect of making Barclay more alert to the dangers of the lunatic fringe in religious movements. Thus, by the age of twenty-five he was aware of the danger of extremes on both sides of any conflict.

Barclay's rapid growth after his earliest controversies is strikingly apparent. At first his style was bombastic, almost in the mood of Muggleton. What is important to note, if we would understand his rapid development, is that there was a marked absence of the strident

[7] *Truth Triumphant,* p. 185.
[8] *Journal of John Gratton, op. cit.,* p. 125.

note after the visit to London when Muggleton was seen face to face.

Some forgiveness for Barclay's apparent harshness of style in controversy is made possible by the recognition that he lived in an age of bitterness and confusion, when persecution was always either experienced or expected. Barclay *did* have enemies and they were pitiless. Furthermore, his was normally the role of answering an attack rather than initiating it. In the Preface to the collected works attributed to Penn, the important distinction is made that Barclay is "rather zealous than heated," and that his sharpness is directed to his enemies' ideas rather than to themselves. His clear rule was to be tough with ideas, but tender with persons, though this was hard to apply in all circumstances. In the Preface Penn says Barclay "rather pities his enemy than triumphs over his weakness and envy."[9] Though all knew that Barclay was a vigorous antagonist, it was the clear consensus of those who knew him that he was a man of kind and friendly disposition. His Scottish neighbor and fellow prisoner, Patrick Livingstone, evidently spoke for many when he wrote, "He was a man of a sweet, pleasant and chearful temper, and above many for evenness of temperament."[10]

The modern reader, who tends to be thrown off by Robert Barclay's debating style, can be helped today not only by noting the radical nature of the changes which occurred in his rapid growth into maturity, but also by attention to the reports of those who knew him best, which have fortunately been preserved. It is impressive to read the words of Andrew Jaffray when he says, "I can truly say I never saw him in any peevish, angry, brittle or disordered temper, since ever I knew him." William Sewel, who wrote on the basis of firsthand acquaintance, gave the most balanced report of Barclay's character which we have. "He was so skilful in school learning," says Sewel, "that he was able to encounter the learned with their own weapons, and of such quick apprehension, as not to be inferior to the refined wits; his meekness also was eminent; and these qualifications were accompanied with so taking a carriage, as rendered him very acceptable to others."[11]

[9] *Truth Triumphant,* p. xi.

[10] *Ibid.,* "Testimonies."

[11] William Sewel, *History of the Rise, Increase and Progress of the Christian People Called Quakers* (London, 1722), p. 472.

When *The Anarchy of the Ranters* was completed on October 17, 1674, Barclay was ready for the major theological task. The first step in the grand design was the relatively simple one of presenting to the learned world a set of theses which he declared himself willing and able to defend. He was thereby following a pattern which had been that of scholars for centuries, and which was illustrated by Martin Luther when he nailed his particular theses to the door of the Castle Church of Wittenberg. The *Theses Theologicae,* as they were called, were fifteen in number and were addressed "to the Clergy of what Sort soever, unto whose hands these may come; but more particularly to the Doctors, Professors and Students of Divinity in the Universities and Schools of Great Britain, whether Prelatical, Presbyterian, or any other." He was aiming for the elite of the intellectual world, so far as religion was concerned, and his purpose was to change minds.

The propositions were presented a full year in advance of the first publication of the *Apology* in which Barclay reprinted and defended them. Indeed the *Theses* provided the table of contents of the *Apology*. Barclay's evident purpose was to whet the appetite of potential readers and thus to prepare scholars for the reception of his major work. That the Latin *Theses* were taken seriously is shown by the quick response elicited from people of prominence, including the Dutch ambassador, Adrian Paets, to whom Barclay wrote from prison and whom he later met in London when the ambassador was one of the commissioners of the Dutch East India Company. Dr. Nicolaus Arnold, a Dutch professor of divinity, replied to the *Theses,* and Barclay issued a rejoinder in Latin at Rotterdam in 1675.[12] When Arnold's criticism reached Barclay in Edinburgh on May 14, 1675, the author of the *Theses* sat down and wrote his answer in two days. In it he referred to the forthcoming *Apology* as containing a fuller answer. This shows that the book was well developed by late spring of 1675. From then until its completion in December, he must have given most of his time to it even though we know that some time was taken out for public debate.

The *Theses* were published in two forms early in 1674, one being a folio broadside in Latin, printed in Amsterdam "anno 1674" by

[12] See Benjamin Rhodes, *Three Apostles of Quakerism* (1884), p. 99.

Christophorus Conradus, and the other being presented in parallel columns of Latin and Low Dutch, with a preface by Benjamin Furly. To this latter Furly attached extracts from the writings of Francis Howgill and Isaac Penington, obviously trying to make his publication an instrument of Quaker evangelism. Furly's publication, a quarto pamphlet of twenty-eight pages, was, according to his own subsequent account, published "about the middle of the year 1674."[13] A second edition of the Dutch version, in thirty-two pages, was published later in 1674 in Amsterdam. In 1675 editions of *Theses Theologicae* were published in English, French, and High Dutch or German.

The advance which the *Theses* represent over the *Confession of Faith* of a year earlier is evident. The arrangement is much simplified, with a more logical order, and the number is reduced from twenty-three articles to only fifteen propositions. Furthermore, though it is easy to see that Barclay's mind is steeped in the Bible, the *Theses* are less limited to Biblical terminology than is the case with the previous articles. In the *Theses* Barclay showed that he did not think it was required of him to mention all points of Christian doctrine, because there was much unanimity which he could assume. Points of uniqueness were therefore stressed, while points of resemblance with other Christian groups were either omitted or touched upon in a cursory fashion.[14] The most vivid contrast between the *Catechism* and *Confession of Faith,* on the one hand, and the *Theses* on the other, is that involved in the growth of Barclay's mind about the human condition. Though in the earlier work he does refer fleetingly to the "Love of God toward fallen and lost man,"[15] he tends to be fundamentally optimistic and certainly is not explicit about the "condition of Man in the Fall" which provides the sole content of the Fourth Proposition in the *Theses*. Those who feared that Quakers might, like Socinians, be glorifying the Natural Light or basing their hope on natural human goodness, were bound to have their fears removed by Proposition IV, though they might not have been equally

[13] William I. Hull, *Benjamin Furly and Quakerism in Rotterdam,* "Swarthmore College Monographs on Quaker History," No. 5 (Lancaster, Pa.: Lancaster Press, 1941), p. 73*n*.

[14] I am indebted to George Hayes, whose doctoral thesis is listed in the Bibliographical Note (p. 256), for insight into this contrast.

[15] *Truth Triumphant,* p. 123.

relieved by any of Barclay's previous writing. In short, the experiences which led up to the writing of the *Anarchy of the Ranters* influenced Barclay's position, not only on Church government, but on fundamental theology as well. Already in the *Theses,* Barclay has arrived at the combination of realism and hope which is central to his entire position. He is not in the least naïve about what man naturally is, and therefore not surprised at human self-centeredness, yet at the same time he has boundless hope concerning what man, by God's grace, can become.

We tend to be perplexed by Barclay's decision to write his major book in Latin, but upon further thought our perplexity is dispelled. He used Latin because it was the one sure way of reaching the best-educated minds, regardless of geographical location. Though he wanted to reach his neighbors, he was not willing for Quakerism to be merely an Anglo-Saxon movement. Since Latin was the common daily language of the Scots Theological College, Barclay used it easily, and consequently did not have to write first in English and then translate into Latin. The Notebook shows how he could, with no hesitation, write in Latin directly. Dr. Anna Brinton, who is more able to appreciate Barclay's Latin style than are most contemporary Quakers, says of it, "Barclay's Latin style is easy, fluent and vivid. Its lineage is traceable to Jerome through the Western Fathers and the Scholastic tradition rather than through Bembo to the Romans or direct to Cicero."[16] Voltaire said Barclay's was the finest Church Latin he knew.

While some of our surprise at Barclay's production may be dispelled by explanation, there is reason for amazement at the way in which he improved so much and so rapidly. His first works have very little value, but in writing the *Apology* the young man of twenty-six was already a veteran writer and thinker, careful in most instances not to overstate his case, and equally careful to see that the entire work was marked by inner coherence. Each point is provided with a cumulative defense, in that he appeals to (a) Scripture, (b) reason, and (c) authority. Elbert Russell explains his reason for this threefold approach.

[16] *Children of the Light,* Howard Brinton, ed. (New York: The Macmillan Co., 1938), pp. 169, 170.

By this method Barclay makes an appeal to three great divisions of Christendom. The appeal to Scripture is for the benefit of Protestants to whom the Bible is the ultimate authority. The appeal to reason is for the benefit of Socinians and other rationalists. The appeal to the Church Fathers is for the benefit of the Roman Catholics to whom tradition embodied chiefly in their writings is the final authority.[17]

Even when Barclay's style seems to the modern reader stilted and verbose, it is not difficult to see that he was striving always for clarity. He believed that he was dealing with something capable of appealing to any thoughtful person, provided the writer disciplined himself sufficiently to present the ideas in a clear form. The fact that a special Quaker language developed so rapidly in the seventeenth century made Barclay's task far harder; he had to try to avoid jargon.[18] An editorial writer in the London *Times* (for Nov. 17, 1966) put the problem succinctly when he said, "Groups in societies always seek to protect themselves from the mass, and one way of doing that is to become partly unintelligible." That Barclay was aware of this danger and was consciously avoiding it is obvious to his careful reader. This is the fundamental reason for his taking the extra trouble to make his own translation from the original Latin into English.

The English edition of the *Apology,* which appeared in 1678, is now a collector's item and is much admired. Comparison of the Latin and English editions has been undertaken and is, at some points, instructive. For example, in the Latin (first edition) Proposition II, ii, the writer, in stressing the necessity of the direct inspiration of the Holy Spirit, says that this is the foundation on which the primitive Protestants and Reformers built (*Primitivi Protestantes & Reformatores*). However, in the English edition he leaves out Protestants and says, "This was the very *basis* and main foundation, upon which the primitive Reformers walked." *Truth Triumphant* followed precisely the first edition in English in this matter, though in later editions editors have substituted "built" for "walked." The best explanation of a minor change of this kind is that Barclay was

[17] Elbert Russell, *The History of Quakerism* (New York: The Macmillan Co., 1942), p. 177.

[18] We may be reminded of the observation of Leon Trotsky that revolutions are always verbose.

moving rapidly to the conviction that Quakerism was neither Roman nor Protestant, though definitely Reformed. His growing objection to Protestantism, as he observed it, was his conviction that it had departed from its earliest position, and had begun to emphasize apostolic succession in essentially the Roman manner. "But now," he says, "Protestants having gone from the Testimony of the Spirit, plead for the same Succession" (*Apology,* Prop. X, viii).

The part of Barclay's *opus* which has been more admired than any other is his opening letter to King Charles II. This is, emphatically, not a dedication. Leslie Stephen, in mentioning the *Apology* in the Barclay article in the *Dictionary of National Biography,* says, "It opens with a singularly dignified letter to the king." Stephen's word "dignified" is well chosen, because the author shows himself to be respectful without a touch of servility. Since he believes in a single standard of address to all men, whether they be servants or rulers, he uses the singular form of the second personal pronoun in addressing royalty, as he would in addressing any other human being. He does not hesitate to call the King's attention to the fact that his position is not merely the result of his own actions or merits. "God," says Barclay, "has done great things for thee, he hath sufficiently shewn thee that it is by him Princes rule." Above all, Barclay implored the ruler to apply himself to the Light of Christ shining in his conscience, "which neither can nor will flatter thee, nor suffer thee to be at ease in thy sins, but doth and will deal plainly and faithfully with thee, as those, who are followers thereof have also done." This was not the tone which was usually taken by those who spoke to Charles II after the Restoration, but there is reason to conclude that it was a tone which the King honored. At last someone spoke to him as man to man, and it was the Apologist of the Quakers who did so.

The fact that George Fox supported Barclay in his careful writing is really significant, for the mind of Fox was not only untrained, but unorganized. He did not and, in fact, *could* not present a coherent system of religious ideas, and did not even feel the need of doing so. He did not hesitate to exaggerate or to go beyond the evidence when this suited his evangelistic purpose. Barclay, on the other hand, after he had become a professional writer, was careful not to make pronouncements without support. It is strange that

Barclay, with his genuine sophistication, admired Fox, but it is stranger still that Fox admired Barclay. His admiration is indicated by his first known letter to Barclay, written from Swarthmore just three weeks after Barclay had dated his *Apology* on November 25, 1675. The letter was in response to one which Barclay had recently written him, evidently giving a report of his literary labors. The most interesting part of the letter is as follows:

> And now Robert concerning the things thou speaks of about thy books, I say, it is well that they are sent, and keep within the Rule of the Spirit of life which will lead into all truth and that all may be stirred up in your nation to walk in it for they have been a long time asleep, for the Gospell bell does ring and sound to awaken them out of sin to Righteousness and so all that have the Instrument to work in God's Vineyard be not Idle, but be diligent that you may have your penny.[19]

Though the early Quakers thought of themselves as living in a time of apostasy, they were actually living in the golden age of English religious literature. That this is true has been recognized by Coleridge and many subsequent readers who are sensitive to greatness, particularly in regard to expressions of the inner life. Men of fanatical temper represented one band in the religious spectrum, but it was by no means the only one. The literary greatness of men like Richard Baxter, Jeremy Taylor, and John Bunyan matched the scientific greatness of Sir Isaac Newton and Robert Boyle, or the purely literary greatness of John Milton. The strangest part of the story is that, however much the Quakers of the period felt that they were out of the dominant stream of thought, there is good reason to include the *Journal* of George Fox and Barclay's *Apology* in the roster of seventeenth-century religious classics. Though these men did not know it, they were very much a part of what Professor Whitehead so aptly termed "the century of genius."

Quakerism arose, not only in a time of religious and political turmoil, but also in the midst of one of the most brilliant periods in the history of the world, so far as science and philosophy are concerned. It was a time of great authors and great men, and Robert Barclay belonged on both accounts. Quakerism survived while other and apparently similar movements withered and died, because it had

[19] *Reliquiae Barclaianae,* VII.

two assets: ideas and men. In Robert Barclay, more than in any other Quaker of the classic period, the two were combined. Great living is the best thing that occurs in the human story, but great writing, though not the highest of accomplishments, stands very high indeed. It was Barclay the scholar whom his contemporaries valued most. George Fox was certainly telling the truth when he said of him that he "Writ many Precious Books in the Defence of the Truth."

It is not easy to know whether Barclay's central vocation was that of writer or thinker. He had to write, of course, if he expected to communicate his thought, but all the greatness of the writing depended upon the thinking. His writing is redundant, and we often feel bogged down in unedifying detail, but if we keep reading, we run into passages of such beauty and clarity that we prize them permanently. As we go along we are startled to read that "nothing makes a man truly a Christian, but the life of Christianity inwardly ruling in his heart,"[20] and we have our reward. It is important to know that Barclay was striving for clarity and that he often achieved it. Certainly he did so when he wrote, "I have felt the evil in me often chained down, and the good reached to and raised."[21] When Barclay set out to construct a system of thought which Christians could accept and defend, he was essaying a hard task, the importance of which was beautifully recognized by his descendant of the same name (1833–1876). His nineteenth-century namesake wrote, "If Christ's religion is to be advocated and defended by faithful souls, will He withhold His Holy Spirit and special blessing from those who cultivate the intellect?"[22] The answer seems to be that He will not.

Barclay's vocation as a thinker involved three important aspects, scholarship, writing, and controversy. These three were always intertwined. The intention was to defend the cause against all adversaries, but this could not be accomplished without literary expression, which gave added clarity to the ideas, and without the scholarship which gave solid substance to what was written. In no one production were the three factors more obvious than in *The Apology Vindicated,* the

[20] *Apology,* p. 276 [X, x].
[21] *Ibid.,* p. 303 [X, xxiii].
[22] Robert Barclay, *The Inner Life of the Religious Society of the Commonwealth* (London: Hodder and Stoughton, 1877), p. 569.

last major work from Barclay's pen. This was written and published in 1679, when the author was thirty years old and just before the striking change in his manner of life which will be described in Chapters VI and VII. *The Apology Vindicated* was written in response to the most thoughtful and sustained criticism of Barclay's theology which appeared in his lifetime. It was in the form of a book called *Quakerisme the Pathway to Paganisme,* by John Brown, "minister of the gospel." It was published at Edinburgh in 1678, with 568 pages. The criticisms were so detailed, and in many places so astute, that they forced Barclay to do some of his best thinking in reply. Accordingly, we have a more careful statement on many questions in the sequel to the *Apology* than in the *Apology* itself.

We are fortunate now to be able to study the Apologist's own copy of the book which attacked him so vigorously and so thoroughly. In the Bury Hill Collection is a copy of John Brown's book, with Barclay's signature and bookplate, and with numerous notes in the margins. Thus we can see how the man's work was undertaken. When, in his text, Brown asks Barclay a direct question, Barclay answers it in the margin. Being asked if he really believes in the resurrection of Christ, he says unequivocally that he does. Some of the criticisms were so familiar and, accordingly, so tiresome that the laconic marginal note is "The old calumny." "He first would have all study, all meditation, all prayer and wrestling with God in prayer . . . laid aside,"[23] writes Brown, to which Barclay replied with one word, "False." The same accusation, with same brief answer, appears in Barclay's own book.[24] As we compare the Apologist's notes with his final literary production we find it easy to picture the Quaker scholar in his study at Ury. That he believed in direct divine inspiration there is no doubt, but he also believed in careful and sustained intellectual labor. Far from shrinking from controversy, he met it gladly with the use of all of his mental powers. For this reason we can be thankful for such an attack as that of John Brown. Robert Barclay might have been reasonably happy in more peaceful times, but he would not have been equally productive.

[23] *Quakerisme the Pathway to Paganisme,* p. 441.
[24] *Truth Triumphant,* p. 848.

CHAPTER IV

PRISONER

God makes a prison more comfortable than a pleasant palace, and fetters of iron far surpassing chains of gold.

William Dewsbury

IT IS HARD to imagine the explosive power of the early Quakers apart from the experience of prisons. Though the imprisonments of men and women Friends were both numerous and harsh, there was one redeeming feature; the prisoners were allowed to write! Thus George Fox wrote his truly wonderful letter of 1656 to "Friends in the ministry" from the foul prison at Launceston. The imprisonment of William Penn in the Tower of London during the exceptionally cold winter of 1668–69, when he was only twenty-two years old, was partly redeemed by the fact that it gave him the opportunity to write the first edition of *No Cross No Crown.* When he was told that the Bishop of London had said that he must either recant or die a prisoner, young Penn sent word to the Bishop through his father, saying, "My prison shall be my grave before I will budge a jot." Though Penn was forbidden to receive letters or food from the outside, the fortunate aspect of the affair was that the young man was allowed to use his pen. The same was true of Robert Barclay in his most severe imprisonment, and because they were of the same type, both made rich use of the literary opportunity.

For a third of a century, imprisonment of Quakers was not only marvelously productive, but also a badge of honor. Far from being ashamed of their imprisonments, those who were denied their liberty of movement took an understandable pride in suffering for what they thought was the truth. Thus there is a genuine dignity in the way in which Isaac Penington wrote to his children and referred to himself as "Your imprisoned father."[1] The imprisoned Quakers naturally felt that they were reliving the days of the early Christians and were heartened by the Apostle Paul's pride in his bonds. It is important to remember that, by the time Robert Barclay experienced his first imprisonment at the end of 1672, there was behind him a long period of Quaker acquaintance with houses of correction and jails, beginning with that of George Fox as early as 1649.

In December, 1672, at the end of his year of decision, Robert Barclay was at Montrose where, at the conclusion of a meeting, he was arrested along with Lord Swinton, his father's earlier fellow prisoner, and four others. Though this imprisonment was comparatively brief, it was notable because it was the occasion of one of the most spirited of appeals to those in authority. This appeared as a joint statement, but there is no serious doubt that young Barclay was the real author.

> As for us [the document says with splendid defiance], we are not afraid of you, nor ashamed of our testimony, and you cannot vanquish us. . . . Our case is committed to Him who judges righteously! We are as regards our testimony and for its sake, well contented, well pleased, well satisfied to be here. Our bonds are not grievous to us: glory to the Lord forever! Who hath not been, who *is* not, wanting to us.[2]

On January 2, 1673 Barclay was released by the action of the Privy Council of Scotland.

Part of the heritage of persecution into which Robert Barclay entered, and which prepared him for his own ordeal, was that of his own father, Colonel David Barclay, who preceded the son behind bars. Six months prior to the Apologist's major imprisonment in the Aberdeen Tolbooth, Colonel Barclay wrote to his son from the same place on May 12, 1676, saying that the number of Quakers at the

[1] Letter of May 10, 1667, *Letters of Isaac Penington* (London, 1796).
[2] John Barclay, *Memoirs* of Scottish Quakers, *op. cit.*, p. 255.

Tolbooth was thirty-one with four out on bond. The sense of spiritual power in this group is unmistakable when we read, "We are all in health and refreshed daily by the Lord's powerfully appearing in amongst us and in a wonderful and unexpected way visiting us by his overcoming love to the gladning of our hearts and making us willing not only to believe but to suffer for his name's sake."[3]

This same letter tells us of the way in which the prisoners suffered as a punishment for preaching through the windows to the people who gathered outside. Andrew Jaffray, Barclay's cousin, "declared to the people in the streets out at them," with the consequence that the prison windows were tightly closed with lead nails, "so that we are barred from breathing the free air." The letter concludes with the request that the Apologist should intercede with the Duke of Lauderdale for a letter to the Council. Outside help was needed because of the threat that, if the same people should be incarcerated again, they would be put high up in the tower, "repenting that they have given us so good a house at this time."

The high tower to which Colonel Barclay referred with apprehension is still in existence and can be viewed by the modern visitor to Aberdeen. There is a spiral stairway of forty-eight steps, opening upon three prison rooms made wholly of stone and devoid of furnishings except for the chains fastened into the walls and a heavy iron bar, to which prisoners seated on the floor were manacled. The walls were four feet thick, with no windows, though a few slits in the wall do let in faint rays of light. In winter, the rooms must have been completely dark most of the time, except for the use of candles. The lower part of the Tolbooth, near the ground level, has been for the most part destroyed, but it was evidently somewhat less terrible. That is why the threat of sending men to the tower for preaching through the windows, which was actually carried out while Robert Barclay was there as a prisoner, was a fearsome one.

George Keith, a fellow prisoner of Colonel Barclay, wrote to the Apologist on the same day, May 12, 1676, saying that most of the prisoners had been at the Tolbooth for about two months. He corroborated the Colonel's account by saying, "we have exceeding sweet and comfortable meetings most frequently wherein the power

[3] *Reliquiae Barclaianae,* VIII.

of the Lord doth mightily appear in the midst of us, so that Friends generally are greatly encouraged, to the astonishing and confounding our adversaries."[4] The letters from prison were sent to Robert Barclay at London, whither he had gone on his return from Holland and Germany, after he had presumably cared for business in Amsterdam in connection with the original publication of the *Apology*. "Remember, my dear love," writes Keith, "to Friends of truth at London, as thou hast freedom especially to William Pen." How rich the spiritual fruits of imprisonment were is indicated when Keith writes of "the power of the Lord so gloriously appearing among us, which is preparing us for some great service."

The Quakers in the Aberdeen prison were strongly upheld, not only by their consciousness of the complete support of their Scottish Friends outside the walls, but also by the known affection of English Friends. The one who could express this best, and who took the trouble to do so, was Isaac Penington, who knew from firsthand experience what the Friends of Aberdeen were suffering. On July 5, 1676 he wrote, addressing "Dear Suffering Friends in Scotland," and concluded by saying, "This is the salutation and tender visit of the love of your brother in the truth, whose breathings are to God for you, and his praises unto Him, through the sense of his being with you, and daily showing mercy to you, upholding and preserving you in the midst of your sore trials and afflictions."[5]

Robert Barclay's first visit to Elizabeth, Princess Palatine, at Herford came while his father and other Quakers were experiencing both a lack of freedom and a great sense of Christ's presence in the Aberdeen Tolbooth. When he reached London he addressed to her the first of many excellent letters, which have fortunately been preserved. In this first letter he referred to her famous brother, Prince Rupert, whom Barclay, more than any other Quaker, felt free to approach. Toward the end of the letter Barclay wrote, "I delivered thy letter to thy Brother, who was civil to me. I also took occasion from thence to employ him to be assisting to me in one address I intend to make to the King, in behalf of my Father and about 40 more of our own Friends that are about some months ago imprisoned in Scotland for conscience sake, in which he promised his concur-

[4] *Ibid.*, IX and X.

[5] John Barclay, *Memoirs* of Scottish Quakers, *op. cit.*, p. 270.

rence."[6] This letter was dated June 24, 1676, six weeks after the letter from the Colonel quoted above.

The address to the King, who was prepared for it by Barclay's earlier reference to persecution, ends as follows:

> It is therefore, on behalf of the said suffering people, with all sincere respect, desired, that it would please the King favourably to recommend their case to the Council of Scotland; that a difference of character may be put upon them who have ever lived and behaved themselves peaceably under the present government, from such that are said to have abused the indulgence; with some present relief to those harmless sufferers, to prevent their utter ruin which in all probability will attend so many of them that live by their labour and trade.[7]

The immediate result of this appeal was Lauderdale's laconic reference, "His majesty is graciously pleased to refer this paper to the right honourable the lords of his majesty's privy council of Scotland." This was dated at Whitehall, August 7, 1676. Unfortunately, the royal intercession did not procure the immediate release of the already long-suffering prisoners of the Tolbooth and also did not prevent the Apologist's own arrest. Indeed, the sufferings and imprisonments at Aberdeen were of such magnitude for a few years that the regular Monthly Meetings were omitted from March, 1676 to November, 1679. The records do not begin again until 1680.[8]

Barclay told Princess Elizabeth, in a letter dated September 6, 1676, that recommendation of the King to the Council was frustrated by the influence of the chief bishops, but his report was not fundamentally discouraging. Of the prisoners, he said,

> . . .they have great reason to be contented, for the glory and heavenly majesty of the Lord doth singularly every day appear among them and the virtuous life of Jesus doth often flow among them as a mighty stream, that the Praises of the Lord is often sounded forth through young boys and girles to the astonishment of many and streams of Joyful tears are almost always running down the cheeks of the aged and oftentimes it is with them as the Disciples in the day of Pentecoste they seem (through the over-flowing power of God) to the dark world, as men reeling and

[6] *Reliquiae Barclaianae,* 1.

[7] *Some Account of the Life and Writings of Robert Barclay* (London, 1801), p. 27.

[8] See *Journal of Friends Historical Society,* Vol. VIII (1911), p. 55.

drunk with new wine, thus are shut up together 42 men in one great room who not of self will nor their own choice but by the Providence of God are placed for a time together in a heavenly community as Joynt sufferers for the testimony of Jesus, I this day take my Journey towards them not doubting but I shall be taken and shut up with them and with all cheerfulness of spirit am prepared to partake with them of their bonas not doubting but I shall also share of their Joys.[9]

What Barclay predicted in this eloquent passage came true in about two months.

By the time of Barclay's second and really serious imprisonment, that of 1676–77, the mood of the Council had hardened, as the refusal to obey the King's suggestion indicated. It would be difficult to overestimate the advantage, in Barclay's literary work, of almost four years of relative freedom before his worst imprisonment began. He could, it is true, write brilliantly in prison, but he could not do there the kind of writing which the *Apology* required, based as it was upon many works of reference which were not available behind bars. As it turned out, the five harsh months of imprisonment, beginning just before he was twenty-eight, brought the period of his life devoted to authorship to a climax.

The major imprisonment at Aberdeen began November 7, 1676, when Barclay was seized while attending a meeting for worship at Aberdeen. Since it had been long expected, the final arrest was something of a relief. Though separated from his beloved wife and children, he was wholly identified with those who made up the fellowship which he so highly prized. There is no doubt that the long hard winter without adequate heat, light, or air was a flowering time in the religious experience of Quakers in the seventeenth century. This we know because, however restricted the prisoners were in other ways, they were splendidly articulate. The letters which poured out of the prison sound like the report of a new Pentecost.

Among the many glowing accounts of the mood of exaltation existing among the prisoners is that in a letter from Gawen Lawrie, later to be appointed as Barclay's deputy in East Jersey.

Many a blessed night and day have I felt when the body hath been in bonds; and I know the same life is with you. . . . Oh! how I have been

[9] *Reliquiae Barclaianae,* 5, 6.

filled with joy when I have heard how God's power hath broke forth amongst you in prison, and how the glory of the Lord hath filled your vessels! No news was so welcome to me. Yea, I have tasted of that joy with you. Dear friends, I could write much; but I know God's presence is *your all,* and is above *all* words.[10]

It was, indeed, an ironical consequence that the frantic effort to avoid "conventicles" produced a situation where, behind bars, the accused persons engaged in conventicles almost continuously.

We know what the hardships of prison life were because we have Robert Barclay's own firsthand report in the dignified statement he drew up and addressed to the King's Council. He was carefully detailed in the description of grievances, reporting, among others, the following living conditions: "They have thronged up fifteen of us in two narrow, stinking holes, where each of us have not so much as could not be denied us in the grave-yard, and so are forced to lie one above another with boxes, notwithstanding the vault below, and not water-tight." He pointed out that many had endured the indignity of these conditions for over a year.

The paradox of creative writing in prison, illustrated by so many authors, including the Apostle Paul, Boethius, and Bunyan, is not as strange as it appears to be at first sight. When the confinement is not sufficiently severe to prohibit writing entirely, it provides a unique opportunity for single-minded attention to a subject, with freedom from normal interruptions of daily life, and often with a sense of spiritual elation. One surprising feature of the Aberdeen imprisonment was that Barclay was allowed to employ the service of a secretary. Thus the officials, though harsh in some ways, were lenient in others. We know of the secretarial service because, in the postscript to one letter addressed to Princess Elizabeth, Barclay spoke of his dear brother, George Keith as "husband to the Authour of these letters."[11] He spoke in the same letter of Keith's wife as "albeit but a young Woman, yet one, who through great Inward exercises and a sound work of Judgment in her heart, hath attained not only an excellent understanding but also a good measure of discerning & a sound & steady place in the truth."[12] How the imprisoned Barclay

[10] John Barclay, *Memoirs* of Scottish Quakers, *op. cit.,* pp. 286, 287.
[11] *Ibid.,* p. 21.
[12] *Ibid.,* p. 19.

could make use of a secretary, who was presumably outside, we do not know, but some way was found. Perhaps Elizabeth Keith was allowed to enter the Tolbooth for this express purpose.

The five months of imprisonment gave Barclay time for three short but important literary productions. The first of these was his careful letter to Adrian Paets, a theological treatise so well done that Barclay's literary executors printed it as the last essay of *Truth Triumphant,* immediately preceding his "Testimony" to his father. The occasion of the Paets letter was the Dutchman's request that Barclay consider the strength of the arguments which he had raised against Barclay's arguments in the *Apology*. The beginning of imprisonment evidently gave the Apologist the time he needed to meet this request. He wrote the letter in Latin, but later, after he had met Paets in London (and Paets had admitted that he had been mistaken in his notion of the Quakers, because he found they could make a reasonable plea for the foundation of their religion), Barclay put the letter into English.[13] Over a hundred years later, the Apologist's biographers said of the letter that it "has been considered by such as have read it with attention, to be as accurate a piece as was ever produced by its accurate author."[14]

The letter was signed by "R. Barclay" and dated November 24, 1676, "from the prison of Aberdeen in Scotland, where I am confined for the sake of the testimony of Jesus." It was delivered into the hands of the ambassador by Benjamin Furly, but, in order to give the recipient full time to answer, was not published by Furly until March 28, 1678. The dating shows that Barclay had seventeen days in prison to complete this closely reasoned work of more than 7,000 words. A careful analysis of Paets' argument, 3,000 words produced jointly by Barclay and his fellow-prisoner George Keith, was sent in advance of the main letter.

As he wrote in prison to his eminent Dutch critic, Barclay rose to great spiritual heights, especially in his full acceptance of the ultimate self-evidence of religious experience. The passage in which this is stated advances, in some degree, beyond the corresponding passages in the *Apology*.

[13] The English translation is also printed in Sewel's *History*, pp. 537–47. The pages in *Truth Triumphant* are 894–906.

[14] *Life and Writings of Robert Barclay, op. cit.*, pp. 120, 121.

But an example of an inward supernatural sense is, when the heart or soul of a pious man feels in itself divine motions, influences, and operations, which sometimes are as the voice or speech of God, sometimes as a most pleasant and glorious illustration or visible object to the inward eye, sometimes as an heavenly and divine warmness, or (so to speak) melting of the soul in the love of God.[15]

Barclay held that, because such an experience is self-validating, "there is no need of outward miracle." It is not reasonable to support the more certain by the less certain and the direct divine experience has about it a degree of certainty which finite human beings do not know in any other connection. Barclay was willing to use all of the evidence which he could adduce, but he saw clearly that the final stand is that of self-evidence. The truths of God's love, Barclay recognized, are contingent rather than necessary, but, just as we can know a contingent truth by the relation of another person, usually by means of the outward senses, there is no good reason for denying the possibility of knowing a contingent truth about God by His own supernatural and immediate revelation. Why not, Barclay asks, "since God is the fountain of all truth?"[16] The letter gives us the clearest indication we have that Barclay understood very well the distinction between natural and revealed religion, that he held firmly to the latter, and that he maintained that the revelation did not depend for its trustworthiness upon any outward or external evidence.

The second work produced by Barclay in prison, and the largest, was a booklet of five chapters called *Universal Love Considered,* dated in Aberdeen Prison, March, 1677. This is a treatise of about 17,000 words and occupies 29 folio pages in *Truth Triumphant*. The author's intention was to write on the problem of how far charity may and ought to be extended toward persons of different judgments in matters of religion. In short, Barclay wanted to know how far toleration can reasonably go. He realized that this was a difficult question, but he felt ready to face it in prison because there, paradoxically, he found "a true freedom and liberty" in his spirit. He began, not surprisingly, with a brief account of his own acquaintance with various types of Christianity. He then went on to show that love is highly ambiguous, since, instead of being the love of God, it may

[15] *Truth Triumphant,* p. 897.
[16] *Ibid.,* p. 896.

equally well be the love of self or the love of the world. He saw likewise that zeal, though a necessity, can be dangerous, for "as there is a true zeal, so there is a false one; and it is not more needful to have the one, than it is to avoid the other." Barclay recognized that those engaged in persecution of others were often zealous men themselves.

After some brief analysis of the departure from true love on both the right and the left, i.e. among Romanists, Protestants, and Socinians, Barclay went on to insist upon the central significance of the fellowship. The first Quakers, he maintained, were brought wonderfully into "unity and community." The fellowship in Christ, he indicated, was the root of which the "universal preaching of this power to all" was the fruit. In short, they came together for power, after which they scattered for service.

In this small and relatively unknown work, Barclay accepted with pride the nickname given reproachfully to him and his associates, and provided a fuller explanation of the origin of the name than had already been expressed in the *Apology* (XI, viii). He was proud, he said, that his people did not have that well-known mark of a sect, the derivation of name from a particular man. Much as he admired Fox, Barclay was glad that he was not a Foxite.

> But as the ungodly will always be throwing some Name or Reproach upon the Children and Servants of God; it being observed, that through the deep and inward Operation of this Power in them a Dread took hold on them, not only to the begetting of God's Fear in their Hearts, but even to the reaching and instructing of their outward Man; hence the name of Quakers or Tremblers hath been Cast upon them; which serveth to distinguish them from others, though not Assumed by them. Yet as the Christians of Old, albeit the Name of Christian was cast upon them by way of Reproach, gloried in it, as desiring above all things to be Followers of Christ: so they also are glad, that the World Reproacheth them as such, who Tremble before the Lord, and who work out their Salvation in Fear and Trembling.[17]

Barclay's unapologetic acceptance of the supposedly derogatory nickname was supported, in his own mind, by the Biblical references to trembling, particularly that of Jeremiah 33:9.

[17] *Ibid.*, p. 698.

The imprisoned author was insistent in his denial of any sectarian bias to his convictions. Members of a sect are self-aggrandizing, seeking to increase their own power or personal prestige, whereas those scornfully called Quakers were trying to be followers, not of man's inventions, but "of Christ alone, waiting to follow Him, as He acts and moves them by his own Spirit and Power." Quakers, he concluded, were not sectarians, "but meer Christians." It was in this spirit that the Apologist's famous descendant, Joseph John Gurney, expressed his own faith, though he may not have been acquainted with the treatise on *Universal Love.*

Were I required to define Quakerism [Gurney said], I should not describe it as the system so elaborately wrought out by Barclay, or as the doctrines or maxims of a Penn, or as the deep and refined view of a Penington; for all these authors have their defects as well as their excellencies. I should call it the religion of the New Testament of our Lord and Saviour Jesus Christ, without diminution, without addition, and without compromise.[18]

If Gurney had been aware of his ancestor's definition of Quakerism as "mere Christianity" he would surely have made use of this vivid expression.

The final point of Barclay's longest prison production was his insistence on the genuine universality of Christian love, understood in such a way that "no Man is altogether excluded from it." As he had said in the *Apology* already, there is abundant reason to believe that the love of God as revealed by Christ may be extended to *any* human being, "even to such, who by the Disadvantage of Education, and the Remoteness of their Habitation are Ignorant of the Name of Christ."[19] Again he made it clear that the outward knowledge of Christ in history, though very "comfortable," is not an absolute essential to being a Christian. If it were, the universal love of God would be denied. Furthermore, if God's love is truly universal, the ministry cannot reasonably be confined to the "narrow compass" of education and sacerdotal ordination. The universal love of God "excludeth none from ministering his Gift, as he hath it, albeit a poor Trades-man, or Mechanick Men." In like manner, the universal

[18] J. G. Gurney, "Brief Remarks on Impartiality in the Interpretation of Scripture," p. 16.

[19] *Truth Triumphant,* p. 700.

love of God is inconsistent with the limitation of God's grace to ceremonial acts. The central conviction here is not the negation of the sacraments, but the affirmation that "the life of Christ is Conveyed unto the Souls of all those, that are Faithful," even though they have not participated in any liturgical act. Like the *Apology,* this short treatise ends with the utter rejection of hatred, even to enemies, and asks the candid reader to decide which Christian group most nearly meets the test of veracity in both faith and practice.

Since the nailing up of the prison windows was not considered by the commissioners to be a sufficient guarantee against the prisoners' preaching to the people outside, the decision was made to remove five of the leaders to an auxiliary prison which was beyond the city limits and called, preposterously, the "Chapel." The five chosen were Patrick Livingstone, George Keith, Robert Barclay, John Skene, and Andrew Jaffray, but when the plan was executed on March 17, 1677, David Barclay was sent in place of Patrick Livingstone. Though it was claimed that living conditions for these men would be better at the Chapel, they turned out to be actually worse. The *Memoirs* of Scottish Quakers describe the harsh new conditions as follows:

> Here there was very little room more than to contain their beds, and only one window, so small, that the inmates could not see, even to eat their food, unless by candle-light, or whilst the door was set open by the keeper, at the times when he came to let in their provisions. On these occasions it was usual for a servant to come and sweep out the place; and when, to make room for him to do this, some of the prisoners would step a few paces on the outside of the door, the provost sharply reproved the keeper, for letting them have that liberty for a few minutes breathing. The little room they were confined in, had a chimney, but very subject to smoke. They would occasionally have a fire; but being obliged to send each time into the town for fuel, it was proposed to allow them the use of a small place under their chamber, to lay some peat in. This the gaoler dare not to do without the consent of the provost, who, when applied to, roughly chid the man that kept the key for offering to mention it. Another window might have been readily opened, to give them a little more light; but this suggestion, when made, was rejected with indignation.[20]

[20] John Barclay, *Memoirs* of Scottish Quakers, *op. cit.,* p. 290.

Meanwhile the crowding in the Tolbooth was even worse than it had been, with no facilities for decency. Burnett, the bailie, boasted he "would pack them like salmon in a barrel, and though they stood as close as the fingers on his hands, yet they should have no more room."[21]

To do serious writing in the restricted space of the Chapel prison might seem humanly impossible, but Barclay produced one more short piece after his removal to this place. On March 26, nine days after the transfer to more restricted quarters, Barclay completed a remarkable letter to James Sharp, adding in loyalty to his principles, "Archbishop of St. Andrews (so called)." As in the famous address to King Charles II at the beginning of the *Apology,* the prisoner again used the pronoun "thee" in addressing his exalted correspondent. In a most straightforward manner Barclay said that the Archbishop was reputed to be the "principal author" of the policy of religious persecution. The most eloquent part of this truly great letter is the following paragraph, which is all the more amazing in the light of the physical circumstances in which it was composed.

> And thou may assure thyself, that the utmost rigour that can be used to us, shall never be able to make us doubt of, or make us depart from that living, precious Truth, that God in his mercy hath revealed to us, and by us is embraced:—nor yet fright us from the public profession of it;—yea, though we should be pursued to death itself, which by the grace of God, we hope chearfully to undergo for the same; and we doubt not, but God would out of our ashes raise witnesses, who should outlive all the violence and cruelty of man. And albeit thou should thyself be more inexorable and violent towards us, thou mightst assure thyself, not to receive any evil from us therefore; who, by the grace of God, have learned to suffer patiently, and with our Lord and Master, Jesus Christ, to pray for and love our enemies. Yet, as thy so doing to an innocent and inoffensive people, would be an irreparable loss to thy reputation; so, the God of truth, whom we serve with our spirits in the gospel of his Son, and to whom vengeance belongs, (so we leave it,) would certainly, in his own time and way, avenge our quarrel; whose dreadful judgments should be more terrible unto thee, and much more justly feared, than the violent assaults or secret assassinations of thy other antagonists.[22]

[21] *Ibid.,* p. 291.
[22] *Life and Writings of Robert Barclay, op. cit.,* pp. 42, 43.

The legal basis for the imprisonment of the Barclays and other Scottish Quakers was that the Scottish Parliament had passed acts against what was termed "keeping of conventicles, and withdrawers from divine worship." What this meant was that, however peaceable the Friends might be when they gathered at their meetinghouse, they were liable to arrest by the mere act of being there. Because the harshness of this legal effort to establish conformity in worship was resented by others who were not Quakers, the Archbishop was assassinated in 1679. The importance of Barclay's letter to Archbishop Sharp lies in the fact that it is a milestone in the struggle against persecution on account of religious conviction. The statement is so convincing that it gives some credence to Voltaire's exaggerated claim that Barclay, by the use of his pen, "put a stop to the persecution." Though Voltaire, in the celebrated statement, was referring to Barclay's address to the King, he might have referred even more appropriately to the author's address to the Archbishop.

While Barclay and his associates were enduring the long Scottish winter of physical hardship and spiritual elation, forces outside were exerted for their release. One who worked for their freedom was Princess Elizabeth of the Rhine, who had heard, in her home in Herford, Germany, of the imprisonment of the man who had visited her only a few months before, and with whom she was beginning a voluminous correspondence. The news came to her by December 11, 1676, through Benjamin Furly. On December 19, she wrote again to her brother, the dashing Prince Rupert. The letter is so important in the record of the effort to overcome religious persecution that we are justified in reproducing it in full.

Dear Brother,

I have written to you some months ago, by Robert Barclay, who passed this way, and hearing I was your sister, desired to speak with me. I knew him to be a Quaker by his hat, and took occasion to inform myself of all their opinions: and find they were (accustomed) to submit to magistrates in real things, omitting the ceremonial, I wished in my heart, the king might have many such subjects. And since, I have heard, that, notwithstanding his majesty's most gracious letters in his behalf to the Council of Scotland, he has been clapped up in prison with the rest of his friends, and they threaten to hang them, at least those they call preachers among them, unless they subscribe their own banishment; and this upon a law made against other sects that appeared armed for the maintenance of their heresy; which goes directly against the principles of those which are ready to suffer all that can be inflicted, and still love and pray for their enemies.

Therefore, dear brother, if you can do any thing to prevent their destruction, I doubt not but you will do an action acceptable to God Almighty, and conducive to the service of your royal master: for the Presbyterians are their violent enemies, to whom they are an eye-sore, as being witnesses against all their violent ways. I care not though his majesty see my letter. It is written out of no less an humble affection for him, than most sensible compassion for the innocent sufferers. You will act herein according to your own discretion, and I beseech you still consider me as

Yours,
ELIZABETH[23]

Though there was some imprisonment in subsequent years, as the letter from George Fox of March 5, 1679, to Scottish prisoners indicates, the worst was over when the appeals of the Quakers brought results in the spring of 1677. On April 3 Colonel David Barclay, by an order of the commissioners of the Scottish Council, was released from prison and confined to his house at Ury, where he was prohibited from holding meetings. The veteran soldier's response was that he accepted his liberty, but as to the announced restrictions, he would act as he saw fit. Robert Barclay was ordered removed from the Chapel prison, along with several other men, to Banff. By this time the Order in Council by which the father was released seemed to help the son, for there was no one to take charge of him. He and a few others, accordingly, went before a notary and protested that they "themselves were freemen, and should pass away about their lawful occasions." By this means Robert Barclay regained his freedom on April 9, 1677.

All of Barclay's imprisonments, subsequent to the long and productive one of 1676–77, appear to have been brief. We know of them only because of passing or incidental references. Thus, when Barclay wrote to Sarah Fell from Ury, 27th of 8th month, 1678, he said, "I have been a prisoner since I left thy sister, but was kept

[23] *Ibid.*, pp. 29–31.

only two nights."[24] We have no way of knowing the exact date of this experience. The only evidence which we have for another imprisonment is the fact that Barclay dated his "Vindication" of *The Anarchy of the Ranters* "Aberdeen Prison the sixth of First Month, 1679."[25] This, we conclude, refers to March of that year. Since there are no other references, this experience must have been brief and relatively unimportant. On November 4, 1679, Barclay and sixteen other men were taken from the last Quaker meeting of Aberdeen from which attenders were conveyed to prison.

Fierce as it was while it continued, the persecution of Quakers in Scotland ended with marked suddenness when the combined pressure of Barclay's several lines of attack was felt. "Not a single reference to Quakers appears in the records of the Privy Council for the years 1678–1680."[26] The end of all legal persecution in Scotland came in 1687, with the proclamation which granted the right of public worship to all nonconformists. The fight for religious freedom waged by Barclay and many others ended in victory, though the price was high.

The paradox of vitality under persecution is wonderful to behold. The sorrow, however, is that as soon as Friends had won their battle against imprisonment, their vitality began to dwindle. In swift succession came the end of imprisonment and the deaths of the two leaders, Barclay and Fox. Together, these events signaled the end of an age of greatness. Quakerism exhibited explosive power for forty years and then became little more than another small though respectable sect. It is hard to avoid the conclusion that there was a causal relationship involved in this historical sequence. So long as hundreds were in prison, some of them dying there and some actually being executed, the fire of Quaker life and letters burned as a fierce flame, but it began to smolder once the element of tragedy was removed. Of the new period, Professor Nuttall has said, "Toleration had come, and the missionary exaltation had grown cooler."[27] Depressing as the radical decline may be, subsequent generations can be

[24] *The Fells of Swarthmore Hall* (Philadelphia, 1896), p. 342.
[25] *Truth Triumphant,* p. 237.
[26] *Reliquiae Barclaianae,* 149.
[27] George Fox, *Journal,* (Cambridge, Eng.: The University Press, 1952), p. xxx.

helped by the record of great days when the fire of commitment was really hot. It was never hotter anywhere than in the prison at Aberdeen. Hugh Peters, chaplain to Oliver Cromwell, when he heard of the most terrible of the imprisonments of George Fox, told the Protector that they could not do Fox a greater service for the spreading of his principles in Cornwall than to imprison him.[28] The same could have been said later of Barclay in Scotland. What Barclay and his imprisoned associates did was to demonstrate again the familiar possibility of the best things in worst times.

[28] *Ibid.*, pp. 254, 255.

CHAPTER V

MINISTER

It is a living ministry that begets a living people; and by a living ministry at first we were reached and turned to the truth.

—William Penn

THE MINISTRY of Robert Barclay began very early. Almost as soon as he became a Quaker, he was recognized as a minister or Public Friend, for it seemed to him only reasonable that a Christian should try to share what he had come to prize in his own experience. Therefore, he ministered in many ways, but especially in four: in writing, in speaking, in visiting, and in corresponding. All of these went on, in one way or another, until his early death, but sometimes one was the focus of his efforts and sometimes another. Thus, as we have already seen, he devoted a concentrated period of four years to writing, just as later he was to employ another concentrated period in traveling in the spoken ministry. Thus each part of Barclay's rich, brief life was given prominence for a period, though no part was ever wholly neglected.

The speed with which he moved into his ministerial vocation comes to us vividly as we read the Record Book of the meeting established at Ury. The date of his public acknowledgment as a Quaker is given with adequate precision, and seems to have been in February, 1667 (New Style). Here is the record:

> At the end of the fors[d] year [1666] Robert Barclay eldest son of the s[d] David Barclay having forsaken poprey In which he was educate In France and fallen In love with some general notions of friends principles came by the power of God to be reached and bow to the Testimony of Truth to whom also the said John Swinton and James Holliday were Instrumental.[1]

What is most remarkable, as we study the chronology, is the rapidity with which the eighteen-year-old convert became also a missionary. The record says that, at the beginning of May, 1667, Robert Barclay "went north" with John Swinton and George Keith, "and had a large meeting at Bayliston upon the first day of the week where the most part of freinds and freindly people In the north were gathered together."[2] Most of the traveling ministry was done by teams and Barclay entered heartily into such teamwork. With persecution a constant threat, nominal membership was unthinkable. A similar visit was made in 1669, when the new Quaker, now twenty years old, joined with Patrick Livingstone and James Holliday, and "travelled to the Orknays In the service of Truth and had many good opportunities by the way."[3]

As we read the details of these gatherings we soon note that people were "convinced" at almost every one of them. In any case, the expectation was clearly evangelistic. Barclay and his able teammates were seeking converts and were intent on making a difference. It is delightful to know that in the gathering in 1667, when Barclay undertook his first recorded journey in the ministry, his future wife, Christian Molleson, was "convinced." Two and a half years later they were married.

By the time that Barclay came into a position of leadership, the Quaker pattern of the traveling ministry had already been firmly established. Since there were no local pastors, some method was required to stir up and sustain the life in local groups. The chief method of accomplishing this was that of constant visitation. The period of Barclay's life in which he entered most fully into such visitation was that immediately subsequent to his longest imprisonment. In spite of being only twenty-eight, he already had prestige in

1 *Journal of the Friends Historical Society*, Vol. VII (1910), p. 91.
2 *Ibid.*, p. 92.
3 *Ibid.*, p. 93.

Quaker circles, partly because he was beginning to be recognized in the outside world, particularly the world of learned men. He had already written and published the Latin edition of his major lifework and was entering into correspondence with famous people. Moreover, he had proved himself to be a courageous sufferer in prison. Since the Aberdeen experience had both deepened and matured him, he was ready for another new development in his rapidly moving career.

Soon after his release from prison in April, 1677, Barclay traveled to London to attend the Yearly Meeting. Presence in London gave him an opportunity to have his direct confrontation with William Rogers, which has already been mentioned. He was tempted to return to Scotland when the Yearly Meeting was over, but was persuaded, chiefly by Princess Elizabeth, not to do so. She looked upon his release from prison as a splendid opportunity for wider service and urged him not to lose it. In a letter from Germany, dated early in July, she wrote saying that it was a cross to her "that you will not make use of the liberty which God miraculously gave you but will return into Scotland to be clapt up again in Prison for which we have neither precept nor example."[4] In this the Princess was referring to Barclay's letter to her, dated in London, June 15, 1677, in which he said he had no prospect of seeing her soon, because he meant to return home in a few weeks. "I expect," he wrote, "I shall very quickly be shut up again in Prison in which place it will be comfortable to me."[5]

Elizabeth's advice prevailed, and Barclay decided to join the strongest ministerial team which Quakers have ever sent anywhere. It is clear that the leaders had decided, in the summer of 1677, that the time had come for a really aggressive missionary thrust to the European continent. Already there were good connections in Holland, where both the *Theses* and the *Apology* had been published, and where some solid Quakers resided. Barclay's library at Ury included a volume, with his personal bookplate pasted in it, which is a collection of Dutch Quaker pamphlets, including his own *Catechism* in Dutch. The harvest seemed to be ready, waiting only

[4] *Reliquiae Barclaianae,* 23.
[5] *Ibid.,* 22.

for able and willing laborers who could reap it. Accordingly, the "first team" was put into the field.

We have more ample sources of knowledge of the missionary journey of the summer of 1677 than we have of most seventeenth-century projects. The major sources are four, viz.: (1) the travel diary of William Penn, the best available edition of which is that edited by John Barclay with the title, *William Penn's Journal of His Travels in Holland and Germany;* (2) Fox's *Journal* as presented in the Ellwood text of 1694; (3) letters of Barclay and others, particularly Princess Elizabeth; and (4) the travel diary of Edward Haistwell (c. 1658–1709).[6] Though Haistwell was a young man of only nineteen, he was already sufficiently mature to act as amanuensis for George Fox, who employed him from March, 1677 to June, 1678. This remarkable young man, like Margaret Fox and Robert Barclay, knew and used shorthand, though most of his diary for the foreign travel was written in a highly legible longhand which is still a delight to read, and which was available to the committee appointed to prepare the *Journal* of George Fox for publication in 1694. One attractive feature of the diary is the use of the left-hand margin of each small page for the number of miles involved in each particular journey. For example, the marginal notation gives the distance from the English coast (Harwich) to Rotterdam as ninety-six miles.

One of the signal advantages arising from the examination of the diary,[7] the shorthand portions of which have at last been deciphered by Douglas G. Lister, is that we learn from Haistwell, as we do not learn from the principals, of the careful preparation for the assault on the Continent. This preparation took the form of an extended house party at the home of William Penn, at Worminghurst in Sussex. It is evident that George Fox was Penn's guest for at least

[6] See *The Short Journal and Itinerary Journals of George Fox* (Cambridge, Eng.: The University Press, 1925), pp. 225–73.

[7] All of the diary, except the parts in shorthand, is printed in *The Short Journal,* cited above. This was edited by Norman Penney. For an article on the diary see the *Journal of the Friends Historical Society,* Vol. XIX (1922), pp. 59–62. Fox mentions his amanuensis, not by name, but as a young man "who travelled with me and used to write for me," *Journal,* tercentenary ed., p. 341.

three weeks. Though Barclay may not have been present that long, we know that he made Worminghurst his base during the week of July 8-15, 1677. The time was spent, not merely in making plans for the missionary journey, but in holding meetings in the area. The relevant portion of the Haistwell diary is as follows:

> And on ye 8th of ye 5th moth being ye 1st day of ye week: There was A meeting at WPs: where there was many ffrds as also severall hundreds of people: at uch meetinge G ff: & Isaac Penington, and Geo: Keith, & Jno Burnyeat & W P: declared ye truth, all being very peaceable.
>
> (And ye week following W. P.: and G. K: & Robert Barclay & S: Smith: had meetings up and down ye Country. Amongst ffrds many people coming in to meetings Inso much that yee Justices threatened to psecute ffrds).

After nearly three hundred years, it is still possible to catch the mood of feverish activity. Apart from Haistwell's account we could recognize this in the efforts in Holland, but now we know that the spirit of excitement began before the journey started. These powerful men were clearly stimulated by one another and, as a result, were the exact opposite of quietistic. They preached every time they got a chance, it being reported of William Penn that when he attended the meeting near his home in Sussex, he was often so pent up that he started preaching as he entered the building, without the formality of first sitting down.

One task taken up at Worminghurst, when so many leading Quakers were gathered there in July, 1677, was that of preparing an answer to Roger Williams who, after the visit of George Fox to Rhode Island in 1672, had published his partisan account of the debate with Quakers under the title *George Fox Digged out of His Burrowes,* the pun referring to Edward Burrough. The book which emerged from the Worminghurst gathering was entitled, *A New England Fire-brand Quenched.*[8]

The Quaker team which set sail from Harwich on July 25, 1677 included all of the major living leaders of Quakerism, with the exception of Isaac Penington, who had recently been with them in preparation for their effort. There were two women and two "servants" in the

8 See Rufus M. Jones, *Quakers in the American Colonies* (London: Macmillan and Co., 1911), pp. 114–18.

Ury: Robert Barclay's Home

Gordonstoun: Robert Barclay's Birthplace
(Photograph by Virginia Trueblood)

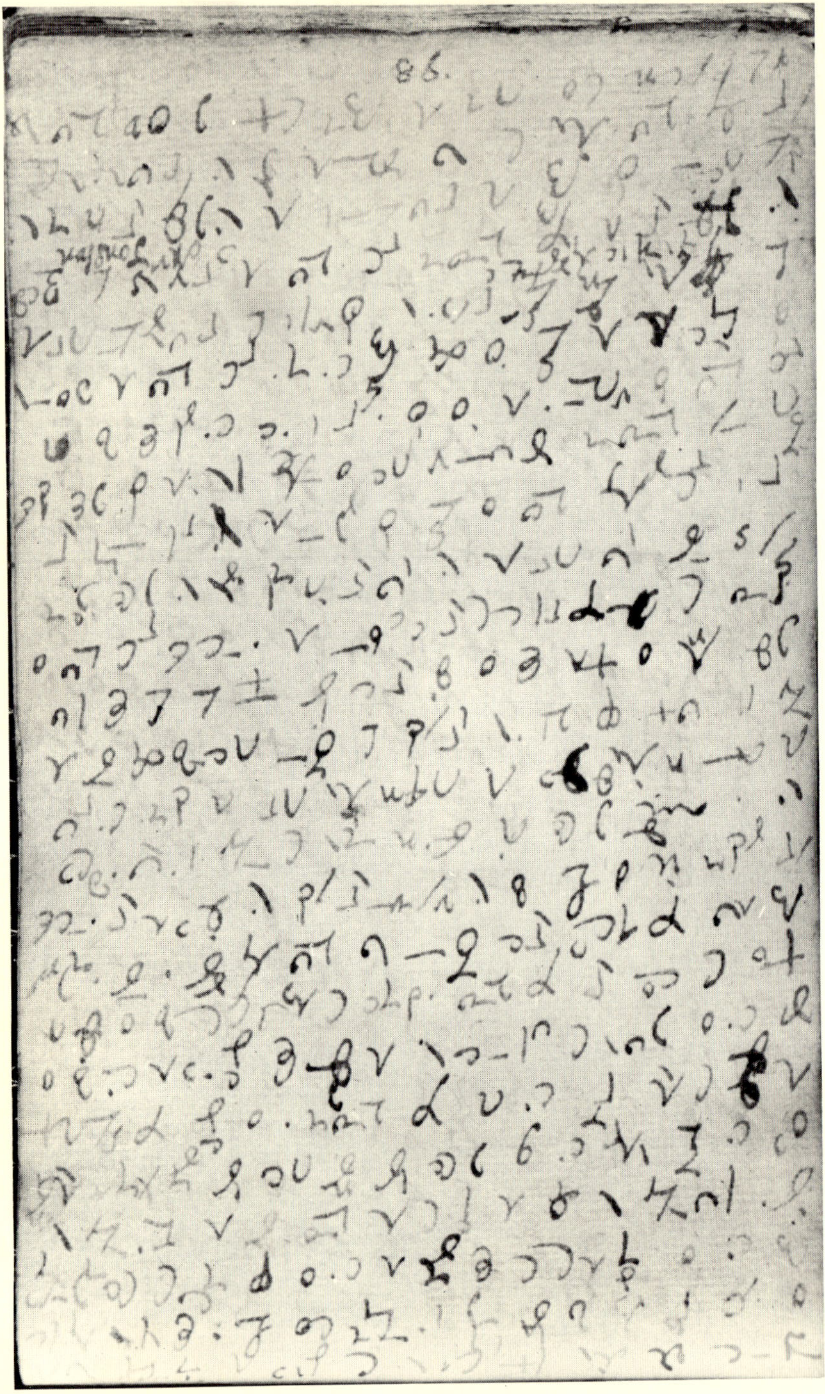

One Page of the Shorthand Notebook

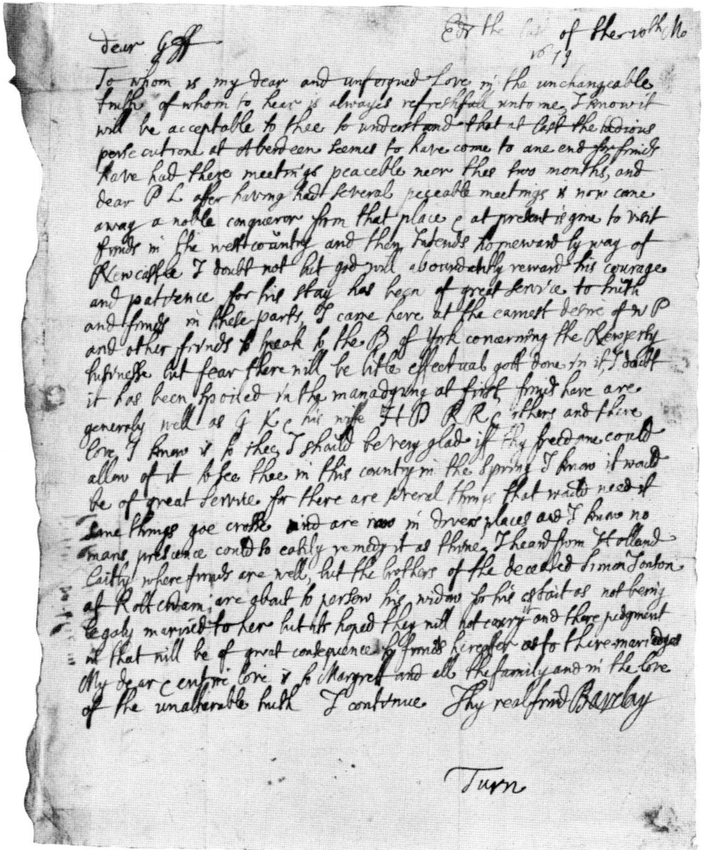

Letter to George Fox, 1679

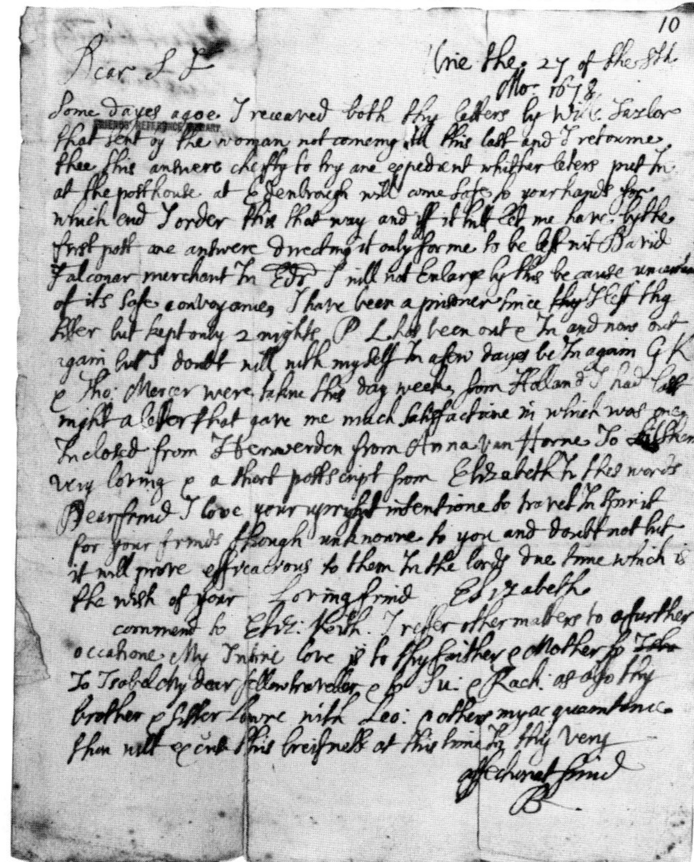

Letter to Sarah Fell, 1678

Princess Elizabeth
of the Rhine

The Barclay Coat of Arms

party. One of the latter was evidently Edward Haistwell, who kept a diary of the entire time, except when he was ill for three weeks. The two women were Isabel Yeamans, a married daughter of Fox's wife, and Elizabeth Keith, the wife of George Keith, who had already been Barclay's amanuensis. The entire party probably numbered twelve persons.[9] William Penn left such a faithful record of the ambitious Quaker enterprise that we know more of Barclay's doings in these few weeks than we know of any other period of his life.

The relevant portion of Penn's chronicle is as follows:

> Those that came over were *G. Fox, R. Barclay, G. K., G. Wats. J. Furly, W. Tallcoat, I. Yeamans, E. K.*, Myself, with two of our Servants.
>
> We set sail about Three in the Morning, being the Fifth Day of the Week; and got the Sixth Day at Night within half a League of the *Briel*.
>
> We had good Service those two Days in the Ship with several Passengers, *French* and *Dutch:* And though they seemed at first to be Shy of us, and to Slight us, yet at last their Hearts were much Opened in kindness towards us, and the Universal Principle and place.
>
> The next Morning Friends were fetcht on Shore by a Boat of Rotterdam, with some Friends of that City that came to the *Briel* to meet us. The Friends that came were *A. Sonneman, B. Furly*, and *S. Johnston, Vettekeuken*, with three Young Men that live at *B. Furly*'s House.
>
> After we had Eaten, we took Boat immediately for *Rotterdam;* where we arrived about Noon, and where many Friends came to see us, among whom we were comforted.
>
> The next Day, being the First Day of the Week, we had two Meetings at *B. Furly*'s House; whither resorted a great Company of People, some of them being of the considerablest Note of that City. And Oh, blessed be the true Word of Life that never failed them that rest upon it, and abide in it! The Gospel was Preached, the Dead were Raised, and the Living Comforted; and God, even our God, bore Heavenly Record to his only begotten Son in us: And Truth is honourable in the Eyes of several in that place.[10]

Penn's ecstatic references to the powerful meetings that were held in Holland are substantiated by similar reports from others, particu-

[9] The twelfth, Thomas Rudyard, was not listed by Penn or Barclay, but was mentioned in the Haistwell diary. Rudyard was later appointed deputy governor of East New Jersey, though he served only briefly. For more on Rudyard, see Alfred W. Braithwaite, *Thomas Rudyard, Early Friends' "Oracle of Law"* (London: Friends Historical Society, 1956).

[10] *William Penn's Journal of his Travels, op. cit.*, pp. 3, 4.

larly the captain of the team, George Fox, who reported a subsequent occasion as follows:

> The next day, being the First-day of the week, we had a very large meeting again, there coming to it a great concourse of people of different opinions, as Baptists, Seekers, Socinians, Brownists, and some of the Collegians. Robert Barclay, George Keith, William Penn, and I, declared the everlasting truth among them; opening the estate of man in the fall, and shewing by what way man and woman might come into the restoration by Christ Jesus. Indeed, the mystery of iniquity and the mystery of godliness were very plainly laid open.[11]

We have no doubt, as we look back from today's vantage point, that the four men mentioned spoke eloquently and abundantly, but there was nothing in the consequences to support their sanguine expectations. In spite of publications and many missionary visits from British Quakers, Quakerism never took deep root in Holland and what there was eventually withered, though there has been a slight renewal in the twentieth century. Norman Penney gives a just report when he says, "A multitude of flying visits were paid to Holland during many years, but despite these and the work of Dutch Friends the Quaker Church dwindled."[12]

Barclay clearly did his best in preaching to the Dutch, but his main target was in Germany.[13] Though the fundamentally modest man cannot reasonably be accused of snobbery, he was always an aristocrat and consequently was more at home with privileged people than with the rude populace. He believed that one of the chief ways of spreading the truth, as he saw it, was that of first reaching the makers of

[11] *Journal,* tercentenary ed., p. 338.

[12] *Fox's Short Journal, op. cit.,* p. 361. In the light of the relative weakness of Dutch Quakerism it is, indeed, a paradox that the first two histories of Quakerism were produced by Dutchmen. The first author of a Quaker history, in any language, was Gerard Croese, whose *Historia Quakeriana* was first published in Latin in 1695. Soon afterward it appeared in English and in German. Croese was not himself a Quaker. The second historian of Quakerism was William Sewel of Amsterdam, a Friend. His *History* was published in Dutch in 1717, in English in 1722, and often later and in other languages.

[13] The best modern account of the 1677 Quaker effort in Holland and Germany is that of William I. Hull, *William Penn and the Dutch Quaker Migration to Pennsylvania* (Swarthmore, Pa.: Swarthmore College, 1935), pp. 21–57. Professor Hull gives the names of Quakers who visited Herford prior to the major visit arranged by Barclay and Penn.

opinion. This accounts for his interest in Lady Conway and in the Stuart kings. If he could win one such he might, consequently, win many more. He may even have thought of his letter to King Charles II as a genuine effort to accomplish the conversion of the reigning monarch. However that may be, there is no doubt about his tremendous effort to enlist in the Quaker fold the King's cousin, Princess Elizabeth, of the Palatinate.

Princess Elizabeth was born in the castle of Heidelberg in 1618. Like Charles II, she was a grandchild of King James I, her mother being the sister of Charles I and Queen of Bohemia. Her father was Frederick V of the Palatinate. It is difficult for us to realize today how celebrated a person Elizabeth was in her time.[14] In the words of Rufus M. Jones, she was a "combination of philosopher and saint," who took far more satisfaction in the entertainment of ideas than in the pursuit of court life, which was always available to her. It is impressive when John Evelyn, writing to Samuel Pepys in 1689, mentions among the "illustrious of our owne nation of both sexes . . . Princesse Elizabeth, eldest daughter of the unfortunate Queen of Bohemia, to whom the great Des Cartes dedicated his books."[15]

Elizabeth's portrait hangs today in the National Portrait Gallery in London, and is much admired. It was painted during her years of residence at The Hague, where her mother maintained a small court. The latter was attractive to a number of both fashionable and intellectual people because of the "virtue and beauty" of the four princesses. It was at this court, in 1640, that Descartes met and admired Elizabeth when she was twenty-two years old. Elizabeth remained single throughout her life, Penn attributing her choice of a single life to her conclusion that such a life was "freest of care, and best suited to the study and meditation she was always inclined to."[16] Some measure of the family interest in philosophy is indicated by the fact

[14] In Letter IV, "Concerning the English Nation," Voltaire says of the Quaker missionaries, "Their labors were crowned with success in Amsterdam; but a circumstance which reflected the greatest honour on them, and at the same time put their humility to the greatest trial, was the reception they met with from *Elizabeth,* the Princess of Palatine, aunt to George of Great Britain, a lady conspicuous for her genius and knowledge."

[15] *Critical Essays of the Seventeenth Century*, J. E. Spingarn, ed. (Bloomington, Ind.: Indiana Univ. Press, 1957), Vol. II, p. 315.

[16] William Penn, *No Cross No Crown,* Chap. XXI, sec. 34.

that Elizabeth's brother, Charles Louis, when he ruled at Heidelberg, in 1673, invited Spinoza to occupy the chair of philosophy at the university. While Elizabeth was residing with her brother at Heidelberg in 1659, a Quaker missionary, William Ames, paid a visit to the castle and was received with marked favor. This was probably her introduction to Quakerism.

Elizabeth's public reputation was much enhanced by the fact that Descartes dedicated his *Principles of Philosophy* to her, affirming that she understood his philosophy better than did anyone else. The beginning of the famous dedication is as follows:

> The greatest advantage I have derived from my writings is the honour of becoming acquainted with your highness, and of being permitted at times to converse with you, and thus becoming a witness of your rare and estimable qualities; and I am sure that I shall render a service to posterity by holding them up as an example.

Nine years later, at the age of thirty-five, Elizabeth's religious interest had grown so much that she began to take an active interest in the affairs of the Protestant Abbey of Herford, in Westphalia. In 1667 she became its Abbess.[17] The Quaker missionaries of 1677 had very good connections with the Abbess, since William Penn had already visited her in 1671, and Barclay, whom she counted a distant cousin, had made a brief visit in 1676 before his major imprisonment. In 1677, two separate groups proceeded to Herford from Holland. In the second were Elizabeth Keith and Isabel Yeamans, by whose hand Fox sent a letter. The fact that Fox went to this trouble gives some indication of how great the prize before them appeared to Friends. The letter from Fox was dated at Amsterdam, August 7, 1677, and was filled with advice on the development of Elizabeth's religious experience. The leader of the team revealed the hope which all of the members felt, when he said, "I have heard of thy tenderness towards the Lord and His holy truth, by some Friends that have visited thee."[18]

[17] Several accounts of Elizabeth's life are available in both German and English. See the note in *Journal of the Friends Historical Society*, Vol. 42 (1950), p. 86. The note describes the work of Von Bernhard Rang who has made a general survey of the present state of knowledge about the life of the Princess. German Quakers have published Dr. Heinrich Otto's *Pfalzgrafin Elisabeth* (Bad Pyrmont: Verlag Leonard Friedrich, 1940).

[18] See *Journal*, tercentenary ed., pp. 339, 340.

There is little doubt that George Fox, like a number of other Quakers, believed that the famous and devout woman, though not yet a Friend, was already traveling on the Quaker road. The impression had gained ground in England that all was ready in Germany for a great new burst of Quaker life. Sarah Fell, stepdaughter of George Fox, wrote that her sister Yeamans "would entreat (if thou please) to have coppy sent her of thy letters from Princess Elizabeth or Countess Hornes, being desirous to hear how 'tis with them, in that remote part of the World, where the Lord is making himself known unto a few scattered ones."[19] Quakers thought that they had a big opportunity to lead a second wave of the Reformation in Germany, and Barclay himself, in a letter to David Van den Enden, a merchant on the Rhine, said that the purpose was to reform Protestantism as Luther had reformed popery.[20] Part of the expectation arose from the existence of a group of followers of an ex-Jesuit, John De Labadie (1610–1674), who had some characteristics in common with Quakers, and who for a while received protection from the Princess at Herford. The Quaker missionaries tried at first to win the Labadists to Quakerism, and failing that, to separate the Princess from a too close association with them. The general public tended to identify Labadists and Quakers. After De Labadie's death, Anna Maria Van Schurman became, until her death in 1678, the spiritual leader of the Labadists. Barclay spoke hopefully of her possible conversion to Quakerism in a letter dated March 16, 1677.

There is evidence that Barclay shared, at first, the lively hope that Princess Elizabeth might publicly join his despised and persecuted movement. In a letter addressed to Stephen Crisp, dated at London, July 3, 1676, he had written, "I have notice from some that have lately been with Princess Elizabeth, that she speaks much to Friends advantage, and saith that the Friends have been falsely reported of."[21]

The joint visit of Barclay and Penn to Germany contributed to the interest of both men in colonization. It has even been claimed that Elizabeth was the person who first gave Penn the idea of founding a colony, which he did only five years after the notable visit. Be that as it may, the consciousness of the existence of many persecuted Ger-

[19] *Reliquiae Barclaianae,* 45.
[20] *Ibid.,* 25.
[21] *Friends Library,* Vol. XI, p. 387.

mans, which he could not miss in 1677, remained with the admiral's son and influenced his crucial decision, once the colony was founded, to provide an asylum for such people. The contemporary importance of the "Pennsylvania Dutch" is a vivid reminder of the way in which Penn's ideas led to practical consequences.[22]

With the large meetings of Amsterdam behind them, Barclay, Penn, George Keith, and Benjamin Furly began their journey "in the common post-waggon to Osnaburg," where they arrived on the evening of Thursday, August 8. "We passed through a very dark country to that place," wrote Penn, "yet I felt not so great a weight and suffering in my spirit as six years ago, when I went through the same places." The traveling ministers, eager never to miss a single opportunity, left with the innkeeper Quaker books in High and Low Dutch. They reached Herford, "where Princess Elizabeth Palatine of the Rhine hath her court," the next evening, August 9. They occupied public quarters and even refused Elizabeth's invitation to dinner on August 10, but after they had dined returned to her for a meeting, which was attended also by her friend the Countess of Hornes and others. "It was at this meeting," wrote Penn, "that the Lord in a more eminent manner began to appear. The eternal Word showed itself a hammer at this day, yea, sharper than a two-edged sword. . . . Yea, this day was all flesh humbled before the Lord! it amazed one, shook another, broke another: yea, the noble arm of the Lord was truly awakened." Thus the enthusiastic Penn went on for many sentences, undeterred by the jumble of metaphors. It is not wholly surprising that the Princess, being eager to have some private conversation with Robert Barclay, urged Penn on August 11 to round up the servants in order to have a religious opportunity with them, which he did with his usual alacrity.

Penn's reference to Princess Elizabeth in the enlarged edition of *No Cross No Crown* is calmer in tone, but it still conveys the impression that the meetings shared by Barclay and Penn at Herford were times of creative power. Of Elizabeth, Penn wrote after her death,

[22] Many of the best consequences were, however, long delayed. The Schwenkfelders, for example, did not arrive in Penn's colony until 1733. The Moravians arrived at the "Forks of the Delaware" to establish Bethlehem and other communities in 1740. The ancestors of the "Pennsylvania Dutch" were Germans.

"Being in some agony of spirit, after a religious meeting we had in her own chamber, she said, 'It is an hard thing to be faithful to what one knows: Oh the way is strait! I am afraid I am not weighty enough in my spirit to walk in it.' "[23]

Penn tells us that on August 13, along with George Keith and Benjamin Furly, he prepared to begin their journey to Frankfurt, but that "Robert Barclay prepared himself to return by the way we came, directly back to Amsterdam." The meeting with the group at Herford had been Barclay's main purpose, which was now accomplished. He never saw Elizabeth again, though their correspondence continued until shortly before her death in February, 1680.

Because Barclay could not secure passage straight to Scotland, when he left the Dutch coast after separating from Penn at Herford, he went to London. From near London he wrote, on September 12, to his illustrious hostess, dealing for the most part with his interview with her cousin, the Duke of York. The Duke was gracious to Barclay when he asked him to use his influence to stop the persecution of Scottish Friends, "and said he would so write, as I desired, for my Father and me, but not for the general."[24] This response casts some doubt on the future king's complete acceptance of the principle of religious freedom for all.

The ministry of Robert Barclay was directed both to groups and to individuals, that involving Princess Elizabeth being the most intense example of his personal evangelism. It seems odd that he should undertake to be her spiritual advisor when he was only twenty-eight and the great lady was fifty-eight, but there is no doubt that Barclay relished this curious role. His letters to her were full of spiritual and moral advice, including much concerning the temptations to which her station in life made her subject. He admitted that being a princess was not absolutely inconsistent with being a Christian, but went on to say that dignities were often hurtful. In short, he told her from prison, it is not impossible for those of the nobility to be saved, but it is very hard. There is not the slightest evidence that there was any romantic attachment between Barclay and his noble correspondent, though their friendship was certainly deep. In the beginning the salutation was "Dear Friend," but on March 5, 1677 it was "Dear and well

[23] *No Cross No Crown,* Chap. XXI, sec. 34.
[24] *Reliquiae Barclaianae,* 29.

beloved Elizabeth." Writing from prison, Barclay certainly put on the pressure, but she resisted it saying, "I must not do anything from perswasion of others nor out of my own oppinion untill I have the light of faith for my conduct which I suppose you will not require from your true Friend." Barclay replied to this by giving a challenge to the effect that people would think being a Quaker was inconsistent with her station. Had she the courage to oppose opinion to this manner? In writing to William Penn, relative to a letter which she had written without effect to a duchess, Elizabeth said, "But since R. B. desired I should write it, I could not refuse him, nor omit to do anything that was judged conductive to his liberty, though it should expose me to the derision of the world." Barclay's last letter to her was written a few months before she died, dated at Rotterdam, July 6, 1679. In this final letter Barclay seemed to be aware that he had been overzealous in his effort to win the Princess to Quakerism, for he said, "I have over-charged thee with my letters, but knowing it is not the will of man that bringeth about the work of God, I choosed rather to be silent than forward."[25] Barclay had received the message!

After his arrival at Ury in 1677, Barclay wrote an epistle addressed to the members of the peace conference assembled at Nijmegen, trying to make them see the vast importance of their deliberations and reminding them of those Christian principles without which their efforts were sure to fail.[26] The plan of writing to them came to him, he said, while on his summer visit to Holland and Germany. "And as I was crossing the sea, and being the last summer in Holland, and some parts of Germany, the burden thereof fell upon me, and it several times came before me to write unto you, what I then saw and felt from God of these things, while I was in those parts." He advised the ambassadors to seek the deeper causes of conflict. Since the troubles were deeper, he said, than was commonly supposed, the cure would likewise be more radical. Barclay finished this essay on November 2, 1677, and on the 23rd and 24th of the following February Latin copies of it were delivered to all of the principal dignitaries at the peace conference, together with an equal number of copies of the *Apology*. It was a noble gesture, nobly executed.

[25] *Ibid.*, 33.

[26] George Fox also wrote an epistle to the ambassadors, dated September 21, 1677.

There is an important sense in which the climactic Quaker year of 1677 was also the high point in the career of Robert Barclay. He was not imprisoned again, except for brief and inconsequential periods; he wrote no more major works; and his intellectual development was complete. If he had died at the age of twenty-nine, his intellectual reputation would have been the same that it now is. The reader is surprised to note that nearly all of the writings collected in *Truth Triumphant* were produced in his twenties. The exception is his "Testimony Concerning his Father," written in 1686, immediately after his father's death. Even the important letter to Heer Paets, published in English in 1686, was originally written in Latin in 1676.

The years of silence are almost as impressive as are the years of intense intellectual activity. Why did the writing come so suddenly to an end? The candle had burned fiercely and brightly from 1673 to 1677, but with the end of personal persecution and the appearance of the *Apology* in English, this phase of his life was over. Indeed, his entire life, after infancy, was divided into three approximately equal parts. The first was the period of preparation, the second the period of theological authorship, and the third the period of public service.

Part of Barclay's ministry was that of friendship, expressed both by his numerous personal letters and by his visits. In his traveling ministry he visited many homes, inclining, as has already been suggested, to see people who were influential. We know for example that in October, 1677, on his way from London to his home in Scotland, he made a point of stopping at Ragley Hall near the present city of Birmingham, to give spiritual strength and comfort to Lady Conway, who had openly espoused Quakerism. The spiritual adviser of Lady Conway was Dr. Henry More (1614–1687) of Cambridge, though in the end the aristocratic lady seems to have followed Barclay more closely than More, whom Barclay had met in London in 1674.[27] Barclay refers to Lady Conway in three of his letters to Princess Elizabeth.

Another home which he visited was Swarthmore Hall, the grand house in northwest Lancashire which was the home of George Fox after his marriage to Margaret Fell, and the retreat center of so many

[27] See F. J. Powicke, "Henry More, Cambridge Platonist; and Lady Conway, of Ragley, Platonist and Quakeress," *Friends Quarterly Examiner*, Vol. 55, pp. 199–220.

Quaker missionaries in the first turbulent generation of Quaker history. Barclay went far out of his way to stop at Swarthmore on his journey north in 1687. Ury and Swarthmore had much in common, since both were great estates and both were dedicated to the furtherance of the Quaker faith. Margaret Fox's daughter, Sarah, kept an account book which is revealing at some points. Thus, under date of February 2, 1677 we read, "by m° p^{d} for 2: Guinnies to John Swinton & David Barclay."[28] Why should this money have been paid at this time? Was it a loan repaid? Was it a gift to Scottish Friends? We do not know. Sarah Fell's correspondence with Robert Barclay gives some reliable contemporary evidence of the speed of the mails in the seventeenth century. Thus she wrote, on January 21, 1679, saying Barclay's letter had taken twenty-three days from Ury to Swarthmore. She considered that it came "pretty readily," though it moved "by way of London by post direct from Edinburgh."[29]

The contemporary reader is often mystified by the reference to Quaker ministers because of the widespread modern belief that Friends have no ministry. This assumption could hardly be more erroneous. Friends of the seventeenth century opposed the system of employing clergymen, with all the rights, emoluments, and honors of their position, but this by no means meant a rejection of the necessity of the ministry. On the contrary, the "Quaker preachers," as Princess Elizabeth called them, were the most obvious among the many evidences of Quaker vitality! George Fox, most influential of them all, preached frequently and volubly to the very end of his life. Just before he died, he attended the meetinghouse on Gracechurch Street in the City of London where, we are told, he "declared a long time very pretiously & very audably & went to prayer."[30] We know, through the use of shorthand reporting, that sermons, like the last one preached by Fox, were often long and were frequently followed by vocal prayer from the same minister, sometimes at equal length.

Because it is our good fortune to have a shorthand report of such a sermon and prayer from Robert Barclay, we have a good idea of his oral style. This sermon was delivered at Gracechurch Street meeting-

[28] *The Household Book of Sarah Fell of Swarthmoor Hall,* Norman Penney, ed. (Cambridge, Eng.: The University Press, 1920), p. 455.
[29] *Reliquiae Barclaianae,* 45.
[30] *The Short Journal, op. cit.,* p. 222.

house. An eighteenth-century painting of the interior of that structure hangs today in the Quiet Room of Friends House, London, the arrangement being the same as in Barclay's day. The "minister's gallery," from which a man of Barclay's prominence naturally spoke, was raised high in the front of the building. The recorded sermon of 1685 is on the theme of which Barclay never tired and which seemed to him to be the major message of a Christian: that of the actual possibility of the presence of the Living Christ in the experience of anyone who was willing to be open to His coming. This was the message which had appealed to Barclay as a youth, and it was the message which he was still delivering when he had reached full maturity. A characteristic passage is the following:

> And this is the Living Manifestation of Christ whereby he cometh into the Soul and into my Soul. This is the Gift of God. We receive God's Gift, that we may receive Life from and by him, that we may Live this Life; This is that which makes the Yoke of Christ easie, and his Burden Light, and his Commandments are not Grevious to us.[31]

If the twentieth-century reader is surprised to learn of abundant Quaker preaching, he may be even more surprised to learn of the practice of ending a sermon with prayer, but there is no doubt about the recorded fact. Barclay conformed, in this regard, to the quickly established Quaker pattern in public worship. He understood that worship without prayer, whether spoken or silent, is a contradiction in terms, and he had no quarrel whatever with the value of spoken prayer as something which can draw seeking souls together. In this regard Barclay was following very closely the example of George Fox, whose leadership he never challenged. Normally Fox was as powerful in praying as in preaching. We must remember that Penn said of Fox, "The most awful, living reverent frame I ever felt or beheld, I must say, was his in prayer." The most appealing part of Barclay's recorded prayer, which amounted to more than 1500 words, is as follows:

> And O blessed God thou hast been graciously pleased to begin a good Work, a glorious Work of Righteousness in our days and times, Blessed God and Father, we humbly pray thee carry it on and make it prosper.

[31] *The Concurrence and Unanimity of the People Called Quakers* (London, 1694), p. 3.

Prosper the Souls of thy People in it that they may be a growing, thriving, and increasing People in thy Holy ways, and in thy blessed Work; and as thou hast sown in precious seed, and Planted a noble Vine. . . . Lord keep thy People sensible of it, that they may mind it and wait upon thee, and be preserved in that Root of Life wherein thy Blessing is.[32]

The public ministry of Robert Barclay went on to the close of his short life. In his last month, he was engaged in the traveling ministry, visiting Friends and others at Aberdeen. In the faded old Record Book of Ury we are told that he was "a faithful preacher of the Everlasting Gospell to the end of his days."

[32] *Ibid.*, pp. 8, 9.

CHAPTER VI

GOVERNOR

A mere literary man is a dull *man; a man who is solely a man of business is a* selfish *man; but when literature and commerce are united they make a respectable man.*

—*Samuel Johnson*

WHATEVER ELSE we may say of Robert Barclay, one thing which we cannot say is that he lived his life in cloistered solitude. He was a man of the world, with a sense of magnitude about all that he did. "He was," said Patrick Livingstone, "a man of the publick spirit, and laboured for the publick good of all." With his literary career behind him, Barclay was ready to employ his remarkable powers in new ways. In spite of the recorded dream of 1672, which seemed to suggest the necessity of choice between incompatible vocations, his life came to be remarkable for its very variety. He actually had four different vocations, and this was possible chiefly because of his decision to follow them one at a time. Each was approached with such astonishing vigor that his accomplishment in less than forty-two years was greater than that of many men who lived twice as long. This is the point of his grandson's remark, "As though he had had a view of the shortness of his time in this world, he posted through all the affairs of this life he thought incumbent upon him."

Beginning in 1678, Barclay gave himself assiduously to financial affairs. It is significant that his two diaries deal more with finances than with anything else, and that the first of these was begun in September, 1678, when the already famous author was approaching thirty years of age. The diaries continue to 1690 and thus cover the last twelve years of his extremely active life. Page after page tells of money borrowed, money spent, money loaned, money given. Why was this? We get a sufficient answer when we learn from the diary that the Ury estate was deeply in debt. The debt apparently increased during the years when both the Apologist and his father were sometimes in prison, and when the major effort went into literary production. Able as he was, the man could not do everything at once. At the end of Diary I we find an entry which is highly revealing:

> This pocket book began in the month called September, 1678; was ended thus in the month called March, 1685, being about 7 years during which time by the good blessing of God, I cleared of my estate of debt about 20,000 Marks, Scots. If it be his blessed will, he may enable me that in the next 7 I may do as much for the honor of his name. In the first place the good of my children and in a measure of submission to his will however he pleases to order things for me, yet not without the hope of his blessing. I have noted this the second of the month called November, 1685, at Ury.

Barclay went about worldly affairs with the same intensity which had already been exhibited in both his thinking and his writing. One result was that, as he increased his patrimony, he was able to be generous in giving. He gave a large part of the money needed to build the meetinghouse at Aberdeen and persuaded Lady Conway to give the remainder. When, in the winter of 1683/4, he received payment for an old debt from the Earl of Mar, he promptly gave half of it to George Keith.[1]

We know now, even better than we knew when the diary was not easily available, how great was the business burden which the affairs of the colony put upon Barclay. Many of the items listed have to do with his effort to help the other proprietors, as well as prospective colonists, to get their financial affairs in order. As we study the accounts we see how natural it was that many of the Apologist's descendants became bankers.

Barclay's interest in New Jersey was not at all strange in the light of

[1] *Genealogical Account,* p. 52.

his increasing contact with William Penn, with whom he had such abundant opportunity for conversation in 1677, and also in the light of his desire, for the sake of religious freedom, to cultivate the good will of the Duke of York. He was aware that, for the most part, New Jersey had been little more than a place of investment for wealthy men, by whom the interests of the poor settlers were sadly neglected. Since both Penn and Barclay were desirous of finding ways in which honest men could escape or avoid both persecution and grinding poverty, the existence of new land to the west seemed to them an answer to their prayers and hopes.

It is important to emphasize the fact that the intense interest in colonization on the part of seventeenth century Quakers was closely associated with their hatred of religious persecution. Increasingly, it seemed to the leading Quakers that the only hope of release from constant harassment lay in establishing new communities, without the entrenched inequities of the old world. They longed to set up colonies in which religious freedom could be assured by the law of the land. If toleration had come sooner in Britain, it is highly probable that the Quaker colonies would never have been founded. It is possible, of course, that other motives, including that of political ambition, entered into these bold new undertakings, but it has not been suggested that Barclay exhibited any self-interest at all. More than two years before Barclay's deep involvement in colonial affairs, George Fox had appealed to him for help because he was thought to have the ear of the Duke of York, who had a special interest in the largely unsettled land between the Delaware and Hudson rivers. Fox wrote from Swarthmore, January 18, 1680 saying, "And it would be very well if thou couldst do anything with the Duke of York concerning our poor Friends in New Jersey."[2]

Fox was already familiar with some of the New Jersey terrain, having crossed the area twice in 1672, prior to any substantial white settlement. "Then," said Fox in his *Journal,* "had we that wilderness country to pass through, and wildwoods where it was said it was never known before any man to ride, since called West Jersey, not then inhabited by English; so that we have travelled a whole day together without seeing man or woman, house or dwelling place."[3] When a

[2] *Reliquiae Barclaianae,* p. 51.
[3] *Journal,* tercentenary ed., p. 286.

few Friends did begin to settle in New Jersey, they entered upon a confused and perplexing political situation. This helps to explain the words of Fox, in the letter mentioned above, where he says, "And it is true enough the ground or beginning of that business about New Jersey was bad enough, but do what thou canst for the things they should have settled before any had gone over, for it will be worse to settle after, so that was wrong I am sure, but for the poor people's sakes that are gone do what thou canst." Just nineteen days prior to the date of this letter, Barclay had written to Fox from Edinburgh, saying, "I came here at the earnest desire of William Penn and other Friends to speak to the Duke of York concerning the New Jersey business, but fear there will be little effectual got done with it. I doubt it has been spoiled in the managing at first."[4]

The early history of New Jersey was even more confusing than that of most colonies, partly because of the shifts between Dutch and English possession. On March 12, 1664, three years before young Robert Barclay became a Quaker, Charles II in a grand gesture granted to his brother, the Duke of York, all of the territory between the Connecticut River and the eastern side of Delaware Bay, as well as all the offshore islands. The Duke of York, in turn, transferred what we now call New Jersey to Lord John Berkeley and Sir George Carteret, keeping what we call New York for himself. The official name given to the territory west of the Hudson, was "Nova Caesarea" in honor of Carteret, who had governed the Isle of Jersey from 1643 to 1651.[5] The name was derived from the fact that "Jersey" is a corruption of "Caesar's Isle." Soon after the grant to these two men, there was new confusion about ownership of land because Governor Nicolls of New York, unaware of the grant, had already approved the sale of Indian lands in the northeastern part of the territory. To solve the problem, the Duke of York declared that the sales made by Nicolls were null and void. After the Dutch had reconquered the territory for a short time in 1673, it was restored to England by the

[4] *The Fells of Swarthmoor Hall, op. cit.*, pp. 343, 344. The letter, which was written December 31, 1679, is also printed in *Letters, etc. of Early Friends* (London, 1841), pp. 257–59.

[5] Sir George Carteret (c. 1610–1680), a strong partisan of the royal cause in the Civil War, had made the Isle of Jersey a refuge for loyalists, including Prince Charles. The granting of American lands was an extreme form of patronage on the part of Charles after he became King.

Treaty of Westminster, on February 9, 1674. The crown ruled that all of the rights reverted to the King.

On June 13, 1674 Charles II officially restored the title and power of Carteret, but not of Berkeley, for Berkeley on March 13, 1674 had sold his interest to John Fenwick and Edward Byllinge, both Quakers. In this period of rapid change Byllinge, because of financial difficulties, sold his share to three other Quakers: William Penn, Gawen Lawrie, and Nicholas Lucas, who later acquired Fenwick's share as well. Carteret, having been persuaded by the Duke of York to surrender his royal grant of 1674, entered into what was called a "quintipartite deed," dated July 1, 1676. By this instrument a line of partition was made between "East" and "West" New Jersey, the line to begin at Little Egg Harbor, on the Atlantic Coast, and to run north to the Delaware River at 41^0 40′ N. The western portion was to go to the Quaker associates and the eastern portion to Carteret.

In March, 1677, shortly before Penn and Barclay began their ministerial visit to Holland and Germany, Penn and his colleagues set up an enlightened frame of government for West Jersey, a forerunner of the more famous one established five years later in Pennsylvania. The assurance of religious toleration was an important and not very surprising feature of the plan. In August, 1677, while Penn and Barclay were in Germany, the ship "Kent" arrived in the Delaware River with 230 Quaker colonists from London and Yorkshire. In order to give a royal blessing to the undertaking, the barge of King Charles II had drawn up alongside the "Kent" when the colonists sailed.

Though both sections of New Jersey suffered troubled times, the development of colonization in East New Jersey was made even more turbulent by the death of Sir George Carteret on January 13, 1680. Governor Andros of New York, in an attempt to assert governmental authority, on April 30, 1680 had Philip Carteret taken from his bed and carried to New York as a prisoner. Finally, after Andros had been recalled to England and his authority cancelled, the territory, having been put up to auction, was purchased early in 1682 by William Penn and eleven associates. The original documents are among the Bury Hill manuscripts. In order to share their responsibility, the twelve Quakers added twelve more to their number, including Robert Barclay and some who were not Quakers, especially the Earls of Perth and Melfort. Thus the Scottish influence in the proprietorship became dominant at the start. Barclay went to London in September, 1682, where "the Earls of Perth and Melfort, with the other proprietors, elected him Governor of East Jersey, and to induce him to accept thereof, they gifted him a propriety, with five thousand acres more, for him to bestow as he should think fit, the government being confirmed to him during life, by K. Charles II."[6] He accepted the appointment on the condition that he would not be required to go to the colony himself. The laconic entry in the diary is: "The proprietors of East Jersey would have me a partner with them and did choose me their governor."

What this means is that Barclay's leadership and probity were so highly prized that he, in return for the acceptance of responsibility, became a partner in the large enterprise without any financial investment. Though Barclay received no salary, the privilege of granting an extra five thousand acres to others at his own discretion was a great inducement to a man of his character. He was also given the right to appoint a deputy governor at a salary of £400 a year.[7] In 1683 the Duke of York gave a patent of the province to the proprietors, and Barclay's governorship began officially. One of his greatest reasons for giving attention to the colony was his hope that it might, like Penn's larger experiment, become a practical application of the Quaker theory of toleration and thus provide an asylum to all who suffered religious persecution. The Duke of York, concerned as he was for the Catholic minority in Britain, was delighted to have his colony of New York adjoined on the south and west by a colony devoted to religious liberty. One important reason for the appointment of Barclay as

[6] *Genealogical Account,* pp. 51.

[7] The first deputy was another proprietor, Thomas Rudyard, who was succeeded in July, 1683 by Gawen Lawrie. Lawrie was a London merchant, who had already endeared himself to Barclay by sending a truly moving letter to the Apologist and other imprisoned Friends of Aberdeen on February 11, 1677. Lawrie's letter is printed in John Barclay's *Memoirs* of Scottish Quakers, *op. cit.,* pp. 360–63. Rudyard was a London lawyer, once a close friend of William Penn, a proprietor of West Jersey and a "first purchaser" in the colony of Pennsylvania. He was deputy governor for only ten months, partly because his administration was unsuccessful. A moral lapse may also have been a factor in his dismissal. In his will he made provision for a "natural" son. See Alfred Braithwaite, *Thomas Rudyard, op. cit.*

Governor was that he neither desired nor sought the position. The official document of appointment, dated July 17, 1683, is as follows:

> The Proprietors of the Province of East New-Jersey, To our trusty and well beloved fellow Proprietor Robert Barclay, sendeth Greeting.
>
> Whereas the Power of Government of the Province of East New Jersey, is devolved upon us, and assigned to us by James, Duke of York . . . and we having heretofore, out of the confidence we had of Robert Barclay, his skill, Prudence and Integrity, constituted and appointed him Governor of the said Province, to appoint a Deputy during his absence therefrom, to be approved by sixteen of the Proprietors, upon the same Reason and Confidence, we do hereby confirm to him the Government of the said Province during all the Days of his life, as to have the Power of the Government of all the said Province . . . according to the Laws and constitutions made or confirmed by us, or to be made, which he himself is to observe and follow, as unto his Duty and Office doth appertain. And whereas we have agreed and are satisfied, for certain good Reasons and Considerations moving us thereunto, to commit this Trust unto him, and to give him this Character, without laying any necessity upon him to repair to the said Province; so likewise we have and do hereby give him Power from time to time as need Shall be, during his absence, to name and constitute and grant Commission to a Deputy Governor, to serve in the said Province, he being always approved by sixteen of us the Proprietors.[8]

It is difficult for us today, nurtured as we are on the stories of New England, to realize the intensity of the interest in the middle colonies. Actually, there was for a long time more general interest in the islands than in the mainland, even Bishop Berkeley expecting to establish his dream university on an Atlantic island. James Truslow Adams has helped us to see this. "The New England colonies," he comments, "were not nearly so popular among emigrants as the other continental and West Indian ones, about as many persons having gone to the one island of Barbados alone as had settled in all the Puritan colonies together."[9] In any case the backing of both King Charles II and his successor on the throne helped to keep New Jersey in the public eye.

The importance in the new government of the Earl of Perth is

[8] *New Jersey Archives,* I, 423.

[9] James Truslow Adams, *The Adams Family* (New York: Literary Guild, 1930), p. 5.

indicated by the name Perth-Amboy for the new capital of the colony. It was the Earl of Perth who pressed Robert Barclay to accept the governorship, largely because, after all of the confusion, he wanted the ambitious scheme to have moral respectability. But moral stature was not all that Barclay provided. Though his governorship was always nonresident, he contributed greatly to the success of the venture by enlisting settlers, and by the collection of supplies for the ships which sailed from Scotland to New Jersey. Most of the Scottish settlers were not Quakers, but it was a Quaker who did more than anyone else to give a Scottish character to the northeast part of New Jersey, a character never wholly lost. It is no accident that Princeton University, which has had closer academic connections with Scotland than has any other American university, is located in the area Barclay governed. G. P. Insh has collected evidence to show that Barclay threw himself into the colonization scheme with characteristic intensity and concludes that "the success of the settlement was due largely to his energy and enterprise."[10] The family record helps to confirm this by saying, "About this time he much employed himself, and was at much pains, in shipping servants and provisions at Aberdeen for East Jersey; about which I find him more assiduous than most of his concerns."[11]

During the summer of 1684 two ships left the east coast of Scotland for East Jersey, one from Montrose and the other from Aberdeen. The formidable task of supplying them, in preparation for life in an area where there was practically nothing except the land, fell largely on Barclay's shoulders. A diarist of the time records, under date of August 13, 1684, "There is a great meeting of the proprietors of the New-East-Jersey plantation where the Earle of Perth, Chancelor, is the main undertaker (the Town being called New Perthtown); there are sundry Quakers also ingadged; and particularly Robert Barclay of Ury, who has got from the King a Palatine power ther."[12]

As was expected from the beginning, Barclay used his political power and position to try to make the colony a means of emancipat-

[10] G. P. Insh, *Scottish Colonial Schemes* (Glasgow: Maclehose, Jackson and Co., 1922).

[11] *Genealogical Account,* pp. 52, 53.

[12] Fountainhall, *Historical Notices,* II, 550.

ing prisoners. On his thirty-sixth birthday he was hard at work at this task, though without immediate success, as the following account vividly shows.

> 23 December 1684. At Privy Councell a petition was presented by Robert Barclay, for the proprietors and planters in East New Jersey, desiring that such of the phanatiques as they thought fitt to banish, or who finding themselves uneasy at home, ather from poverty or principles ware willing to remove, might be delivered to them, they standing much in neid of tradesmen and labourers of the ground. The Chancelar and Register ware for it; but the Treasurer stopped it, (being no friend to thisse plantations,) till they should consult the kings pleasure anent it.[13]

Later, fortunately, Barclay's efforts were rewarded with some success. On July 29, 1685 he petitioned the Privy Council of Scotland to allow a ship to take twenty-four prisoners to East Jersey. He was wise enough to use an argument which the councilors might appreciate, viz. that the prisoners involved both trouble and expense to the government where they were, which would not be true in New Jersey. Furthermore, the ship which could take them was ready at Leith. On July 31 the Council ordered that the men be delivered to Barclay.[14] The ship sailed from Leith in September, 1685 on what was a tragic voyage, because the passengers, while at sea, suffered an epidemic of malignant fever, and nearly half died *en route*. In 1686, the Earl of Perth arranged for two hundred oppressed Scots, most of them Presbyterians, to emigrate to what is now Perth Amboy.

Endless administrative work was required, in order to provide transportation to the new world. An example of this is the letter Barclay wrote to Sir John Gordon, Advocate of Edinburgh, dated at Ury, March 4, 1684. The letter begins:

> DEAR COUSINE,
>
> I suppose thou hast wrott ere now, to London, to thy brother George, and proposed to him to bring down his veshell here to carry passengers to East Jersey. . . . There will not want passengers, besides those that fils another ship to be hired, and one that is goeing from Glasgow.[15]

[13] *Ibid.*, 585.

[14] The names of the men may be seen in *Proceedings of the New Jersey Historical Society* (1940), p. 210.

[15] M. Christabel Cadbury, *Robert Barclay* (London: Headley Brothers, 1912), p. 71.

No vessel that sailed meant more to Robert Barclay than the ship "America" which left Aberdeen in August, 1685, for one of the passengers was the Apologist's youngest brother, David, who died during the voyage. He had with him when he died goods valued at £150, with seven or eight servants. David, the youngest son of the Colonel, had bought a propriety and meant to settle permanently in the new world, as his brother John succeeded in doing. According to the father's will, all property designed for David was to revert to the Apologist as the eldest son, but Robert decided to convey it all to his brother John, who had already emigrated. Even before David's death, on July 10, 1684, John Barclay had received from Robert an estate of 500 acres in East Jersey, called "Plainfields," as part of the first division of 10,000 acres. There is preserved among the valuable records of the State Historical Library at Trenton, New Jersey, the record of the interesting "Conveyance" of property to John, "With the consent of his father and out of love and affection." The date of the document, which may be read with some difficulty, is March 8, 1686. In this, John Barclay is described as "planter and inhabitant in said province." A part of the expressed consideration for this transfer was the "extinguishment" by John Barclay of the balance due on a bond for 1350 Scotch marks which Robert had given him in 1684.

The diary provides a deeply human touch in the fact that, at the end of the first volume, there is a careful account of what Robert Barclay expected of his much-loved brother David, in the new colony. Because news came back so slowly, the words were probably written after the latter's death, but before Robert knew of it. The notes for a message to David included the Governor's great desire that the land should be surveyed. This led to the appointment of George Keith as surveyor-general. Keith's most important professional duty was to run the line between the two parts of New Jersey, a boundary which naturally produced a great deal of bitterness. At one time Princeton was west, at another time east, of the line. The two parts were not consolidated into one colony until 1702. The original document confirming the "Keith's Line," which is part of the Quaker Collection of Haverford College Library, is an impressive one. It is dated, London, September 5, 1688 and begins as follows:

> It is Agreed this Day between D^{r}. Daniel Cox Governour of the Province of West Jersey on Behalf of himself & all the rest of the Proprietors

of that Province on the One part, and Robert Barclay, Governour of the Province of E. Jersey on behalf of himself and all the Rest of the Proprietors of that Province on the other Part as followeth viz[t].:

For the finall Determination of all the Differences Concerning the Deed of Partition & all other Disputes and Controversies about dividing the Land and Settling the Bounds between East and West Jersey. . . .

At the end Robert Barclay, as Governor, set his seal. The seal of the proprietors of East Jersey shows a hand with equal balances, and beneath is a sheaf of grain between two ears of Indian corn. A few months after the signing of the above document, the close collaboration of the Apologist's brother and George Keith was increased by the appointment of John Barclay as deputy surveyor of the province, to serve under Keith.

Without Robert Barclay's moderating influence, the brilliant George Keith, who was always a debater, became ever more disturbing in the New World, particularly because he was so censorious. After he had turned Anglican he organized a debate with a young English Quaker minister, Samuel Bownas (1676–1753), who was traveling in America. This was held at Hempstead, Long Island. Bownas, to Keith's chagrin, won the crowd, but Keith succeeded in getting the young man sentenced to prison "for speaking lies and reflections against the Church of England." Bownas, consequently, was held in prison in New York for nearly a year.[16]

The kind of public life which Barclay lived in his final years involved many strains and even the possibility of dissension. The letters of the period show that, for example, personal difficulty arose in connection with colonial affairs. There are four letters from Barclay to Penn dated from September 7, 1685 to December 9, 1687 which reveal both the strain that existed and Barclay's determination to overcome it.[17] Barclay had been accused by Penn of ingratitude, Penn evidently referring to the fact that, had it not been for him, Barclay would never have been made Governor of East New Jersey. Barclay's reference to this is as follows:

[16] See Elfrida Vipont, *A Faith to Live By* (London: Bannisdale Press, 1965), chapter on Samuel Bownas.

[17] These letters, which are preserved in the Bury Hill Collection, are printed as an Appendix to Mrs. Colquhoun Grant's *Quaker and Courtier: The Life and Work of William Penn* (London: John Murray, 1907).

It came neer to me yt that I was forced to go out of towne without having more time with thee, for there were several things as to thy letter and mine which I had great desire to have discoursed further with thee concerning, being confident I could have convinced thee of some mistaits especially as to yt metter of gratitude, which graited most upon me. But I am resolved for my part yt love shall cover all, untill Providence give a further opportunity of seeing thee.

The major problem was continual pressure from New York, with real danger of annexation. Penn favored some kind of appeasement, perhaps even the giving up of part of East New Jersey in order to save West New Jersey, but Barclay held that this would be only temporizing and would fail in the end.

I am of the mind [writes Barclay] the same unjust apytit [appetite] will recurr again and E. Jersy will not satiat it, and as its like the same reasone of there not advancing in there trade may hold after they have devo[u]red E. Jersy so it may be suggested and prevail when thou may not be so neer; or perhapps not so well Harted to fence it of[f] so that a joint defence now seems to me saifest for all.

In all this, Barclay's great concern was that he should be fair to the other partners and not sacrifice them to Penn's personal interest or political needs.

The strain on the friendship between Penn and Barclay was increased by the insistence with which Penn, hard-pressed financially as usual, demanded the money which he had invested in East New Jersey. Barclay finally had to inform Penn that it was the general rule in Europe never to pay for anything "eer it be receaved." There is no doubt that this remark was intended as a rebuke. When we combine it with other statements in the letters, including those which express genuine affection, we get the most comprehensive revelation of Barclay's character available anywhere. The letters show that, however loving, he was not in the least naïve about the human predicament. Two examples of his salty wisdom are: "Compliments to princes are often forgot," and "I have all along seen the vanity and unfixedness of human assurances." Here, then, is shown a remarkable combination of tenderness and toughness. On the one hand, he did not let Penn think that he accepted his proposals of expediency, but on the other, he made Penn know how deep was his affection. In

Letter III, before Barclay dealt with their "transmarine" affairs, he made sure that his honored correspondent knew that he had been refreshed by receiving the salutation of his love. He went so far as to say "thy brotherly embraces reached and affected my soul." The outcome was completely successful, especially in the fact that the friendship remained unspoiled. Consequently, the most eloquent of all testimonies to the character of Barclay, after his untimely death, was that of his fellow courtier and colonist.[18]

One unfortunate source of tension was that the glittering prospects of new life in Penn's colony made recruitment for East Jersey harder. It must be emphasized that the problem of convincing desirable colonists of the wisdom of going to the new land was not an easy one, even when conditions at home were bad. The propaganda literature issued by the East Jersey Company was of four types.

1. *A Brief Account of the Province of East Jersey in America.* A pamphlet issued in 1682 by the first twelve proprietors.

2. Individual letters from deputy governors and other early colonists.

3. A broadside, 1684 (apparently written by Barclay).[19]

4. Scot of Pitlochie's *Model of the Government of the Province of East New Jersey in America.*

The first publicity material, the *Brief Account,* in which Barclay undoubtedly had a hand, is remarkable for its honesty, a virtue which the following paragraph illustrates:

> Lastly, Although this country, by means of its being already considerable inhabited, may afford many conveniences to strangers, of which unpeopled countries are destitute, as lodging, victualing, etc., yet all persons inclining into these parts must know, that in their settlement there they will find their exercises; they must have there winter as well as summer, they must labour before they reap, and, till their plantations be cleared (in summer time) they must expect (as in all those countries) the musketos, flies, gnats, and such like, may in hot and fair weather give them some disturbance, where people provide not against them, which as land is cleared, are less troublesome.

Apparently this disarming candor was not sufficient to stop malevo-

[18] Quoted in Chap. I.

[19] "It bears every evidence of having come from Barclay's pen," Insh, *Scottish Colonial Schemes, op. cit.,* p. 150.

lent gossip about the new country. Unless something could put an end to harmful tales, the chance of securing good colonists was slight. Here was an undertaking well suited to a man who had disciplined his mind, for a dozen years or more, with careful dialectic. Accordingly, the problem of New Jersey was attacked by a precise statement of particular allegations with specific answers to each. The broadside of 1684 meets the three principal objections.

First, they allege that it is a long and dangerous voyage thither! To which it is answered that ordinarily it is not above 6 or 7 weeks sailing from Scotland, which in a good ship well victualled and with good Company in the Summer Time is rather a pleasant Divertissement than a Trouble or Toyl. . . .

Next, they say, there is no Company to be had save Barbarians, Woods and Wilderness! To which it is answered that this Country has been Peopled and Planted these several years by gone. . . . Nor are the woods there anything so wild and inhospitable as the mountains here. . . .

Lastly, they object that far fetcht Fowls have fair Feathers, and they do not believe the half that is written and spoken in Commendation of these Countreys. To which it is answered, they may as easily deny the truth of everything which they have not seen with their own eyes, for all these things are as verily true as that there is any such pleasant Country as France, Italy, Spain, etc. The things being matter of Fact are confirmed by letters from persons of undoubted credit, living on the place, and by certain Information of many Eye-witnesses, who having once been there. can never after be induced to live in Scotland, nor can it reasonably be imagined that the persons above-written are all fools, to be imposed on by lies and fancies.

In addition to such specific rebuttal, Barclay was at pains to make a general appeal on high moral grounds.

There is nothing more strange than to see our Commons so besotted with the love of their own misery, that rather than quit their Native Country, they will live in much toyl and penury so long as they have strength, being hardly able all their life to acquire so much Riches as can save themselves from begging or starving when they grow old: meantime their children (so soon as they are able to walk) are exposed to the Cruelties of Fortune and the Charity of others, naked and hungry, begging Food and Rayment from those that either cannot or will not help them: and yet can hardly be perswaded to go to a most profitable fertile and safe, Country, where they may have everything that is either necessary, profitable or pleasant for the life of man with very little pains and industry.

We have had the good fortune, in recent years, of having made available to us several scholarly studies of the period of New Jersey history which included Robert Barclay's governorship. These are part of what is called the New Jersey Historical Series, handsomely recognized by Governor Richard J. Hughes. The volumes have been planned and produced as part of the tercentenary celebration, by the New Jersey Tercentenary Commission. The most valuable of these, for Barclay studies, is *The New Jersey Proprietors and Their Lands,* by John E. Pomfret.[20] Valuable helps to the contemporary reader are the reproduction of the seal of East Jersey (p. 38), an Appendix giving the names of proprietors and governors, with their dates, and a frontispiece map, showing the Keith line of 1687, as well as the Lawrence survey line of 1743, which ran east of Princeton.

The New Jersey State Historical Library is rich in relevant materials. For example it contains, under date of September 1, 1701, a deed by "Robert Barclay of Urie, son and heir of Robert Barclay of Urie." It recites the dates of the original patents, by and to whom granted, the names of the original twelve proprietors, the other twelve to whom they sold half of their holdings, and other historical facts connected with the province of "Nova Caesarea."

Altogether we may truly say that the East Jersey episode was one of the richest experiences of Barclay's life, though it is the part of his life which is least known. Many who have heard of Barclay as the major Quaker theologian do not connect his name with colonial history at all. The fact that he could accept, unselfishly, such heavy responsibilities is important for the total understanding of a great man. He was great, in part, because his life had truly balancing aspects. Being an upholder of a philosophy based ultimately upon experience, he was convinced that there is little value in theory when it is not tested in practice. His work as a colonial statesman gave him a laboratory test

[20] Princeton, N. J.: D. Van Nostrand Co., 1964. For other relevant information see John E. Pomfret, "The Proprietors of the Province of East New Jersey, 1682–1702," *Pennsylvania Magazine of History and Biography,* Vol. LXXVII, No. 3 (July, 1953).

of some of his most cherished ideas. Accordingly, the relatively unused term, "Governor Barclay," is not really as strange as it at first appears.

The work of colonization, in which both Penn and Barclay were deeply involved, constitutes one important difference between the Quaker Movement of the seventeenth century and the other religious movements which, in spite of some similarities, soon withered and died. These others had none of the boldness of vision which is necessary if colonies are to be made into successful ventures. William C. Braithwaite, the distinguished historian of early Quakerism, was convinced that the new Utopias overseas provided the extra element, beyond organization and intellectual elaboration, needed for wholeness and therefore for survival. "Without colonization," he said, "Quakerism would not have vindicated itself as a Faith able to reshape the whole of life."[21]

[21] William Braithwaite, *Second Period of Quakerism, op. cit.*, p. 414.

CHAPTER VII

COURTIER

I look on the bearer, Robert Barclay, to be well affected to me.

—James II

One of the factors which made Barclay's life in his thirties markedly different from his life in his twenties was the friendship with James II, first as Duke of York and then as King. The open friendliness of the Duke of York is well illustrated by the following brief letter, dated from Windsor, June 27, 1680:

I send you here inclosed a letter to the Lord Advocate as you desired. I choose to write to him because I had spoken to him of it when I was in Scotland, you see I do my part, & I make no doubt but that he will do his, & then you will have no further trouble in that affair.

—JAMES[1]

On October 13, 1680 the Earl of Perth wrote to Barclay, "The Duke speaks wonderfully kindly of you."

The paradox of an affinity between Robert Barclay and King James II is acute. Though the men were distant relatives, the contrasts between their characters and ways of life were enormous. In the first place, Barclay was a strong family man, never doubted in his fidelity, whereas James was an unblushing libertine, both before and

[1] *Reliquiae Barclaianae,* p. 52.

after his marriage to Ann Hyde. Indeed, he had a number of acknowledged illegitimate children. In the second place, Barclay was one of the leading Quakers, outspoken in his criticism of popery, while James was fanatically devoted to Roman Catholicism. In the third place, Barclay was a man of peace, while King James both before and after his coronation was a vigorous upholder of the military, particularly the naval arm, of which he was twice appointed Lord High Admiral.

What is most strange is that any man of Barclay's sincere piety and unchallenged probity would even be acceptable in Stuart court circles. After the Restoration, especial ridicule was heaped upon those who were foolish enough to let their religion affect their conduct or limit their private pleasures. Such ridicule "was considered a kind of test of loyalty to the then sovereign and government." There were, of course, people who maintained an unapologetic piety, but these were not conspicuous in court circles. Barclay's acceptance in such circles is both a mystery and a revelation of the man's character. Sewel's explanation may be best, when he says, "Besides, he was of a friendly and pleasant, yet grave conversation, and eminently fitted for composing differences; and he really lived up to what he professed, being of an unblameable deportment, truly pious, and well beloved of those he conversed with."[2] There is a good reason to know that King James II did not admire Quakerism, but there is equally good reason to know that he admired the philosopher of Quakerism.

The contrast between James and Penn was also great, though not equally great. The King and William Penn were brought together, as were the King and Barclay, by their common interest in religious toleration, but on purely political issues they were poles apart. This is made evident by the effort of Penn to strengthen parliamentary government, even to the extent of upholding Algernon Sidney, who had been a member of the Long Parliament and who had been driven into exile at the time of the Restoration. Yet Penn, like Barclay, was a close associate of King James up to the time of the King's final flight from England on Robert Barclay's fortieth birthday. So close, indeed, was Penn to the Roman Catholic monarch that he lived under a cloud after the "glorious revolution," being confined, for a

[2] Sewel's *History, op. cit.,* p. 628.

time, to his own home. This is what led to the writing of the book, *Fruits of Solitude*.

King James II was a complex and mystifying human being. On the one side, he was capable of great loyalty, as his support of Barclay and Penn proved, while on the other he was capable of deceit and intrigue. After he joined the Roman Church his governing policies always followed from this connection. One of these was the emancipation of his fellow Roman Catholics, while another was the recovery of England for Catholicism. He would ally himself with any who seemed useful in the accomplishment of these purposes. That he was a man of commanding appearance is shown by his portraits in the National Portrait Gallery and by the large bronze statue by Grinling Gibbons. This presents James in Roman habit, and was first erected in Whitehall on Christmas Day, 1686, but now stands in front of the National Gallery, facing Trafalgar Square. Whether James II was sincere has often been debated. Barclay evidently thought that he was, but there is a strong body of contemporary opinion to the contrary. Trevelyan gives the mature judgment of the modern historian when he says, " . . . it was only when the breach with Episcopacy drove him to dissemble, that he took into his mouth Penn's noble doctrine of universal Toleration."[3]

Because the Catholicism of James was so extreme, those who were known to be friendly to him were naturally suspected of leanings in the same direction. Thus, William Penn was frequently supposed to be a Jesuit in disguise. It was confidently reported that he had received holy orders at Rome, and that he regularly performed Mass in the royal chapel at Whitehall. The problem presented by the obvious fact of his marriage was easily met by the hypothesis that he had been given a papal dispensation to have a wife and children. Though Penn denied the rumor, his denials were not believed,[4] but actually, of course, there was not the slightest truth in the allegation. Penn was hated for his closeness to the King, but he seems not to have used his opportunity for his own advantage. For this reason, argued William I.

[3] G. M. Trevelyan, *England Under the Stuarts* (16th ed.; New York: G. P. Putnam's Sons, 1933), Vol. V, p. 428.

[4] Even Dr. John Tillotson, Dean of St. Paul's and later appointed by William III as Archbishop of Canterbury, helped to spread the report that Penn was a Jesuit.

Hull, it would be better to call him "mediator" than "courtier." The same can be said for Barclay. In Professor Hull's language, it is fair to say, "Amidst so many false and doubtful courtiers, and without apparently any other real friend, even a king might welcome the friendly companionship of a great and kindly man like Penn, who had no axe of his own for the royal grindstone and sought no favours for himself."[5]

While Barclay was not suspected of Roman Catholic leanings to the degree that Penn was, he sometimes had to face the charge. The fact that he had studied, as a boy, in a Roman Catholic School in Paris, where his uncle was rector, helped to make the accusation plausible to many minds. A characteristic blast was that of the Aberdeen students: "It is well known that R. B. was brought up in a Popish College, and it is thought by many that he is a Jesuit Emissary, which we are the rather induced to believe of him, because his practices agree so exactly with the Jesuit morals."[6] The chief practice referred to was that of urging, as Penn did, complete freedom of action to Roman Catholics, along with all other dissenters. Barclay supported such a policy, not because he admired Roman Catholic theology or practice, which he did not, but because he saw no valid point at which to draw the line, once the principle of religious freedom was adopted. He admitted difficulties in this, but he was convinced that the difficulties of compulsion were greater than the difficulties of toleration.

It may be wondered how a man of Barclay's firm principles, which included the rejection of flattering address, could be acceptable at court functions. He must have appeared eccentric in a setting in which sickening adulation was regularly expressed, especially by those seeking favors. One mode of speech for all, which the opening address of the *Apology* illustrates, was clearly unfashionable. We have some idea of how the honest Barclay handled this problem when we read, "but being known not to be a man of form, I hope, my reader will excuse me."[7] In the practice of refusing to overstate gratitude, Bar-

[5] William I. Hull, *William Penn, a Topical Biography* (New York: Oxford University Press, 1937), p. 245.

[6] *Quakerism Canvassed*, p. 57.

[7] From the sentence which ends the "Advertisement to the Reader" preceding the letter to Adrian Paets. See *Truth Triumphant*, p. 893.

clay was supported by his fellow Quakers in Scotland. Thus, after they were assured in 1687 of toleration, the Scottish Friends, having received from Barclay a letter urging them to express thanks to the King, replied that Barclay, himself, was the one who should write the letter. They requested at the same time, however, that he not offer *humble* thanks, "we judging them only proper to God (and not to man) who is the alone fountain of all Goodness even as it streams through man as one Instrument."[8] Barclay prepared the statement at once. His letter shows that he believed, as we have already said, that the King was sincerely devoted to liberty of conscience and to freedom of worship, in which judgment he was possibly wrong. The strongest evidence that he may have been mistaken in his generous judgment is the fact that James permitted the most horrible persecution of the Covenanters, immediately after his accession to the throne in 1685. In contrast, Barclay, as has been shown in the preceding chapter, did all that he could for the unfortunate victims of this particular persecution, and helped them to emigrate to New Jersey. That he was not naïve, however, is indicated by his remark to Penn, mentioned in Chapter VI, when he said that "compliments to princes are often forgot, and seldom have the desired effect."

One of the best accounts of Barclay's style at court is that written by George Keith, who though critical, at the time, of Barclay's theology, nevertheless contrasted Barclay favorably with Penn. Penn, Keith said, "is known to bow very Genteely when he has occasion to come before Persons of Honour," whereas Barclay "was more Observant of what he professed to be his Principle than most of them, for when he came before the greatest of his Superiors, he would stand as straight as a Post, or Pillar, (as I have observed him to do) tho' otherwise, and in his Natural Temper very affable, and discreet."[9] Penn upheld his own particular practice by the comment, "I know no religion which destroys courtesy, civility and kindness."[10] Barclay tried, as much as Penn did, to be courteous, and indicated that it was for him a personal hardship to give up courtly manners.

Barclay's life as a courtier may be said to have begun in 1676, after his first visit to Princess Elizabeth and before his long imprison-

[8] *Journal of the Friends Historical Society,* Vol. VIII (1911), p. 62.
[9] Keith, *Standard of the Quakers Examined, op. cit.,* p. 466.
[10] Hull, *William Penn, a Topical Biography, op. cit.,* p. 306.

ment. We know that he saw James, then Duke of York, after his return from Holland and Germany. Already he was concerned, not only with the effort to end the persecution of Quakers, but also with lobbying in Penn's colonial interest. As in all such efforts, the way to success lay through men of influence, one of whom Barclay himself soon came to be. From London, on July 20, 1676, Barclay wrote to Penn as follows:

> I have been constantly following my business since I last saw thee and have had occasione to be twice with the Duke since thou art gone. I have found him generous in keeping his bond and I am like to effectuate something by his means. Thy friend Ashtone proved wonderful serviceable to me for which I expect thou wilt thank him: being at present in great haist I have not time to enlarge.[11]

The lobbying in which Barclay was involved in 1676 was with the King's brother and concerned the decision to make a formal division of New Jersey into east and west colonies, a division which was to mean a great deal to him six years later. Part of Barclay's usefulness with the Duke of York arose from his sensitivity about the effectiveness of particular persons. Thus he wrote to Penn, in January, 1680, to warn him that the Duke would listen to some men, but not to others. Penn was advised not to send Edward Byllinge, who had been prominent in colonial affairs, because James had "an ill opinion of him," whereas Gawen Lawrie, who was later to be Barclay's deputy governor, was one of whom the Duke spoke "very advantageously." The Duke, said Barclay, believed Lawrie to be "a Discreet wise man." In the same letter we catch a glimpse of the sordidness of intrigue at court, in which some men were engaged in the effort to undermine the reputations of others. "I perceave," wrote Barclay, "some one has not been wanting to possesse him with no good opinion of thee and as one who is not his friend, which conceit perhaps has no good influence in this matter."[12] Whatever the strategy of Penn's political enemies may have been, it is important to remember that the Stuart kings did not dishonor their promise to their dying friend, Admiral Penn, to the effect that they would bestow their favor on his

[11] This letter is in the Penn-Forbes Collection of the Historical Society of Pennsylvania, II, 15.

[12] *Ibid.*

son. The history of both New Jersey and Pennsylvania would have been very different, apart from the solemn Stuart promise and the remarkable fidelity with which it was kept. It appears, therefore, that part of Barclay's influence at court arose from his close association with Penn.

The opportunity for Barclay to see James was enhanced when, in 1679, the latter was made High Commissioner in Scotland. The appointment seems to have been made as a means of getting James out of England, where his influence as an avowed Roman Catholic was feared. Once he was established at Holyrood, Robert Barclay not only had easy access to him, but was frequently summoned from Ury. The Duke resided in Edinburgh, not continuously but, with various breaks, from November, 1679 to June, 1682, when, with his resettlement in England, his political ascendancy was established. The consequence was that, in 1684, he was again able to serve as Lord High Admiral.

By the time that the Duke of York arrived at Holyrood as High Commissioner, Robert Barclay's wordly status had been raised by the granting of a charter from King Charles II, making Ury into a free barony, with civil and criminal jurisdiction. The date of the charter was August 13, 1679. In this act the Stuarts paid an obvious debt to the Barclays for loyal support, and made some recompense for unjust imprisonment, while, even more importantly, they provided insurance against future molestation. The charter was ratified and validated six years later, after James became King, by an Act of Parliament of Scotland, A.D. 1685. The ratification is an impressive document, occupying over five pages in *Reliquiae Barclaianae*.[13] It begins:

> Our Soveraigne Lord with advice and consent of his Estates of Parliament for the good and faithful Services done and performed to His Majesty and His most Royal progenitors by Collonel David Barclay of Urie and Robert Barclay his eldest Lawfull Son In times past by thir presents Ratifys approves and perpetually confirms an Chartor dated at Windsore Castle the terteenth day of August 1[oo] vjt seventy nyn years Granted by His late Majesty King Charles the Second of ever blessed memory whereby His Highness with consent of the Lords of the Thesaury and Exchequer of His ancient Kingdom of Scotland, etc.

[13] *Reliquiae Barclaianae,* 61 a, b, c, d, e, f. The original warrant, dated Windsor Castle, August 13, 1679, is extant in the Public Record Office. See *Calendar of State Papers,* under this date.

After James was settled in London the visits of Robert Barclay to the English metropolis became more frequent. His travels increased markedly, and on some occasions he would barely reach home when he would be asked to journey southward again. In one of the letters urging him to return, George Fox wrote, "thou hadst their Ears more than any Friend when here & freedom & liberty on Friends' & Truth's behalf."[14] Fox promised, at the same time, that Barclay need not worry about the expense, since he might consider that he was traveling on official Quaker business.[15] Most of the approaches to the ruling circles were concerned with imprisonment, though some involved the complicated affairs of New Jersey and Pennsylvania. Barclay made a conscious effort not to appeal to the court too often or too much."[16]

In the spring of 1683 he took his wife and his eldest son southward with him. He placed the boy in the boarding school at Theobald's, near London, which was conducted by George Keith, who at that time had not yet emigrated to New Jersey. At the end of the summer, leaving their son with Keith, Barclay started north with his wife, her brother, Gilbert Molleson, and an eminent merchant of Holland, Arent Sonmans, then residing in Scotland. Sonmans, who had met Barclay when he reached the Dutch shore in 1677, and who was also a proprietor of East New Jersey, was accompanied by his wife. Between Huntington and Stilton the travelers were attacked by highwaymen.[17] Molleson was only robbed, but the Dutch merchant was shot in the thigh and died a few days later at Stilton, as a result of his wounds. Barclay succeeded in overawing the dangerous men, so that, when one of them attacked him, he took the man by the arm, "very calmly asking him how he came to be so rude, for he knew his business; the fellow trembling dropped the pistol in great surprise, and did not so much as search or demand anything from him." Robert and Christian Barclay remained to attend the funeral of their murdered companion and then proceeded homeward, arriving there September 5, after what Barclay noted in his

[14] *Ibid.,* 59.

[15] *Ibid.,* 60.

[16] This is indicated by a letter from Sarah Meade to her mother, Margaret Fox.

[17] *Genealogical Account,* p. 52. The son specifically said that he had the account from his mother, an eyewitness.

diary as "a long and tedius journey." This unfortunate experience occurred on the one long absence from home in which Barclay was accompanied by his wife. During most of his long travels she was confined at Ury by pregnancy or by the care of very young children.

The story of the attack north of London has often been told and has, indeed, become a favorite Quaker anecdote.[18] What is not generally known, however, is the subsequent story of the son of the man who died as a result of the attack. Sonmans was intending to emigrate to East New Jersey when, as a member of Barclay's party, he was shot. It has been suggested that he was attacked, not from the motive of theft, but by an emissary from Holland on account of political animosity. On August 14, 1684, his only son, Peter, matriculated at the University of Leyden, where he apparently studied both mathematics and law. Later Peter Sonmans emigrated to America to claim 5¼ proprieties, more than any other, and refused to surrender to the lawful heirs, descendants of his Scottish stepmother. Peter turned out to be a scoundrel, apparently fathered an illegitimate child, and became bitterly anti-Quaker, even though he owed so much to the Quaker governor.[19] The hypothesis that the attack by robbers had political or sinister motivation is an interesting one, but it does not seem likely that it can be verified. The value of the story in Quaker folklore has been to show how, in an unexpected crisis, Barclay's practice accorded with his principles, and that his personal nonviolence was successful.

Barclay's life was full to the brim. Late in 1685 he attended, in Edinburgh, the wedding of his sister Jean to Sir Ewen Cameron of Locheill, and then went to the court at London by way of York. He started home, reached Edinburgh, but was recalled to London by urgent affairs. On February 13, 1686, he received news of his brother's death at sea. That spring his youngest child was born, his wife had a severe illness, and later in the same year his father, the old Colonel, fell ill and died.

In 1687 Barclay stopped at Swarthmore as he went north, in

[18] See Richard Pike, *Quaker Anecdotes* (London, 1881), p. 39.

[19] See Milton Rubincam, "The Strange Career of Peter Sonmans," *Proceedings of the New Jersey Historical Society* (1939), pp. 230–51. The spelling of the surname of the Dutch family varies, but "Sonmans" is the spelling found in the Bury Hill manuscripts.

order to see George Fox. From there he went to Edinburgh, then to see the Earl of Perth at Drummond Castle, and then home. Whenever possible he paid some attention to the Ury estate which, as he wrote Penn in 1685, he did not dare to neglect, "Being the subsistence of so numerous a family and 6 children depends upon it." It is not really surprising that Barclay, in his busy thirties, found no time to write books. Moreover, he was seldom robust, mentioning in many letters his "great bodily weakness."

Among the best accounts of what Barclay was doing in the hectic days of the short reign of James II is that provided by one of the leading Quakers, George Whitehead. James became King February 6, 1685, and the official Quaker petition, along with a careful record of imprisonments, was presented to him on March 3. The total of the Quaker prisoners, listed by counties, was 1460. Whitehead felt led to go to the King in person, but he needed Barclay to open the way for him.

> And acquainting my beloved Friend Robert Barclay, with my Intention of going to the King, he was willing to go with me, and accompany me, he being more acquainted with the King than I was, and the King having a particular Respect to him, from the Knowledge He had of him in Scotland, the said Robert Barclay being an Inhabitant of that Country, and having Occasion to visit him when he was there, before he was King.[20]

The direct confrontation with James came on May 26, 1685, at about four in the afternoon. Whitehead's account of the conversation appears to be accurate and complete. We know something of Barclay's style from the fact that, after he had employed his friendship in order to gain entrance, he let Whitehead and the King do most of the talking. At the end, Barclay expressed his satisfaction both with Whitehead's presentation of the case and "the King's Behavior towards us."[21]

From the time of the King's conference with Barclay and Whitehead, events moved rapidly in the direction of total toleration. While there is much reason to believe that James II was motivated chiefly by concern for his Catholic subjects, he may have been influenced, in

[20] *The Christian Progress of that Ancient Servant and Minister of Jesus Christ, George Whitehead* (London, 1725), p. 575.
[21] *Ibid.*, p. 580.

part, by the insistence of Barclay and others, who upheld freedom of conscience as a principle. Finally, in 1687, James took the step which brought religious liberty, but which also drove him from the throne. Without the consent of Parliament, and having prorogued it until November, the King, at the Council in March, declared that uniformity in religion had been proved impossible and that he had now resolved on a declaration of toleration or liberty of conscience to all dissenters. On April 4, 1687, the Declaration appeared.

It would be a great error to suppose that James II had any fondness for Quakers in general or any real appreciation of their system of life and thought. Though it has sometimes been asserted that King James once attended a Quaker meeting with his friends Barclay and Penn, the probability is that he did not do so. The only known evidence of his attendance is that provided by John Barclay after he discovered and edited some valuable historical materials. His report, referring to events in 1687, is as follows.

On his way home from London in the 6th month, Robert Barclay stopped two days at Chester, where the King then was upon a progress. There, in the Tennis Court, he and William Penn had "a most large meeting as he calls it in his Diary; the King himself being present at one of the religious opportunities held in the Friends meetinghouse.[22]

We might accept the truth of John Barclay's statement except for the fact that it is not supported by the record available in the *Genealogical Account,* which would surely have mentioned the royal attendance if it had occurred. The statement from 1740 is, "Having finished his business at that time at London, he took journey homeward in August, 1687, by the way of Chester, where the King then was, upon a progress, where he and William Penn had a large meeting at the Tennis-Court."[23] We are now in the fortunate position of being able to examine Barclay's own diary, to which his nineteenth-century descendant referred and which was evidently found at Ury in 1826. The really clinching evidence that the King was not present at the Quaker meetinghouse is, therefore, that which the Apologist himself provides, as follows: "Arrived at Chester, 26, stayed there (the King being there) till 28. (27 with W.P. at a most large meeting

[22] John Barclay, *Memoirs* of Scottish Quakers, *op. cit.,* p. 344.
[23] *Genealogical Account,* p. 84.

in the Tenniscourt of Chester."[24] John Barclay's statement about the King's attendance was probably his own interpretation. We have good confirmatory evidence in the diary of Bishop Cartwright, who noted, "His Majesty went to his devotion in the Town Hall. I preached to the Corporation in the Cathedral and Wm. Penn held forth in the Tennis Court."[25] The King's devotions at the Town Hall were undoubtedly those of the Roman Catholic Mass. We must remember that James had written, on July 16, 1685, that though he was favorable to Barclay he had "not great reason to be well satisfyd with the Quakers in generall,"[26] and there is no evidence that he changed his mind.

In March, 1688, Barclay made his last trip to London, accompanied by his eldest son and by his brother-in-law, Sir Ewen Cameron. They arrived in the city April 13. Barclay was soon successful, with the King's help, in composing a difference between Cameron and the Duke of Gordon. During this last visit Barclay presented his son at court. He also did a great deal of preaching, including the sermon of May 16, already quoted in Chapter V. He was in London in time to see, at first hand, the danger to the King which was involved in the imprisonment of the seven bishops. Barclay, characteristically, seems to have felt sympathy for both sides of the controversy. Indeed, there are few events in his life which are more revealing than his visit to the seven bishops imprisoned in the Tower of London. The background of their imprisonment was that the King had taken the suicidal step of issuing a proclamation to force clergy and bishops to read the Declaration of Indulgence in their pulpits and thus personally to advocate a measure which they detested. Seven refused.

That the King's action was a mixture of evil as well as good all students of history now agree. Even though it was a good thing to end all restraints on religious liberty, there is no doubt that the King's act was a blow to constitutional government. Conscious that Parliament would not uphold him, James went through with a high-handed act of personal authority and thus strained the royal pre-

[24] Diary II, unpublished, p. 42.

[25] This notation was extracted by Hudson Gurney in 1855.

[26] Historical Manuscripts Commission, Fifteenth Report, Appendix, Part VIII: *The Duke of Buccleuch Manuscripts* (London, 1897), p. 215.

rogative to the breaking point. Those who opposed him on principle, like the bishops who were confined to the Tower, feared a Catholic revolution which would produce such a limitation on the freedom of the majority as should make the current limitations on the freedom of minorities seem mild by contrast. They saw the Declaration of Indulgence as merely one move in a game of power and chicanery. The result was that almost the whole nation, including both Churchmen and nonconformists, felt a common danger, and therefore sided with the bishops against the King.

In all of this, Friends were placed in a difficult situation. They had no more desire than had most of their neighbors to see popery established in their land, but, having suffered so much, they were immensely relieved to be free from legal restraints. What Friends had suffered has been described by a Quaker historian as follows:

> No legal chicanery, no arbitrary proceeding had been too gross if it had served the turn of their oppressors. In a word, they had been treated for a generation as outlaws, living and worshipping on sufferance, and only living and worshipping at all because cruelty is capricious and their honest neighbors refused to aid in their destruction. The law denied the Quakers the common rights of an Englishman. If strictly administered his marriage was no marriage; he was disabled from giving legal evidence or taking up his freedom in the town where he traded; and, in common with other Non-Conformists, public offices were closed to him.[27]

So great was Quaker revulsion to what they had suffered that they tended to excuse the highhandedness of the King. Letters appeared from "A Gentleman in the Country," probably William Penn, putting the best possible light on the royal act. "This Declaration," he says in his third letter, "seems to me no more than a Royal Bill without doors, informing the kingdom of His Majesty's mind, and preparing both Houses to make it the subject of their next session." It is hardly surprising that William Penn was under a cloud and stayed out of public life for several years after the coming of William of Orange.

Barclay seems to have felt the tension of the crisis severely, the best evidence being his personal vindication of his dealings with the King, which he wrote after returning home to Ury. It was in line with Barclay's whole way of life to go directly to the imprisoned

[27] William C. Braithwaite, *Second Period of Quakerism*, *op. cit.*, pp. 131, 132.

bishops who had publicly resisted the King's action. In his interview with them Barclay tried to make them realize how onerous the laws had been, giving them firsthand evidence concerning Friends who had died in prison. What was more remarkable was that he told them that the Quakers had no intention of making the situation of the bishops more difficult by publishing these facts or in any way strengthening the hands of the King against them.

Though the seven bishops were acquitted on June 30, 1688, the anger of the people was so great that the invitation to William of Orange, whose wife was James' daughter, was sent that same day. William landed November 5, 1688, and James' second escape was on December 23, Barclay's fortieth birthday. Barclay's son left a vivid account of the last parting between the two friends who, though they were so different, had nevertheless been involved in some of the same affairs.

> Standing alone with the King in a window, who looking out, said, "the wind was now fair for the Prince of Orange his coming over:" upon which Robert Barclay took occasion to say, "It was sad that no expedient could be found out to satisfy the people" to which the King replied, that "he would do anything becoming a gentleman except to part with liberty of conscience which he never would, while he lived."[28]

After this separation Barclay went north in December, traveling with James Stewart, Lord Advocate for Scotland. This was his last journey of any length, and he stayed chiefly at Ury during the final two years of his life. Though he was not ashamed of his association with James, the flight of the King and the subsequent fighting in Ireland made it wise for Barclay to stay out of political life entirely.

During the years 1689 and 1690 Barclay paid careful attention to the barony over which he had jurisdiction, cared for his family, and preached many sermons. His most significant production was his "Vindication," written at the end of March, 1689. This is a dignified piece of work, not at all apologetic in the present sense of the word. He was not ashamed of his political connections, but because he knew that he was being criticized, he felt that it was only fair to provide an explanation. The essay is not really part of his literary work, which had long been completed, but is rather an

[28] *Genealogical Account,* p. 56.

epilogue to his life at court.[29] Sensing this, the editors of *Truth Triumphant* did not include it in the collected works. Though not primarily literary in intent, the opening lines have about them a tone of simple grandeur:

> To live in this world and escape the censure of it is vain, to imagine, and for any man to pretend to be a Christian, and to expect not to fall under the lash of envy, malice, and slandering tongues, is to forget whose name he bears, and what was his Lord and Masters lot and to repine at it is to repent in some measure, coming under the standart, Who as he forwarned his disciples to expect it, so commandeth them, patience to endure it.

The author, after this noble beginning, applicable to the life of any Christian in any age, went on to say that he had been loaded with calumnies, to which at first he did not reply, except in private correspondence. Since, however, some of his friends had expressed their satisfaction in his private replies to "vulgar stories," and since some of his fellow Quakers were "suffering consequentially in the ruine of my reputation," he thought it right to make a public statement. He understood the human heart sufficiently to realize that some who had engaged in "undeserved malice" might not be convinced, but that was not his responsibility. He was willing, in the end, to "leave the issue to the goodness of God, whom I heartily pray that He may forgive and amend my enemys, though upon a narrow search I find not my conscience chargeable with any just cause given to any man alive to be such to me." His ultimate appeal, he said, was "to the righteous judgment seat of Christ, where no humor or interest will have place and where my record is and shall remain, as to the truth and sincerity of what I affirm in this my vindication."

The chief criticisms to which Barclay addressed himself in 1689 were two: that he was a Jesuit and that, for pro-Roman activities, he had received payment from the King. He answered the first charge by pointing to his family life and by reciting again the story of his conversion, after early years under Roman Catholic influence. "I do sincerely profess in the sight of the searcher of hearts," wrote Bar-

[29] The "Vindication," formerly at Ury, was presented over a century ago by Hudson Gurney to Arthur Kett Barclay. See *Reliquiae Barclaianae,* 62–71, for a printed copy.

clay, "that I am no Papist nor have been these twenty-two years." He referred any reader to his many treatises in which he had already made this plain. He went on to say, however, that he had never hated Roman Catholics personally nor supported persecution of Protestants. "Thou art inexcusable O man whosoever thou art that condemns another and does the same thing." He specifically denied having been "a caballer with Father Peters so called." Barclay affirmed, furthermore, that he had never even spoken to Peters, and knew him only by sight as would any footman at Whitehall. He had kept himself scrupulously free from such connections "even before there was any prospect of the great revolution that hath since happened."

Turning to his connection with the King, Barclay began the account by reference to events of 1676, when, before he had ever seen or spoken to the then Duke of York, and when he had "no design of becoming a Courtier," he was told that the Duke might be influential in persuading Lauderdale, "in whose hands were the sole management of Scots affairs at that time" to put a stop to imprisonment for religious nonconformity. At the first, in 1676, Barclay says he found the Duke "inclineable to interpose in it he having then and always since to me professed himself to be for liberty of conscience." Later Barclay wrote, "I never found reason to doubt his sincerity in the matter." Because Barclay's main interest was the advantage of others rather than himself, he made it a point, he says, not to go to the King to testify his "respects to him on his coming to the Crown."

On the point about money, Barclay's testimony was that, for his many efforts to help others by direct royal appeal, he never received any reward for his labour, loss of time, and neglect of domestic affairs. "And as for the advantages I have had for my attendance at Court at any time I have nothing to boast of, I am sure who frequents the Courts of Princes find often more reason for wearying than pleasure." As for money received, not in excess of three hundred pounds sterling, "was in satisfaction of a debt due to my father laid out in the service of King Charles the first." Most of this debt, Barclay added, still remained unpaid.

It is important, in reference to financial affairs, to distinguish between Barclay's work as Governor of East Jersey and his efforts to stop persecution. For duties of the former sort, the Governor quite properly accepted actual expenses, though he took no salary. The following order was sent out to all proprietors, "by the comittee & Councill of Proprietors in London," under date of June 16, 1685: "*Ordered* that Tenn pounds on every Propriety be payed in Stock for Defraying the Great Charges for Negotiating Our affaires of the Province at Court among Offercers and Ministers Lawyers etc: Robt. Barclay atending here many months and much Expense in Variety of business requiring it."[30]

As for his affection for James, Barclay did not deny it. "I must own," he wrote, "that I love King James," and "wish him well." Furthermore, says Barclay, as a Christian, "I cannot excuse myself from the duty of praying for him." Far from being involved in any military intrigues, Barclay professed himself as committed, personally, to the "Doctrine of non-resistance and passive obedience."

Barclay's work at the end was more truly local than it had been for many years. He is known to have held one meeting of his barony court.[31] Many of his duties on the large estate had accumulated during years of major absence. The man who had done so much in so short a time seemed to appreciate a period of release from the strain of life in London and Edinburgh. He enjoyed himself "in visiting and being visited by his friends and neighbours," until about the end of September, 1690, when on his return from a meeting at Aberdeen he immediately sickened. One who was with him during the last few days was James Dickenson, a Quaker minister from Cumberland, who was asked to remember his love to Friends in Cumberland, at Swarthmore, and *to Dear George* and to all the faithful everywhere. To Dickenson we are indebted for recording his very last words, as follows: "God is good still; and though I am under a great weight of weakness and sickness, yet my peace flows; and this I know, whatever exercises may be permitted to come upon me, they shall tend to God's glory, and my salvation, and in that I

[30] New Jersey Archives, II, 37, 39. See also Hayes Dissertation, *op. cit.*, II, p. 52.

[31] See *The Court Book of the Barony of Urie*, edited by D. G. Barron, printed in Edinburgh in 1892 for the Scottish Historical Society. The manuscript of the Court Book is available in the Bury Hill Collection. The court action signed by the Apologist appears on pp. 82, 83, of the manuscript book.

rest."[32] Thus, after many storms, he had come to a peaceful haven.

Barclay's final sickness, though brief, was very severe, and included a violent fever. He died on October 3, 1690 and was buried where the Colonel had been buried only four years earlier, in the "Howff," on top of a hill on the Ury estate. He was attended to his grave "by several of the nobility, and numbers of the gentry, and greatly lamented by all who knew him."[33]

It is hard to exaggerate the role of Barclay in the entire Quaker Movement of the seventeenth century. More than any other man, he brought the movement into public esteem, so far as thoughtful persons were concerned. The Dutch historian, William Sewel, in reference to Barclay's untimely death, gave an estimate of the man's character which any might envy:

> In the year 1690, Robert Barclay also departed this life; a man of eminent gifts and great endowments, expert not only in the language of the learned, but also well versed in the writings of the ancient fathers, and other ecclesiastical writers, and furnished with a great understanding, being not only of a sound judgment, but also strong in arguments, and cheerful in sufferings.[34]

[32] The words appear to be accurate even though not quoted in Dickenson's *Journal*. See John Gough, *A History of the People Called Quakers,* Vol. III (Dublin, 1809), p. 247.

[33] *Genealogical Account,* p. 57.

[34] Sewel's *History,* pp. 627, 628.

PART II

THOUGHT

CHAPTER VIII

THE AUTHORITY OF EXPERIENCE

And this I knew experimentally.
—George Fox

FAITH, in the nature of things, requires validation. This is because there are many different faiths, some of which are mutually incompatible. Some faiths are little more than superstition, while others, not obviously superstitious, are such that they will not bear full examination. Insofar, therefore, as we care about the truth, we must be willing to submit any faith, including our own, to relentless scrutiny. Once we have heard them, it is almost impossible to argue with the now classic words of Samuel Taylor Coleridge, "He who begins by loving Christianity better than Truth will proceed by loving his own Sect or Church better than Christianity, and end in loving himself better than all." Apart from an overmastering concern for what is true, there is no possible antidote to wish-thinking, and therefore no intellectual integrity. However comforting it may be, if the Christian faith is not true, it is an evil! This is why, as the Biblical injunction puts it, you must always be prepared "to make a defense to anyone who calls you to account for the hope that is in you," but this important task must be done "with gentleness and due deference" (I Pet. 3:15).[1]

[1] "Deference" is John Baillie's translation of *phobos*. See his *Invitation to Pilgrimage* (London: Pelican Books, 1960), p. 12.

It was Robert Barclay's acute sense of the need of validation which led to the writing of his major works, particularly the *Apology*. He believed, of course, in proclamation, but he saw that proclamation is not enough. The Fifth Monarchy Men were strong on proclamation, but, since there was no intellectual justification for what they confidently proclaimed, their utterances were no more than opinions. Though the early Quaker Movement included some adherents of this fanatical type, Robert Barclay saw clearly that it could not survive unless it could win wider assent, and that such assent depended upon the ability to make a thoughtful presentation, in which reasons were given.

Barclay undertook to bring many different items of belief into a coherent system. In doing so, he had to include God, Christ, man, the Holy Spirit, the Scriptures, salvation, Christian behavior, prayer, worship, ministry, and much more. We must always remember that he was trying to state coherently not merely what Quakers happened to believe, but what the truth is and how it may be apprehended. It came to him, as a genuine revelation, that all of the aspects of the spiritual life could be unified by reference to one commanding idea, that of "spiritual empiricism." This is what Maurice Creasey means by calling Barclay "the Newton of Protestantism." In no other way can we understand him. He was Newtonian because, "in his fearless application of the test of 'experience' and his attempt to bring everything within the scope of a single, simple comprehensive principle," he was doing something comparable to Newton's work in physics.[2] Each of them could make mistakes, but the grandeur of conception is the same in both. Barclay, says Creasey, "sought and found, a means of bringing the whole body of Christian doctrine into some real relationship with an experimental religion." The word "experimental," which Barclay probably caught from Fox, meant the same to him that "experiential" means to us. The parallel with scientific empiricism, given such a great lift by Galileo, is obvious. Like Galileo, in his answer to the skeptical astronomers, the test was what could be "seen," providing the conditions of sight were fully met. Writing in prison, Barclay said, "And thence can say somewhat experimen-

[2] Maurice A. Creasey, Barclay Dissertation, p. 183 (see Appendix B, p. 256).

tally."[3] When he was little more than a boy Barclay wrote in shorthand that the "finder of truth" must "experimentally feel."

In a mood strikingly akin to that of the natural sciences, which were becoming firmly established in his lifetime, Barclay cut across fruitless argument to point to what had occurred or was occurring. A good illustration of this method is his discussion of the ministry of women. Regardless of the arguments pro and con, he directed his readers to the objective fact that women *do* minister and do so effectively. "And lastly," he wrote, "it hath been observed, that God hath effectually in this day converted many souls by the ministry of women; and by them also frequently comforted the souls of his children; which manifest experience puts the thing beyond all controversy."[4] It would have helped, in Doctor Johnson's famous joke about women preaching, if he had read far enough in Barclay to reach this passage. Barclay's mood is like that of the wise rustic who, upon being asked if he believed in baptism, completed the conversation by saying, "Why, man, I've *seen* it!"

Though Barclay was "Newtonian," he was, in an even deeper sense, "Cartesian." He did not make many direct references to Descartes, but it is obvious that he was familiar with the famous philosopher's ideas.[5] He could not have failed to know that Descartes had dedicated one of his major works to Princess Elizabeth thirty years before the writing of the *Apology* was started. In the letter to Adrian Paets, which is the most strictly philosophical of Barclay's writings, and in which specific mention is made of the Cartesian thought, Barclay was probably denied the advantage of direct quotation because of the fact that the writing was done in prison, without access to a library. But, whatever the reason for the omission, it is not hard to see that he was attempting in theology what Descartes had attempted in general philosophy. Like Descartes, he wanted to get away from the endless balancing of the judgments of authorities and to make a new start on a firm foundation. Like Descartes, he was convinced that he could never proceed with satisfaction unless he

[3] *Truth Triumphant,* p. 678.

[4] *Apology,* p. 314 [X, xxvii]. All references to the *Apology* in Part II of this book are to the Philadelphia stereotype edition of 1908, which is widely distributed. To assist those using other editions I have added, in Roman numbers, the propositions and sections, which are the same in all copies.

[5] See *Truth Triumphant,* p. 900. He calls the philosopher Cartesius.

could first find one solid point, after the fashion of Archimedes with his famous fulcrum. Like Descartes, Barclay was prepared to doubt all that could be doubted, in search for something, no matter how simple, that could be recognized as existing beyond doubt. In short, he was searching for the theological counterpart of *cogito ergo sum*. What is more, he believed that he had found it! Just as Descartes recognized that he had to begin with method, Barclay saw that he should start, not with knowledge about God and man, but with the way in which such knowledge can be reached.

The first proposition of the *Apology* requires no long explanation in a chapter, since it only states the obvious point that, in questions of religion, there must be found some adequate ground of knowing the truth. The real enemy is not irreligion, but false religion, because the conflicts between contradictory opinions naturally tend to the conclusion that the whole thing is a matter of groundless opinion. Unless we can find something dependable, no genuine knowledge of God is possible. But how is validation to proceed? Many, in Barclay's day, began by quoting authorities, as is done in deciding legal questions. What so surprised Margaret Fell, when she first saw and heard her future husband, was that he went beyond authority, even the authority of the Bible as she had understood it, to the necessity of an inner experience on the part of each Christian. The arresting words of Fox at Ulverston, in 1652, were, "You will say, Christ saith this, and the apostles say this; but what canst thou say?"

Barclay, in his rejection of authority as ordinarily understood, ran the risk of self-contradiction, in that he quoted others to support his position. He quoted Augustine as saying, "It is the inward master that teacheth." Likewise he quoted Clement of Alexandria, Tertullian, Jerome, etc. Though the captious critic might object, Barclay was really on firm ground here. He was saying that it was the consensus of Christian authorities that there is something better than the authority of men. He did not hesitate to mention, in *Apology II*, "all sorts of professors in all ages." Far from being self-contradictory, this was his way of showing, by skillful dialectic, that even his adversaries *really* adopted his conclusion. If both Papists and Protestants do actually accept the primacy of "inward immediate objective revelation by the Spirit,"[6] where is the argument? When his opponents

[6] *Apology*, p. 69 [II, xvi].

uphold Scripture as primary, and he asks them why they uphold it, their only recourse is to refer to the inward testimony of the Spirit, but that, says Barclay, is what he has depended upon all along. He even quotes Calvin to this effect. Thus his strategy is that of confuting his critics out of their own mouths. If we find that there is something which men are unable to oppose, even when they try to do so, we are catching a glimpse of firm ground.

It is always reasonable to ask "Why?" whatever the subject under discussion. If we depend upon the Scriptures, it is incumbent upon us to give a reason for doing so. We cannot provide this by quoting the Scriptures again, for then the reasoning is patently circular. One of the ablest of contemporary philosophers, particularly in the field of epistemology, has put Barclay's point with clarity, though with no specific reference to him. In his highly respected *The Ways of Knowing,* Professor Montague shows the reason for the impossibility of treating authority as an ultimate source of truth. "When questioned as to why a given authority, say one of the writers of the Bible, should be accepted without question, the answer is almost inevitably a statement that the witness himself did not have to depend on authority, but possessed superior opportunities of acquiring the truth direct through some one of the other sources of belief such as experience or intuition."[7]

This is Barclay's point precisely. Barclay recognized, as Montague and other philosophers have done, that while the authority of the judgment of other human beings is useful and even necessary for practical life, it is not ultimate. Any sensible person depends upon the authority of the expert in his daily life, for the simple reason that he has neither the time nor the skill to become an expert in everything himself. I accept the authority of my dentist, not because he is infallible, but because the only practical alternative would be to depend upon my own judgment, which would surely be worse. But the authority of the dentist, or of any other expert, points back beyond itself and rests finally upon disciplined experience. If the separate reports of the experiences of those whom we have reason to trust are in substantial agreement, the probability of objective truth is correspondingly great. In the realm of dentistry again, it is a significant fact that a group of American experts and a group of

[7] W. P. Montague, *The Ways of Knowing* (London, 1928), p. 40.

British experts, working in complete independence, in an effort to learn the most satisfactory combination of silver, tin, etc., for an amalgam filling, came to almost exactly the same conclusion. Such cumulative evidence is the best that we know, not because it is something other than experience, but because *it represents essential agreement in the report of experience*. In Barclay's clear mind it was soon evident that the logic of religious experience follows the same identical form as does the logic of scientific experience. Both are empirical and both require verification.

Even when he does not mention it, Barclay is concerned with the problem of the authority of Scripture, a problem which he realizes is not amenable to any simple solution. The problem is always close to the surface in *Apology II,* and is dealt with specifically in *Apology III*. What first strikes the reader is Barclay's own love of the Scriptures, as well as his deep knowledge of them. He quotes the Bible voluminously and usually with relevance. Though he was always careful to maintain the position that the Bible is secondary, while the direct revelation which came to its authors is prior, both temporally and logically, it is hard to see how an extreme upholder of Biblical authority could love the Bible more or could use it more reverently than he does. Barclay valued the Bible because it enables us to extend the fellowship of verification to past ages and to see how our direct experiences of God's power compare with the reported experiences of God's power at other times. In an attractive figure of speech concerning the Bible, he said it had the value of a mirror:

> God hath seen meet that herein we should, as in a looking-glass, see the conditions and experiences of the saints of old; that finding our experience answer to theirs, we might thereby be the more confirmed and comforted, and our hope of obtaining the same end, strengthened.[8]

There is no possibility of understanding Barclay's complex view of the Scriptures without a firm grasp of the idea, central to all his thinking, of the help which Christians give to one another. Alone we may be pathetically deluded, but the experience of "answering" one another is the divinely ordered means of avoiding delusion. It is probable that Barclay took over from Fox this unusual use of "answer." Fox had said, as early as 1656, that it is the duty of a

[8] *Apology*, p. 88 [III, v].

Christian to "walk cheerfully over the world, answering that of God in every one."[9] To answer is to *match* and consequently to encourage. As our experience is shown to match that of the saints of old, it is easier to develop a contemporary matching. Thus Fox, in the same letter, urged his readers to have unity both "with the Scriptures and with one another." What Barclay did was to take this important idea of the fellowship of verification and to refine it. Unless they strike a responsive chord in us, the Scriptures, he maintained, do us no good whatever. At the heart of his chapter on the Scriptures Barclay wrote, accordingly, "This is the great work of the Scriptures and their service to us, that we may witness them fulfilled in us, and so discern the stamp of God's Spirit and ways upon them, by the inward acquaintance we have with the same Spirit and work in our hearts."[10]

That Barclay was saying the same thing about the Bible in his spoken ministry is indicated by the report of Christopher Story of a gathering in Cumberland, presumably in 1687, in which the Apologist spoke as follows: "If a man could begin at Genesis and repeat all the Scriptures to the end of Revelation, and was not led and guided by a measure of that spirit by which the Scriptures were given forth, it would avail him nothing."[11] The paradox of the Bible-lover who thus seems to lower its value is similar to that of Socrates, who, though he loved philosophy, was eager not to overstate its worth. Barclay worked out a system in terms of which it was clear, both that the direct illumination in the heart is *primary* and that the witness of others is *contributory*. This makes the Church through the ages not a mere collection of individuals whom God reaches separately, but those who are more likely to be reached because they belong to the *fellowship of witness*. "For though God do principally and chiefly lead us by his Spirit, yet he sometimes conveys his comfort and consolation to us, through his children, whom he raises up and inspires, to speak or write a word in season; whereby the Saints are made instruments in the hand of the Lord to strengthen and encourage one another."[12] It is logically possible for God to reach a

[9] *Journal* (1952), p. 263.
[10] *Apology*, p. 88 [III, v].
[11] "Friends Library," Vol. I, p. 145.
[12] *Apology*, p. 87 [III, v].

man alone, without the Bible, which provides the ancient fellowship, or without the Church, which provides the contemporary fellowship, but it is not likely that this will occur.

Barclay was helped, in his effort to clarify the true relationship between direct experiences and the Bible, by the metaphor of the "fountain." The fountain is the original source of a stream as it "springs out of the bowels of the earth." When we have traced a stream back and back, as we love to do, we stop when we reach the fountain, because we can go no farther. Metaphorically, then, the Word of God in the heart is the fountain, while the Scriptures, being derivative, are the streams. This leads to Barclay's most quoted passage on the subject which we are now considering:

> Though then we do acknowledge the scriptures to be very heavenly and divine writings, the use of them to be very comfortable and necessary to the church of Christ, and that we also admire and give praise to the Lord, for his wonderful providence in preserving these writings so pure and uncorrupted as we have them, through so long a night of apostacy, to be a testimony of his truth against the wickedness and abominations even of those whom he made instrumental in preserving them, so that they have kept them to be a witness against themselves; yet we may not call them the principal fountain of all truth and knowledge, nor yet the first adequate rule of faith and manners; because the principal fountain of truth must be the Truth itself; i.e. that whose certainty and authority depends not upon another.[13]

While Barclay sometimes employed the Bible as an arsenal of proof texts, and even produced a forced exegesis of some passages, he illustrated on the whole what we should call a modern approach to the Bible. He recognized, for instance, that the Scriptures could not tell him whether it was his duty "to preach in this or that place, in France or England, or Holland or Germany."[14] The gospel could give him the major premise of his syllogism, but the minor premise had to be provided otherwise. Barclay even showed that he was not afraid of what was later to be called "higher criticism." He was cognizant of the problems of Biblical authorship, and was well aware of the fact that there were alterations in the Hebrew and Greek texts. This did not, however, worry him, because the alterations had

[13] *Apology*, p. 75 [III, ii].
[14] *Ibid.*, p. 79 [III, iii].

taken place in what was at best a secondary rule. "The principal rule of Christians under the gospel is not an outward letter, nor law outwardly written and delivered, but an inward spiritual law, engraven in the heart, the law of the Spirit of life, the word that is nigh in the heart and in the mouth."[15] The gospel, accordingly, is in one sense *final,* and in another sense *open*. Barclay accepted this paradox in order to deny any break with the historic Christ and yet to be ready for continuous revelation. He solved the paradox by saying that he rejected a new gospel or new doctrines, but accepted "a new revelation of the good old gospel and doctrines."[16] Christ has given the truth for all time, but much that it implies may not be seen until it is revealed to later generations. This is why we need not speak always of revelation in the past tense. Christ may, indeed, reveal truths to us today as he did to the Twelve. The basic proposition, therefore, is "that Christians now are to be led inwardly and immediately by the Spirit of God, even in the same manner, though it befall not many to be led in the same measure, as the saints were of old."[17] This, indeed, is religion in the present tense!

It was central to Barclay's philosophy, as to that of Descartes, that no stability can be found in a process of infinite regress. If *a* depends on *b* and *b* depends on *c,* somewhere the search must end, or it is meaningless. He had evidently learned from Descartes that the ultimate ground of confidence must be something which, in the last analysis, is self-validating. *Unless something is self-validating nothing is validated!* Descartes had said that this final ground must be marked by absolute "clearness." Barclay appears to refer to this when he says that the ultimate principles must be those which we do not "examine by any other principle, but their own evidence and clearness."[18]

Without necessarily allying ourselves with particular conclusions in the philosophy of Descartes, such as his mechanism, we can give assent to his intellectual acumen in pointing to the necessity of both intuition and deduction. Ultimate propositions are reached by intuition, while derivative ones are reached by deducution. Intuition

[15] *Ibid.,* p. 78 [III, ii].
[16] *Ibid.,* p. 94 [III, ix].
[17] *Ibid.,* p. 46 [II, ix].
[18] *Ibid.,* p. 67 [II, xv].

means "seeing" and refers to those truths which we "see" in that they are apprehended without argument. The cogency of any argument rests finally upon such "intuitions," whatever the subject matter may be. If the teacher shows the pupil that his argument, upon analysis, is self-contradictory, and the pupil replies that he cannot see anything wrong with that, the discussion may as well end, for both teacher and pupil are wasting their time. If one cannot "see" that, "if all *A* is *B,* and all *B* is *C,* then all *A* is *C,*" what more can be done? There is no further principle to which appeal can be made. In like manner, if we analyze a moral situation and show finally that an action, such as that of a mob, is unjust to persons, we are brought to an absolute barrier if the other person cannot "see" that injustice is wrong. In a free society final skepticism about there being any such truths at all is a possible position, but it is one which destroys all rational investigation. The absolute skeptic, who doubts even the existence of other persons, cannot be given a demonstration to satisfy him, but he is certainly wasting his time in trying to convince his nonexistent adversaries. Unless we can rely on some fundamental intuitions, we can make no progress in either science or morality. Barclay's conviction was that the same is true in religion. He therefore made it clear that all talk about religion is mere speculation unless, at some point, there is "the inward immediate manifestation and revelation of God's spirit, shining in and upon the heart, enlightening and opening the understanding."[19] Only so can men proceed beyond mere conjecture.

When Barclay made this important analysis of the empirical starting point, he set the standard for subsequent Quaker practice. This has been illustrated by Edward Grubb in the twentieth century, who refers directly to Barclay's beginning and says, "Teachings about God, reasonings about His being and nature, can do no more than prepare the way for the true knowledge, which can only come from His direct touch upon our souls. . . . True religion is quite other than acceptance of opinions or beliefs, or even of a code of laws believed to have come from God; it is an experience and a life."[20]

[19] *Ibid.,* p. 28 [II, i].

[20] Edward Grubb, *Authority and the Light Within* (London: James Clark and Co., 1909), p. 73.

Not surprisingly, Grubb quotes, "I have heard of thee by the hearing of the ear, but now mine eye seeth thee."

The part of Barclay's logic which refers to the ultimate ground of religious truth is unimpeachable. His difficulty comes, however, not in regard to *necessity,* but in his reference to *certainty*. He was searching, almost feverishly, for something which would stand in clear contrast to all of our normal experiences, by being "infallible." This, indeed, is a word which Barclay used often, and it is easy to see why he did so. If the fulcrum of Archimedes is not absolutely stable, how can any lifting be done? He was not satisfied, in our world of mutability, with the "most nearly certain," because he thought that the whole effort required that which is *absolutely* certain. Herein lies one of the greatest contrasts between Barclay's mentality and the prevailing mentality of the last third of the twentieth century. Today, we are acutely conscious of the fact that there is no proposition that is amenable to complete and absolute proof. The person who asks you to prove your position beyond the shadow of a doubt is asking for the impossible. This is because all proof is either deductive or inductive or a combination of the two, and both stop short of certainty. Deduction, we say today, cannot be sure of its premises, while induction cannot be sure of its conclusions. Certainty is indeed possible *within* the deductive system, but how are the premises supported? Even the starting point of Descartes does not hold, except upon the assumption of the validity of the law of noncontradiction, but how is that to be proved?

It is not to Barclay's discredit that he had no awareness of these difficulties which are commonly understood by contemporary philosophers. He was not satisfied, therefore, as we recognize that we must be, by degrees of probability. The only alternatives which Barclay was able to recognize were certainty and skepticism. "To deny infallibility," he said, "is a bad way to make a Reformation: since they who do reform had need to be certain that they are doing so."[21] His mistake here was his unargued assumption that, if you are not certain, you cannot proceed at all. At this point he was never wholly free from his Roman Catholic boyhood teaching. It would have been

[21] *Truth Triumphant,* p. 893.

wonderful if he could have proceeded boldly, without feeling the need of infallibility, but perhaps this is asking too much.

How greatly Barclay feared a general and crippling skepticism was shown before he wrote the *Apology,* while he was writing the *Anarchy of the Ranters.* The important passage is:

> And if any will plead, that there is now no infallible judgment to be expected from the Spirit of God in the Church, it (no doubt) will leave the dissenters as much in the mist, and at as great a loss, as those they do dissent from; both being no better than blind men, hitting at random; which will turn Christianity into skepticism.[22]

Because it was skepticism he feared, he was convinced that, having abandoned the infallibility of both Rome and Geneva, he had to find another. But here the problem of human error raises its head. Barclay argued that the "true" follower will not be deceived in his immediate revelation, but how can he know which one is true? Muggleton thought *he* had direct revelations, and yet he was patently in error! How, then, is any third ground of infallibility to be discovered or defended?

The mistake which Barclay made about infallibility is genuine, but not crucial. His mistake lay in the fact that he did not distinguish, with sufficient sharpness, between the objective truth and the subjective awareness of the truth. There is, of course, no flaw at all in the truth itself. There is an absolutely reliable truth about how many people are now in the building, providing we are clear about what we mean by "building," by "people," and by "now." What we think, or what we wish, makes no difference at all. In this sense the truth is "infallible," and it is equally so whether we are talking about the character of God or what is really right or how many apples there are in the barrel. If this were not the case, there would be no possibility of genuine error and no reason to try to avoid it. Confusion enters at the moment we transfer any of this infallibility to the finite recipient, but this is what occurs whenever infallibility is claimed in practice. To apply the term to the truth itself is really a matter of fundamental confusion, because the claim to infallibility, when it is made, always refers to human judgments or to human productions. This is because, with all of our efforts, we never transcend subjectivity, in science

[22] *Truth Triumphant,* p. 235.

or in anything else. The laws which are discussed in natural science are presumably objective and unbreakable, but we never know laws "in themselves." All that we ever know, or can know, is what finite men *think* that the laws are. And it is in what we think that we can make mistakes. There is no probability whatever that our liability to error, which is intrinsic to our finitude, will ever be overcome. It is part of the price of our creaturehood.

This is what Barclay might have seen, but did not. Consequently, he contrasted Quakerism favorably with both Catholicism and Protestantism, and did so by a kind of trick. It was easy for him to show that any claim to infallibility in the judgments of the Church Fathers or of the Pope was vulnerable because of actual mistakes or contradictions, to which it is possible to point. In the same way, it is not difficult to show that any conclusion about Biblical infallibility is undermined by the conflicting interpretations of the same passages. By contrast, Barclay held that the leadership of the Spirit is an infallible source, because God does not lie, and also because the truth cannot cease to be true. But such a conclusion is only possible if Barclay omits the obvious fact that there is no experience of the leadership of the Spirit that does not depend upon the human instrument, which, in the nature of the case, is always far from perfect. He should have been able to see that immediate inspiration, which is undoubtedly prior to both Bible and Church tradition, requires human interpretation, exactly as both Bible and tradition require it.

There was a sense in which Barclay understood this, especially after his visit to London, with its introduction to the absurd fanaticism of some of the men who believed themselves to be in direct contact with the Holy Spirit. As an apparent result of this shocking revelation of human finitude, Barclay made some perceptive statements about the possibility of error in understanding the divine leading. In such passages, he was really denying infallibility, for only one instance is needed to destroy an absolute or universal claim. In spite of this, however, he still spoke of infallible guidance. How, the reader is bound to ask, was this possible? I think the answer is that, in the speed of his youthful writing, he never took the time to bring the two parts of his thought together. I think I detect layers in the *Apology,* especially in the development of the second proposition. It is the sort of failure which might have been overcome if, ten years later, Barclay could have brought out a revised edition of the major work. But he was hindered from doing this by the fact that he lived his life in chapters. When the more mature revision, producing greater coherence, might have been undertaken, Barclay was fully employed in political affairs and in responsibilities at court.

Many have tried to catch Barclay in intellectual mistakes of this kind, but the undertaking is not really profitable. We can learn from him without being bound by every word which he wrote. If we follow his most mature insights, which are found in the upper layer of his writing, we can neglect the others without condescension. Taking the major emphasis of Barclay as our key, we see that in most instances, he recognized the finite human predicament and, in practice, sought to learn how ways could be arranged for the validation of claimed revelations.

Barclay was recognizing the human liability to error when he mentioned the aberrations which have occurred among Christians who have claimed direct inspiration for their acts. "I confess I do," he says, "with my whole heart abhor and detest those wild practices which are written concerning the Anabaptists of Munster."[23] I consider this to be a part of the later and higher level of Barclay's thought. He limits himself to saying that equally monstrous events have come among those relying on the infallible Church or the infallible Book. This is true, but it has only negative effect and provides no positive support for the third kind of infallibility, which he asserted in other passages. But we are far, in any case, from the mood of the naïvely dogmatic passages which presumably represent his earlier and less critical position. An example of such naïveté is: "We then trust and confide in this Spirit, because we know and certainly believe, that it can only lead us aright, and never mislead us."[24] He combines this with an assertion of the infallibility of science which sounds strange to modern ears and which no scientist claims. An adequate reason for thinking of this as an earlier layer of thought is its striking similarity to what is found in the Notebook, clearly representing the precritical period.

The truly critical and presumably later mood is demonstrated when

[23] *Apology,* pp. 62, 63 [II, xiv].
[24] *Ibid.,* p. 68 [II, xv].

Barclay admits that any particular claim of revelation may be erroneous. The most sophisticated passage is that in which he says,

> For it is one thing to affirm, that the true and undoubted revelation of God's spirit is certain and infallible; and another thing to affirm, that this or that particular person or people is led infallibly by this revelation in what they speak or write, because they affirm themselves to be so led by the inward and immediate revelation of the Spirit. The first is only asserted by us, the later may be called in question.[25]

This may be confidently stated to be Barclay's mature conclusion. This judgment is supported by his insistence that the infallible judgment is dependent upon the existence of a genuine loving fellowship. The dependable leading comes, says Barclay, not to men in solitude or in contention, but "where there is any Gathering or Assembly, which truly and properly may be called the Church of Christ."[26]

Though Barclay suffered from inner confusion and conflict on the subject of infallibility, this did not affect his main contention. What rings true and clear is his major conclusion of what it is on which the knowledge of God rests. There are many good reasons for believing in God, including those based upon the order of the universe and the objectivity of the moral law, and these no sensitive person will neglect or minimize, since God has reached men in various ways, but all of these are instrinsically inferential. They may profitably be compared to the highly respectable reasoning of astronomers who conclude, on the basis of careful reasoning about the movements of other and known bodies, that there *must* be a new planet which has not been seen. This, which is rational speculation at its very best, provides some glorious chapters in the history of astronomy, but there is a world of difference between the rational inference and the actual perception. It is the latter which provides the ultimate verification of the accuracy of the speculation and, at the same time, introduces something which is different in kind. We can be grateful for the rational, but we are even more grateful for the empirical.

This explains Robert Barclay's approach to religious knowledge. He does not despise the rationality of the great theistic thinkers, but

[25] *Ibid.*, p. 58 [II, xiii].
[26] *Truth Triumphant*, p. 227.

he says that the very best evidence for God is that men actually *meet* Him. One of the most exciting facts about the world is that thousands of people, of many ages and of both sexes, have reported that, in their own experience, the Living God has reached them and has made them into new men and women. The skeptic may try to explain all of this as a psychological aberration, but when he does try, he is probably unaware of the magnitude of the task which he undertakes. His task is made greater by the fact that so many of those who provide a firsthand report are persons of both high intelligence and moral probity. Many, moreover, are critically minded. Over and over the report is verified by the most amazing life changes, not for a moment, but for all of the rest of their lives.

Some of these may be deluded, and this Barclay, like any reasonable man, is willing to admit. But what, we have a right to ask, is the chance that they are all deluded? This would, indeed, be a large order. The point is that either God really is, or *all* have been deluded. Barclay cannot believe this, because he knows something of what has occurred in changed lives. It is by reference to these that Barclay rests his case. Like a good scientist, he makes his report and allows others to make their own judgment. Of this gospel he says, God "hath raised up a few despicable and illiterate men, and for the most part mechanics, to be the dispensers of it; by which gospel all the scruples, doubts, hesitations and objections above mentioned are easily and evidently answered."[27] In the end Barclay does not reject authority; instead he points to the authority of experience.

The philosophy of Robert Barclay is thus deeply empirical, if we broaden the concept of empiricism to include spiritual experience and not merely, as has sometimes been done, limit the conception to physical or sense experience. There are, of course, people who reject the inclusion of direct religious experience in their empirical approach to reality, but they do so only by a dogmatism which they do not even attempt to defend. Though Barclay may, therefore, reasonably be called an empiricist, he did not hesitate to employ a variety of means of knowing the truth. We have our best understanding of the truth, he thought, when we use cumulative evidence, in which each strand in the rope of evidence confirms

[27] *Apology,* p. 131 [V and VI, x].

the others, until the total effect is greater than the mere sum of the parts. In this vein, Barclay speaks of those truths which have "been manifested to us by the revelation of Jesus Christ in us, fortified by our own sensible experience, and sealed by the testimony of the spirit in our hearts."[28] When several lines of evidence point in the same direction, the conclusion may not be absolutely certain, but the evidence is the best which men know or are likely to know.

It is important to realize that Barclay made no attempt to deal with all aspects of Christian theology. For example, he did not set out to prove the existence of God. This was not because he thought such proof was unprofitable or unnecessary, but because he was writing primarily for believing Christians and could, accordingly, assume many things without argument. "I write not to atheists, but to Christians, who already acknowledge; and I judge it not my work to write books to persuade them of that, they already profess to believe."[29]

The point at which Barclay was most sure that he was not wasting his time was that of religious epistemology. This is the central subject of his most meticulous philosophical work, his essay called "The Possibility and Necessity of the Inward and Immediate Revelation of the Spirit of God."[30] It was assumed by his correspondent that knowledge comes to men in only two ways, viz. sense experience and reason. Reason, it was held, can give necessary truths, while only sense experience can give contingent truths. Barclay's great step, philosophically, was to challenge the assumption that these two exhaust the possibilities. It is logically possible, he contended, that there is a third way and that contingent truths can be known by direct contact between God and the human mind. His deepest conviction, which was supported both by reason and by the experience of himself and others, was that there is a *third way* in epistemology. This third way is the way of experience, though it is not experience confined to the use of sense organs. If I know the sunshine because I experience it by visual sensation, why is it not possible to know the love of God through an experience which, though nonsensory, is equally genuine? The heart of Barclay's conten-

[28] *Ibid.*, pp. 131, 132 [V and VI, x].
[29] *The Apology Vindicated,* in *Truth Triumphant,* p. 733.
[30] This was first a letter in Latin addressed to Ambassador Paets of Holland.

tion, which is crucial to his entire system of thought and that of the People Called Quakers, is to the effect that "we may know a contingent truth by a supernatural knowledge, God supplying the place of the outward relator."[31]

In this enlargement of the concept of empiricism Barclay boldly upheld the idea of a spiritual sense. Natural and spiritual senses may be distinguished by their objects. Why, he asks, should one who really believes in God deny the power of God to speak inwardly to the ear of the inward man? That He does so speak is attested by a tremendous body of evidence, made up of the reports of otherwise trustworthy persons. To say that this cannot be, is to be guilty of human arrogance. In this emphasis on direct experience Barclay was going beyond Descartes, because Descartes stressed a natural idea of God in the human mind and sought, inferentially, to prove the existence of its objective source, while Barclay called attention to a direct experience. The big contrast is that between the Cartesian position of mere rationalism and the Barclayan position of spiritual empiricism.

Such careful intellectual examination may seem to be far from the simple proclamations of George Fox, and in some ways it is, but it must be remembered that Barclay was answering an intellectual inquiry and that his inquirer had raised the epistemological question in a direct fashion. If the inquiry could not be answered, the foundation of the faith was undermined. As Barclay was not denying reason, so he was not denying the value of sense experience or the material order; he was merely affirming that these together do not exhaust the possibilities.[32]

What is most surprising, in Barclay's epistemology, is its high degree of sophistication. He recognized that, in sense experience, the subjective interpretation is as important as is the "corporeal motion." Because we add our expectations, every experience is a construct. Thus he denied the validity of naïve realism and upheld the representative character of all knowledge. His chief contribution, here, was

[31] *Truth Triumphant,* p. 896.

[32] This point is almost wholly missed by Dr. Leif Eeg-Olofsson, in his published dissertation, *The Conception of the Inner Light in Robert Barclay's Theology*. He says that Barclay "owing to his theory of knowledge could not see that a spiritual, inner knowledge can be given through outer things" (p. 207). On the contrary, Barclay's point was that spiritual knowledge is not *limited* to what comes by outer things.

the valuable observation that exactly the same structure appears in both natural and supernatural knowledge. In both it is possible, because of subjective interpretation, to make mistakes. The causes of error are in the *receiver*, not in the object. Since this is true of both reason and sense experience, it is not really surprising that it is also true in spiritual experience. "And if there be at any time a mistake, the divine illumination is not the cause of the mistake, but some evil disposition of the mind."[33] Such epistemological dualism is the surest mark of Barclay's intellectual sophistication. That it was his final position is indicated by the fact that he translated his philosophical essay into English and prepared it for publication only four years before he died.

[33] *Truth Triumphant,* p. 902.

CHAPTER IX

THE LIGHT OF CHRIST

The Light who lights every one who comes into the world, is no peculiar tenet of the Quakers.

—*Charles Kingsley*

THE PARALLELS in the careers of Robert Barclay and John Calvin are numerous and striking. Both began in Roman Catholicism, both had vivid conversions, both wrote with rare maturity at the age of twenty-six. There was never any doubt in Barclay's mind, after he saw his vocation clearly, who it was that he had to match. It was John Calvin of Geneva (1509–1564). The similarity of style of the *Apology* to that of the *Institutes* has often been noted. Like Calvin, Barclay wrote first in Latin, to try to reach the learned of all lands; like Calvin, he began with an address to his reigning king; like Calvin, he later translated his work into his own native language. In short, Robert Barclay attempted to state Christian truth for his generation as John Calvin had tried to state the truth as he saw it, one hundred and forty years earlier.

It is obvious that there was much in Calvinistic thought which Barclay admired and consequently accepted. Five major points stand out in this regard. First, Barclay accepted the sovereignty of God, with no tendency to erase the radical distinction between the creature and the Creator. Second, he accepted the reality of human sin, never doubting its factual universality in the race of men. Third, he accepted the necessity of the work of Christ, because of the manifest inability of men to save themselves. Fourth, he accepted the necessity of personal individual salvation, because no one is able to inherit his religion. Fifth, he accepted the idea that the Christian religion must influence all of life, thereby fundamentally denying the distinction between the sacred and the secular.

In spite of this large area of conscious indebtedness and agreement, one aspect of Calvin's analysis shocked Barclay in a radical fashion. On the basis of his own direct experience, and that of others whom he trusted, Barclay believed wholeheartedly in the Living God who was accurately revealed in Christ, i.e. that the God of all the world was like Christ. If He were like Christ, He would undoubtedly reach out tirelessly to every son and daughter of earth. But, to his amazement, Barclay read in Calvin's *Institutes* that God had deliberately withheld His saving power from some men, perhaps even the majority of men. That there was inequality of powers and inequality among humans, some being vastly less fortunate than others, was not the problem. The problem was that such manifest inequality extended to eternal salvation and that it was in accordance with the divine will. Here was a contradiction in the very character of God Himself, an extreme form, indeed, of the problem of evil. The dilemma arises from the agreed fact that many men do not know God. Does this mean that God *cannot* or that God *will not* bring them into fellowship with Himself? Calvin, filled as he was with the sense of God's sovereign power, had chosen the second horn of this cruel dilemma.

It must be clearly understood that the problem which so aroused young Barclay was not that of the occurrence of sin. Being very much a realist, he recognized sin as factual. The human heart, he said, moves toward its own self-centeredness much as a stone, according to the principle of gravitation, tends to move toward the center of the earth.[1] He quoted approvingly "the heart is deceitful above all things, and desperately wicked" (Jer. 17:9). In short, he did not lean, in the least, in the direction of sentimental optimism about the human situation. The revelations of what men do in concentration camps may have shocked many twentieth-century men, indoctrinated by the idea of natural human goodness, but they would not have shocked Robert Barclay.

[1] *Apology,* pp. 100, 101 [IV, ii].

This does not mean that Barclay believed in that version of original sin which sees newborn babes as already corrupt and, for that reason, needing the magic of baptism to avoid eternal damnation, for his realism saved him from this monstrous conclusion. While he admitted that men and women do, as a matter of fact, move in experience into lives of sin, there is no reason for children to be called sinners simply because they are so *potentially*. His statement is that the "evil and corrupt seed is not imputed to infants, until they actually join with it." The very notion that the unbaptized infant could be condemned before self-consciousness has arisen is contradictory to the idea that "no man is ever threatened or judged for what iniquity he hath not actually wrought."[2] Consequently the Roman Catholic's frenzied insistence upon infant baptism, in order to avoid damnation, Barclay did not hesitate to brand as absurd in itself and both cruel and contrary to both God's mercy and justice. The Apologist took actual sin so seriously that he could not imagine the possibility of its being washed away by a mere ceremony.

Barclay's quarrel with Calvin was on the specific point at which later generations have recognized Calvin's vulnerability, his conception of double election. Since Propositions V and VI of the *Apology* were devoted to the "Universal and Saving Light of Christ," the author began the discussion by dealing directly with the particular position which he was out to demolish.

> As for that doctrine which these propositions chiefly strike at, to wit, absolute reprobation, according to which some are not afraid to assert, That God, by an eternal and immutable decree, hath predestinated to eternal damnation the far greater part of mankind . . . and that for the bringing this about, he hath appointed these miserable souls necessarily to walk in their wicked ways . . . yet he justly condemns for disobedience, albeit he hath withheld from them all grace by which they could have laid hold of the gospel.[3]

In the strongest language which he is known to have used in print, Barclay called this a "horrible and blasphemous doctrine." To blame people for what they cannot possibly avoid seemed to him to be the height of absurdity, utterly destructive of any conception of responsibility.

[2] *Ibid.*, p. 105 [IV, iv].
[3] *Ibid.*, p. 112 [V and VI].

The reasons for rejecting the idea of predetermined reprobation are specific. The first is that it lowers the conception of God, by making Him the author of sin. The idea that God would deliberately withhold His saving light and love from any one of His children, who are made in His image, is in direct conflict with the empirical evidence of first-hand religious experience. Barclay and those whom he trusted had experienced God, as the Father of Jesus Christ, always giving because always personal. In the light of this experience he could not think of God merely as an unmoved Mover, in the Aristotelian sense, or as an impersonal Principle. God, as the Apologist knew Him, on the basis of the evidence which he trusted most, was the One who was always reaching out to men, seeking them even more than they could seek Him. A God who would arbitrarily decide to leave some men unreached would be something quite different, and also something not really worthy of reverence. That this was a subject about which the author of the *Apology* felt passionately is shown by the following sentence:

> For if he hath created men only for this very end, that he might show forth his justice and power in them, as these men affirm, and for effecting thereof hath not only withheld from them the means of doing good, but also predestinated the evil, that they might fall into it; and that he inclines and forces them into great sins; certainly he must delight in their death, and will them to die; seeing against his own will he neither doth, nor can do anything.[4]

Another argument employed was that such a doctrine limits the effectiveness of Christ, because it necessarily means that He touches only a small part of mankind. It is idle, then, to say that He died for *all*. The most impressive argument, however, is the practical one that the doctrine in question makes a mockery of the preaching of the gospel. What is the value of bringing the gospel to men who, "by an irrevocable decree," are excluded from the possibility of being benefited by it? The reasonable man, if he were a complete Calvinist, says Barclay, would do nothing, because he would "wait for the irresistible juncture," knowing that what is to come *will* come, regardless of any human action. In short, the doctrine, taken seriously, would cut the nerve of all evangelical effort.

[4] *Ibid.*, p. 116 [V and VI, iii].

We must remember that the dogma which Barclay thus attacked was one with which he was extremely familiar. The Westminster Assembly had been summoned by the Long Parliament in June, 1643, only five and a half years before Barclay's birth, and the mood of its deliberations was the prevailing mood of his early Scottish childhood. However vigorous his attack became, he knew that the dogma was one which intelligent people accepted, and he knew why. Though nobody felt good about double election, thoughtful men believed that they were forced into accepting it by a combination of factors. They observed, for one thing, the factual inequality in both human knowledge and human goodness. It was a fact of history that some had never heard of Christ, while others who had heard of Him rejected Him. When Calvinists coupled this empirical observation with the idea of the absolute sovereignty of God, the intellectual predicament was terrible. They felt constrained to conclude, by the combination of two propositions, that the observed inequality was in accordance with the divine will. Here is a problem which no one wholly solves, but for a man of the temperament of the twenty-six-year-old Barclay it was truly agonizing.

The more Barclay studied the Bible, the more he was convinced that some solution of the problem had to be found, for the New Testament evidence of the intention of universal redemption was overwhelming. The joy heralded by the Judean shepherds was to be "to all people." "The gospel," says Barclay, "invites all; and certainly, by the gospel, Christ intended not to deceive and delude the greater part of mankind, when he invites and crieth, saying; 'Come unto me, all ye that labour and are heavy laden, and I will give you rest.' "[5] Who, Barclay asks, is bound to seek after that which is impossible? What an unbearable paradox it would be for God to give men "a commission to preach the gospel of salvation unto all, while he hath before decreed that it shall not be possible for them to receive it." How strange that we are asked to pray for all men, when "no man is bound to pray for that which is impossible to be attained." Here the clear mind of the logician is at work. Because he finds the situation intolerable, he seeks a solution.

The sharpness of Barclay's problem may be best exhibited in the

[5] *Ibid.*, p. 120 [V and VI, vi].

form of a dilemma. What is a Christian's reaction to Christ's assertion, "No one comes to the Father but by me" (John 14:6)? If Christ is the *only* Way, as He says, and if most men have not had the opportunity of knowing that Way, the dilemma is as follows: Either it is a fact that most members of the human species have been condemned without a chance, or we must conclude that Christ was wrong in His assertion. Since Barclay found that he had to reject both of these possibilities, his only hope lay in further thinking, which might make him conclude that the two unacceptable propositions did not exhaust the logical possibilities.

As has so often occurred in human thought, the problem was solved by questioning, and consequently discarding, a premise which, if retained, makes a solution impossible. The making of the premise explicit is an important step in the intellectual effort because, once it is clearly seen, the premise is by no means self-evident. The premise which Barclay examines is that the work of Christ is limited to His earthly appearing. Once Barclay scrutinized this he realized that there is no adequate reason for accepting it as true. With the consequent intellectual freedom, Barclay saw the way in which both horns of the dilemma could be avoided. The essence of his solution lay in the double affirmation as follows: It is true that men cannot be saved apart from Christ; it is likewise true that any spatial or temporal limitations on His saving power must be rejected. *All men need Him; but the good news is that all men may have Him.*

The key to this new approach was, of course, one which had long been known, the Logos doctrine, which is so eloquently expressed in the prologue to the Fourth Gospel. Therefore, Barclay's solution was by no means original, though he was the first Christian thinker to make it both explicit and central. Earlier Quakers had already made so much use of "That was the true light which lighteth every man that cometh into the world" (John 1:9), that it was known as the "Quakers' text." Barclay differed from them only in the systematic way in which he presented the solution. So much did he value the text just mentioned that he presented it, along with John 3:16, even in the original *Theses Theologicae*. His own statement of the position, which brought such relief to his troubled mind and which is one of the most important in all of Quaker thought, appears in the *Apology* as follows:

> That God, who out of his infinite love sent his Son, the Lord Jesus Christ, into the world, who tasted death for every man, hath given to every man, whether Jew or Gentile, Turk or Scythian, Indian or Barbarian, of whatever nation, country, or place, a certain day or time of visitation; during which day or time it is possible for them to be saved, and to partake of the fruit of Christ's death.[6]

By taking the idea of the eternal or Living Christ seriously, in the mood of John's Gospel, Barclay was able to see that Christ has been reaching out to men, not only in Palestine during a few years of human history, but from the beginning, as will be the case until the end. If this is not accepted there is no escape from the idea of divine injustice. Unless we accept some such position as that stated by Barclay, we cannot escape the conclusion that Socrates is in hell! But, if Barclay's thesis is accepted, the gospel is indeed good news, since it means that Socrates, when he listened so obediently to the inner voice, clearly had what Barclay calls his "day of visitation." There is still human inequality, even if this liberating idea is seen as true, and such inequality is a mystery which neither Barclay nor any other honest thinker can fully explain, but if the new insight is a valid one, the absolute barrier to belief in God's outgoing love is removed.

We have not, even by Barclay's great forward step, solved all of the problems, and it is not likely that we shall ever do so, but we have made a genuine advance when we choose the least evil among available alternatives. Two distinguished Christian thinkers, whose presence we sorely miss, H. G. Wood and John Baillie, expressed independently the conception that, since no solution of any profound problem is free from difficulties, the path of wisdom is to accept the solution with the least difficulties. In a valuable autobiographical preface H. G. Wood wrote:

> When, at the University, the difficulties of Christian theism were forced on my attention, I did not feel inclined hastily to throw over theism, because I knew that the difficulties of other positions might prove more serious than those I was asked to recognize in theism.[7]

In estimating the value of Barclay's central conviction, we need to

[6] *Ibid.*, p. 132 [V and VI, xi].

[7] H. G. Wood, *Christianity and the Nature of History* (Cambridge, Eng.: The University Press, 1934), p. xviii. Compare John Baillie, *Invitation to Pilgrimage, op. cit.*, pp. 20, 21.

keep in mind the difficulties inherent in any known alternative. At least, Barclay avoids ascribing to God the condemnation of men for failures for which they are not responsible. If there is any revelation at all, outside the limits of historical Christianity, this, says Barclay, "sufficiently exonerateth God of every man's condemnation."[8]

Because the revelation to most of mankind is necessarily an inner experience, and because Barclay like other Quakers made abundant use of the metaphor of light, the doctrine of universal hope came to be known by the designation "Inner Light," though this was not Barclay's characteristic usage. The Quaker theologian was well aware that he was dealing with the deepest kind of mystery, for which no language is or can be adequate. All that we have is experience, plus some power of intellectual organization. It is not surprising, therefore, to find the employment of various forms of language. One term, which Barclay possibly took over from Keith, was *Vehiculum Dei,* but it was not much used, partly because it sounds forbidding. One of Barclay's favorite metaphors was that of the "seed." The seed is in all, but it does not always mature. In the long run, however, it was the term "light" which prevailed, largely on account of John 1:9. Because light is outgoing, as the Word is, the expression seemed appropriate, in reference to the divine self-giving. As light penetrates darkness, the eternal Christ is seen as illuminating the darkness of men's minds, though they, if they will, can erect barriers to His reception. Christ, by coming also in the flesh in the course of human history provided, not a contrast to the Light which has always been shining in men's hearts, but a highly visible demonstration of that same Light. Though the Light "strives and wrestles" with men to save them, a man cannot have the vision merely by deciding to have it. This was Barclay's way of facing the problem of free will and predestination. A finite man cannot initiate the encounter, though God has made Himself vulnerable by allowing man the right to resist it.

Barclay's defense of the universality of the Light of Christ did not depend merely upon reason and Scripture, though both were persuasive. It rested, in addition, on the record of men's lives. Though he was always Christ-centered in his faith, he could not, as a superbly honest man, avoid admitting that there has been a high level of

[8] *Apology,* p. 136 [V and VI, xii].

religious experience on the part of some non-Christians. This ceases to seem strange if Christ's revelation has been independent of temporal limitations. It pleased Barclay to learn that this was no new idea of his, but was known in the age of primitive Christians. "Hence Justin Martyr stuck not to call Socrates a Christian, saying that 'all such as lived according to the divine word in them, which was in all men, were Christians, such as Socrates and Heraclitus, and others among the Greeks,' etc. 'that such as live with the word, are Christians without fear or anxiety.' "[9] He referred also to Augustine's suggestion, in the *Confessions,* that he had read in the writings of the Platonists statements which helped to confirm the conception of the eternal Word.

Barclay's generous recognition of the fruits of the Christian life, wherever he found them, led him into one celebrated mistake. This was the minor fact that he gave a few lines to the life of a man who is now generally supposed to have been a fictional character, Hai Eben Yokdan. The story of Yokdan, a prototype of Robinson Crusoe, became popular at the very time that Barclay was doing his major writing. It depicted a man who, though living on an island, separated from infancy from all other human beings, nevertheless was reached by the divine Light in spite of his obvious handicap. Here, it seemed, was an extreme form of the evidence which Barclay was seeking to assemble. With rare restraint, however, he limited himself to the following paragraph:

> Yea, there is a book translated out of the Arabic, which gives an account of one Hai Eben Yokdan; who living in an island alone, without converse of man, attained to such a profound knowledge of God, as to have immediate converse with him, and to affirm, "that the best and most certain knowledge of God is not that which is attained by premises premised, and conclusions deduced; but that which is enjoyed by conjunction of the mind of man with the supreme intellect, after the mind is purified from its corruptions, and is separated from all bodily images, and is gathered into a profound stillness."[10]

This brief account appeared at the end of *Apology* V and VI, xxvii, in the Latin edition and also in the English translation of

[9] *Ibid.,* pp. 187, 188 [V and VI, xxvii].
[10] *Ibid.,* pp. 188, 189 [V and VI, xxvii].

1678, as well as *Truth Triumphant* and several eighteenth-century editions.

The account came to Britain in the form of an Arabic book by Abi Jaafar Eb'n Tophail, described in one translation as "a philosopher by profession, and a Mohemetan by religion." It was translated into Latin and published in 1671 by an Oxford scholar, Edward Pocock, with the help of his father. A Dutch translation appeared in 1672 and one in English in 1674, when Barclay was already writing the *Apology*. Though the title page of the English version does not carry the name of the translator, it is now agreed that he was none other than George Keith, Barclay's stormy friend and literary collaborator, who evidently brought the tale to Barclay's attention.[11] The story so delighted the readers of the period that it appeared in many editions, the most famous of which was produced in 1708 by Simon Ockley, with the title, *The Improvement of Human Reason Exhibited in the Life of Hai Ebn Yokdahan.* It is easy to see how such a tale was accepted uncritically by those who were devoted to the romantic idea of the "noble savage." Though subsequent scholars have long concluded that the orginal work was a romance, it appears that the seventeenth-century translators looked upon it as an historical account. If Barclay made a mistake, it was the mistake of taking their judgment.

As the eighteenth century advanced there was increasing doubt as to whether the Arabic Robinson Crusoe had ever existed, and Quakers, consequently, decided to be careful. In the highly legible Minutes of the Morning Meeting for February 14, 1780, we learn that Friends had discussed with care the question of "the propriety of making any alterations or remarks on Robert Barclay's Apology." The practical decision was that it be reprinted according to the last octavo edition, leaving out the story of Hai Eben Yokdan. The deletion was inconspicuous, Article xvii of Propositions V and VI simply being shorter by one paragraph in some subsequent editions. For ex-

[11] In Antonio Pastor, *The Idea of Robinson Crusoe* (Watford, Eng.: Gongora Press, 1930) it is asserted unequivocally that Keith was the translator. Henry J. Cadbury says the anonymous translation of 1674 "is now definitely proved to have been the work of George Keith." See "Early Quakerism and Uncanonical Lore," *Harvard Theological Review,* Vol. XL (July, 1947), pp. 195, 196. See also *Journal of Friends Historical Society,* Vol. XXVII (1930), pp. 65, 66.

ample, the tale is omitted from the three-volume edition of *Truth Triumphant* (New York, 1831) though it was retained in the stereotype edition of the *Apology* (Philadelphia, 1908).

The short paragraph in the *Apology* might have been forgotten, had it not become a weapon in theological controversy among nineteenth-century Quakers. The chief furore arose as a reflection of the strong evangelical reaction to the influence of Elias Hicks, especially among those known as Beaconites. These partisans, who already feared Barclay, used the Arabic tale as a means of attacking the standard of Quaker thought at what they supposed to be a vulnerable point. They spoke of the tale as though it were a conscious forgery, when actually the worst that can be said was that Barclay trusted Keith and others by whom the story came to him.

The most vicious attack on Barclay's use of the disputed tale was that of John Wilkinson (1783?–1846). The latter left the Society of Friends in 1836 because he believed that Friends minimized the Scriptures and the mediation of Christ. He told vividly how he was affected by the news that the Arabic tale was probably fictitious:

> I was informed that, in the later editions of the *Apology,* the story of Yokdan had been omitted, because it was found that it had a fabulous origin. I am not likely to forget the effect this information had upon my mind, in breaking the spell under which I was bound by Barclay, and it gave me also a pretty strong caution with regard to laying much stress on immediate revelation.[12]

When Joseph Smith, Quaker bookseller and collector, gained possession of the book which Barclay had evidently seen, he published a broadside in which he offered to make it available in a reprinting. His purpose, he said, was to "vindicate the character of Robert Barclay from the odium which has been cast upon it by some adversaries."[13] Even before Smith's spirited defense of Barclay, writers in *British Friend* had suggested that much was being made of little. In the issue of August, 1847 it was pointed out that, since "the author's argument receives but little additional support from the passage," it "consequently is but little weakened by the omissions." "It is evidently

[12] John Wilkinson, *Quakerism Examined* (London, 1836), pp. 82, 83.

[13] A copy of the broadside is preserved in the Friends House Library. The date is 1862.

a most incorrect assumption," the article goes on, "that the apologist laid much stress on this case, as, in addition to 26 sections preceding his allusion to it, chiefly founded on the Holy Scriptures, the 27th is almost wholly employed in giving testimonies to the Inward Light, from both heathen and Christian writers; to shew that it is the *inward work,* and not alone the *outward history and Scripture,* that gives the true knowledge."[14]

Though the controversy has no present significance, it may be necessary to say in passing that the claim that Barclay got his basic idea from a fictitious story is preposterous. There is abundant evidence that his central convictions arose independently of this account, which came to his attention late, and which he used very briefly, as a kind of postscript to a collection of other experiences intended to support his thesis. What is interesting to the Quaker historian, however, is the way in which Quakers, a century or more ago, were divided on the issue of reprinting or not reprinting the paragraph in question. While the extreme evangelical party always wanted it deleted, the conservatives tended to keep it, apparently on the ground that Barclay provided a solid center, away from all extremes, and was therefore worthy of support. Since the problem now has only historical interest, it is wise to retain, insofar as possible, the integrity of Barclay's original text. The issue was once blown up out of all proportion to its true importance. Even if the original Arabic story were a romance, it does no harm. In any case, the citing as evidence of what was fictitious cannot, by any reasonable logic, undermine the doctrine of the universality of Christ's Saving Light. To deny the conclusion because one piece of evidence has been shown to be fictitious, would be to commit the "fallacy of transferred errancy."

The very comprehensiveness of Barclay's position makes it easy to pervert or to misunderstand it. The problem arises when the reader who notes Barclay's emphasis on one side of a complicated issue may fail to note that he also places equal emphasis on another and complementary side. The orthodox Christian may easily suppose that he stresses too much the universality of Christ, while the mystic may be disturbed by his stress on the historic Christian revelation at a particular time and place. The important step, for both and for all others,

[14] *The British Friend,* Vol. V, p. 211.

is the recognition that Barclay sought deliberately to state both aspects of what is necessarily a complex situation. The fact that Christ came in the flesh does not deny the possibility of encountering Him in contemporary experience. At the heart of Barclay's understanding of the central Quaker doctrine is the deep conviction of the identity of the historic Christ and the Living Christ.[15]

If the central point of identification is kept in mind and recognized as valid in Quaker thought, intellectual pitfalls on both the right and the left can be avoided. Above all, we are saved from the danger of interpreting the Light naturalistically or humanistically, as is often done when the phrase "that of God in every one" is made to do duty as a virtual creed.[16] This phrase is welcomed by some precisely because it makes no reference to Christ at all and thus appears to provide emancipation from the confines of a particular historic faith. Though the phrase is from Fox, there is no reason to suppose that the founder of Quakerism ever thought of the Universal Light as separated from Jesus Christ. His fundamental insight, as he was moving over from seeker to finder, was, "There is one, even Christ Jesus, that can speak to thy condition."[17] This is why Geoffrey Nuttall says, unequivocally, "George Fox's Lord was no mere light within."[18] It was in accordance with the teaching and experience of Fox that Barclay, like Penn, spoke characteristically, not of the "Inner Light," but of the "Light of Christ." It is a mark of Barclay's amazing maturity, in spite of his youth, that he recognized so early the opposing dangers and prepared to overcome them. This explains why he did not identify himself with the Cambridge Platonists, though he met Henry More and quoted him briefly. He saw immense dangers in a generalized mysticism, separated from a Christ-centered faith. The late Herbert G. Wood, one of the ablest of modern Quaker theologians, saw this clearly and cxpressed it when he said, "Admittedly, when the early Quaker concern with Christ as an inward teacher is

[15] See *Truth Triumphant,* p. 627.

[16] The phrase was employed, in part, by Barclay in his last letter to Princess Elizabeth, when he wrote of "the answer of that of God," but he was more careful, than was Fox, in avoiding the dangers inherent in its use. In the same sentence he spoke of his testimony "for Christ and his Truth's sake."

[17] *Journal* (1952), p. 11.

[18] *Ibid.,* p. xxviii.

obscured, the doctrine of the inner light becomes an intellectualistic-moralistic mysticism."[19]

The very dualism on account of which Barclay was attacked and dismissed a generation ago, now appears to be one of his greatest strengths. His dualism includes a real distinction between the natural and the supernatural light. The former is the light of reason, which is generically a part of man as man, but the latter is experienced as a divine gift. No man, said Barclay, is either Christ or God, "but God and Christ are in us." The divine Light is in all men, but it is not *of* all men. This is what Barclay meant when he wrote of "this inward gift, grace and light."[20] He had no faith in what is called "natural religion," and said explicitly, "Nature cannot refresh or comfort the soul, nor pour in wine and oil into it when it is wounded with sin."[21] It was not that Barclay was insensitive to natural beauty, but rather that there are some wounds which are too deep to be healed in that way. Nature-mysticism, as later expressed by Wordsworth, would have seemed to Barclay better than nothing, but also far removed from a real encounter with Jesus Christ in the heart. There is much reason to conclude that Barclay's interpretation of the Christian faith in terms of dualism was not, as is often asserted, an unconscious adoption of the thought forms of his day, but rather the result of a profound understanding of the human situation. In any case his philosophical dualism was not something he added to the faith which he espoused, since it was inherent in the experience of Quakers, who lived constantly with the paradox that, though they were themselves unworthy, God in Christ had, nevertheless, reached out to them with His transforming power.

This basic theology may rightly be called the theology of the Holy Spirit. Barclay identified the Holy Spirit with the Living Christ. The Holy Spirit is not spirit in general, but that which is consistent with Christ's earthly life, teaching, death, and resurrection. The historic revelation of Christ gives precision; the revelation of the Holy Spirit in each contemporary life gives universality; and it is the combination which makes vital Christianity possible. The Word, Barclay believed,

19 *Theology,* Vol. LVII (1954), pp. 350, 351.
20 *Apology,* p. 189 [V and VI, xxviii].
21 *Truth Triumphant,* p. 631.

not only became flesh and dwelt among men, but continues today as the contemporary Word. It is a serious mistake to suppose that Barclay, as a Christian thinker, was less than orthodox. On the contrary, he was orthodox *and more!* In this he represented George Fox with great fidelity. Fox accepted every item of the Apostles' Creed, but did not end there. The same can be said of Barclay, the best evidence not being found in the *Apology,* but in the writings in which he answered specific questions. The clearest answers are provided in the manuscript dialogue with his uncle, Charles Gordon, to whom he wrote, "I believe, according to the Scriptures that there are three which bear record in heaven, the Father, the Word, and the Holy Ghost, and these three are one." This is similar to the statement by George Fox who said, in 1673, "As God did then speak by his Son, in the days of flesh, so the Son, Christ Jesus, doth now speak by his spirit."[22]

If any one asked how the historic and living Christ could be identical, Barclay's only answer was that this is a miracle and also a mystery. This did not bother him, for he knew already that he lived in a world full of mystery. In spite of the mystery, he accepted the identity because it had the double evidence of Christ's statement and his own immediate experience. The One whom he knew as his Guide and Teacher in the Aberdeen prison was available to him, as He had been to those with whom He walked on the road to Emmaus. Like those travelers, Barclay's heart burned within him and he sensed directly the identity. Those who had not had such an experience were not, he thought, in a logical position to deny it, while only dogmatism could hold it to be impossible.

The final wonder was that God had shown His outgoing love by making such an experience of the Living Christ available, even to those who could not match it with the helpful knowledge of the Christ of history. "The history then," Barclay wrote, "is profitable and comfortable, with the mystery, and never without it: but the mystery is and may be, profitable without the explicit and outward knowledge of the history."[23]

Barclay's use of the word "mystery" leads to the question whether his interpretation of the Quaker understanding of the Christian faith had any affinity with what is usually termed mysticism. It is well

[22] *Journal* (1952), p. 666.
[23] *Apology,* p. 141 [V and VI, xv].

known that Rufus M. Jones was the archexponent of the thesis that Quakerism was best understood in terms of its mystical roots, particularly those found in Continental mystical movements. Since the death of Professor Jones in 1948, there has been a tendency for scholars to conclude that he was wrong in emphasizing the Continental connection, because there is so much evidence of the influence of purely British and specifically Puritan sources.[24] Referring to the early Quakers, Henry J. Cadbury writes, "It is increasingly clear that we need not look to the continent for their spiritual roots. These could be found in England."[25] Curiously, it is sometimes assumed that this settles the question of any affinity between Quakerism and mysticism, but it does not. Whatever the geographical source of influence may have been, the question of the true interpretation of the Quakerism of the creative period remains.

The relevant point to make, in connection with Barclay's treatment of the Light of Christ, is that much of his emphasis is consistent with what Rufus Jones interpreted as mysticism, i.e. emphasis on firsthand religious experience. Indeed, this is the only way in which Barclay can maintain the identity of the Christ of History and the Christ of experience. "Christ outwardly died but once, but inwardly he dieth in a spiritual and mystical sense as often as any crucify him to themselves by their unfaithfulness and disobedience."[26] It was in his profound essay on "Immediate Revelation" that Barclay dealt with the kind of experience which establishes some affinity between Quakerism and the mysticism for which Rufus Jones contended. Barclay's description of the religious experience which is self-authenticating is as follows:

> Spiritual-minded men do behold the glory and beauty of God, in respect whereof and for which all the glory of this world is despicable to them; yea, even as dross and dung. And they also hear God inwardly speaking in their souls words truly divine and heavenly, full of virtue and

[24] Influential in this alteration of historical judgment is Geoffrey Nuttall. See especially *The Holy Spirit in Puritan Faith and Experience* (Oxford: Basil Blackwell, 1946). Professor Nuttall's thesis has been given strong support by the publication of Hugh Barbour's Yale dissertation, *The Quakers in Puritan England* (New Haven: Yale University Press, 1964).

[25] Henry J. Cadbury, "Revised Views of Quaker Origins," *The Friend* (London), January 1, 1954, p. 6.

[26] *Truth Triumphant*, p. 628.

divine life; and they savour the taste of divine things, and do as it were handle them with the hands of their souls. And those heavenly enjoyments do as really differ in their nature from all false similitudes and fictitious appearances of them, which either the mind of man by its own strength can imitate, or any evil spirit to deceive man counterfeit; as a true man differs from the dead image of a man; or true bread, honey, wine or milk doth from a mere picture of those things.[27]

There was certainly a mystical aspect of Barclay's thinking because the heart of all mysticism is a sense of the insufficiency of a merely historical faith. Barclay qualified for this by his insistence upon the necessity of personal experience, without which historical knowledge of events will not suffice. But the character of his mysticism was limited by the fact that he also saw the necessity of historical revelation and therefore of particularity. This was how his matured mysticism was saved from any taint of pantheism. Barclay was preserved, finally, both by his deep Biblical involvement and by his robust common sense, from the temptation to identify the finite individual with the divine. We know now that Barclay had this temptation and that he learned how to resist it. One of the striking values of the deciphered shorthand is that it shows that he upheld a more extreme mysticism in his youthful jottings, before he had seen its dangers. In his precritical phase he understood Quakerism as an extreme form of mysticism, saying that men "become also a part of God." There is, however, nothing like this in the *Apology*. The words spoken by a visitor at the first meeting at Ury were mystical words, but nine years later the Apologist had come to appreciate ideas of a radically different character. The words "in nothingness there are all things" appealed to him at eighteen, but this was a taste which he outgrew.

Barclay's contact with mysticism, in the popular sense, included his acquaintance with Francis Mercurius Van Helmont,[28] the close friend and personal physician of Lady Conway, of Ragley Hall. He was the son of the famous mystic and alchemist, Jean Baptiste Van Helmont (1577–1644). Lady Conway's physician became a Quaker, as she did, though he was a strange one. One evidence of his eccen-

[27] *Ibid.*, p. 902.

[28] See William Braithwaite, *Second Period of Quakerism,* 2d ed. *op. cit.*, pp. 687, 688.

tricity was that he led George Keith to accept the doctrine of the transmigration of souls. His close touch with Continental cabalists was an aspect of his religion which appears to have repelled Barclay. It was probably one of the influences which led him progressively closer to orthodox Christianity or at least to a kind of Quakerism consistent with such orthodoxy. Accordingly, Barclay did not see Quakerism as a species of mysticism, though he could not deny the validity of some conceptions normally associated with the mystical heritage. What he valued was the mysticism of the New Testament. Dr. Van Dalfsen, in her scholarly study of the Inner Light, indicates how deeply Christian the particular kind of mysticism finally expounded by Barclay really was:

> The Inward Light is with the Quakers another term for the Holy Spirit, by whom God, as the living Christ, is present in man. In other words it is a personal numinous spiritual Substance, in essence Christ, distinguishable from man himself, both cosmic and yet inward, which can as such be experienced, and the influence of Whom is manifest in changing the man in whom He dwells.[29]

Perhaps the most striking difference between Barclay's mysticism and mysticism in general was his emphasis upon power. The Light, though it may illuminate, does not give wisdom so much as energy. The Apologist was, in this regard, faithful to the theology of the Holy Spirit which the New Testament provides. In His last recorded utterance on earth Christ was reported as saying to His feeble followers, "You shall receive power when the Holy Spirit has come upon you" (Acts 1:8). The promise was fulfilled, not only at Pentecost, but according to Barclay on many subsequent occasions. It is revealing that Barclay, when he came to the last sentence of his long chapter on the "Universal and Saving Light," was careful to put the final stress on power. His declared purpose was that all should come "to mind the Light in them, and know Christ in them . . . to be crucified by the Power of his Cross in them, so as they may . . . come to walk in his Light." The verification of religious experience, then, was not mere illumination, but new life.

[29] G. L. Van Dalfsen, *Het Inwaartsh Licht Bij de Quakers* (1940), p. 197.

CHAPTER X

THE CHURCH OF CHRIST

It is impossible for men to meet with God and to love Him without at the same time meeting with and loving one another.

—John Baillie

IN DEVELOPING a philosophy which was both evangelical and rational, Barclay soon recognized that it was necessary to deal clearly with the nature of the Christian fellowship. Indeed, in writing the *Apology,* he introduced the problem of the nature of the Church just prior to his treatment of ministry and worship, two topics which he was obviously eager to handle. He did this because he saw that, unless the character of the Church was understood, it was obviously futile to try to deal with the practical matters which had been central to his thought since he had begun, as a boy, to write in his private Notebook. There is no point in developing the ministry unless it represents the gathered community, and there is no real depth to worship if it is carried on alone. It is preposterous, says Barclay, to speak of the *offices* of the Church, unless we know what the Church is.

Barclay, to the surprise of many, accepted the dictum that outside the Church there is no salvation. By this he did not, of course, refer to the Roman Church or any other particular denomination. His point was that Christianity is intrinsically social, that a person cannot be a Christian alone, and that, when we once know Christ in our hearts we are bound to find or to produce a fellowship to which we can belong. It is a strange irony of history that there has often been a general supposition that Quakers are pure individualists, each going his own way, with no stress on the life of the Church. Any close examination of the writings of early Friends, and particularly those of Robert Barclay, will show the extreme error of this judgment. The reality of the fellowship in the Living Christ was the important element in their lives. It is, indeed, not too far from the truth to say that the primitive Quakers, having abandoned the absolute authority of the hierarchy and the similar authority of the printed book, rested chiefly on the authority of the *group experience*. Certainly they understood that the isolated individual needs the joint guidance of the loving group in order to balance and to correct his own individual judgment.

In no other writing was Barclay more insistent on the necessity of the group life of Christians than in the essay on *Universal Love* which he wrote in Aberdeen prison, when his sense of community was at its highest. It was here that he expressed his acceptance of the ancient Roman Catholic dictum, *extra ecclesiam nulla salus,* though in a different sense than that intended by the Roman Church. What he meant was that isolated salvation is impossible; Christians need one another. With deep feeling Barclay described the way in which the earliest Quakers had formed a genuine group. They were gathered, we are told, not by a mere "unity of opinion," nor by tedious disquisitions, but "by a secret want, which many truly tender and serious souls in divers and sundry sects found in themselves." They could not remain isolated from one another when once they had experienced "the inward peace and joy of the Holy Spirit in the soul." In short, they were united, not by doctrines, but by a felt need, and by the common experience in which that need was met. One of the most eloquent of Barclay's many golden passages bears on this very point:

> And so many came to be joined and united together in heart and spirit in this one life of righteousness, who had long been wandering in the several sects; and by the inward unity came to be gathered in one body: from whence by degrees they came to find themselves agreed in the plain and simple doctrines of Christ. And as this inward power they longed for, and felt to give them victory over sin, and bring the peace that follows thereon, was that, whereby they were brought into that unity and community together; so they came first thence to accord in the universal

preaching of this power to all, and directing all unto it: which is their first and chiefest principle, and most agreeable to this universal love.[1]

Here is one of the best statements found anywhere of the origin of the People Called Quakers. The central observation is that their "unity and fellowship did arise from their mutual sense of this power working in and upon their souls."

Because there is a tendency today to speak of group dynamics as a psychological device, it is necessary to make clear that Barclay meant nothing of the kind when he emphasized the reality of the fellowship. The power of the fellowship, as he had experienced it, was not that of human ingenuity, but rather that of Christ as the head of the group. It was in this sense that he defined membership. Membership, he explained, is what Christ gives "to as many as being turned to his pure light in their consciences, come again to walk in his righteousness and innocent life, and so become true members of his body, which is the church."[2]

Since Barclay equated Christian and Church member, it was necessary for him, in consistency, to enlarge the scope of the latter term beyond its usual connotation. Far from limiting membership to those in communion with the Bishop of Rome, or to those physically baptized in a certain way, the Church, as Barclay understood it, was truly catholic or comprehensive. In includes, he said, all of those to whom the secret life and virtue of Jesus has been conveyed.

There may be members therefore of this catholic church both among heathen, Turks, Jews, and all the several sorts of Christians, men and women of integrity and simplicity of heart, who though blinded in some things in their understanding, and perhaps burdened with the superstitions and formality of the several sects in which they are engrossed, yet being upright in their hearts before the Lord, chiefly aiming and labouring to be delivered from iniquity, and loving to follow righteousness, are by the secret touches of this holy light in their souls enlivened and quickened, thereby secretly united to God, and there-through become true members of this catholic church.[3]

Barclay was naturally criticized for his comprehensiveness, which

[1] *Truth Triumphant,* p. 697.
[2] *Apology,* p. 278 [X, x].
[3] *Ibid.,* p. 263 [X, ii].

stood in direct contrast to the position of most Protestants, as well as to that of all Roman Catholics, who, when they said there was no salvation outside the Church, meant outside their Church. When a certain John Brown produced and published a virulent attack on the *Apology,* Barclay's catholicity was one of his chief points of attack. Barclay replied in detail in 1679, with *The Apology Vindicated,* reasserting that "some of all Sects of Christians may be members of the Catholic Church." He took this position firmly because he could not deny the evidence of new life among all the varied groups which he had met. As a true empiricist, he proposed to sit down before the fact as a little child. If the facts were in conflict with dogma, it was too bad for the dogma. He saw that the Good Shepherd had followers in many folds.

Such a breadth of conception was bound to be shocking to many of Barclay's readers, but his logical mind was driven to this conclusion, once he had decided to depend upon experience as the test. He saw clearly that Christ's influence has not been limited by the barrier of time. It followed, furthermore, that the Church did not begin at Pentecost, early in the first century A.D., but "hath been in being in all generations." Sometimes, he says, it has been "invisible," but not for that reason any less real. Having thus refused to set any arbitrary limit, since the ultimate judgment of who is a Church member is God's and not ours, Barclay went on to admit that the more common meaning of the Church was that of a gathered and visible fellowship. Certainly it was upon such a fellowship that he depended, especially in prison. His definition of the Church as a gathered community is as follows:

> The church is to be considered as it signifies a certain number of persons gathered by God's Spirit, and by the testimony of some of his servants raised up for that end, unto the belief of the true principles and doctrines of the Christian faith, who through their hearts being united by the same love, and their understandings informed in the same truths, gather, meet, and assemble together to wait upon God, to worship him, and to bear a joint testimony for the truth against error, suffering for the same, and so becoming through this fellowship as one family and household in certain respects, do each of them watch over, teach, instruct and care for one another, according to their several measures and attain-

ments: such were the churches of the primitive times gathered by the apostles; whereof we have divers mentioned in the holy scriptures.[4]

We may note that there is no reference, here, to the Church as a building. The definition found in the *Apology* does not differ, essentially, from the one given earlier in *The Anarchy of the Ranters,* in which the clearest statement is as follows:

> A Church then in the Scripture-phrase is no other than a meeting or gathering of certain people, which (if it be taken in a religious sense, as most commonly it is) are gathered together in the belief of the same principles, doctrines and points of faith, whereby as a body they become distinguished from others, and have a certain relation among themselves; and a conjunct interest in the maintaining and propagating these principles, they judge to be right: and therefore have a certain care and oversight over one another, to prevent and remove all occasions, that may tend to break this their conjunct interest, hinder the propagation of it, or bring infamy, contempt, or contumely upon it; or give such, as on the other hand are or may be banded together to undo them, just occasion against them, to decry and defame them.[5]

Such a Church, if it is truly Christian, has a single head, who is Christ Himself. This is why there can be no worthwhile discussion of human heads of the Church. But, though there can be no human head, it is only reasonable that there should be diversities of gifts. Some should be recognized as wiser than others when there is an effort made to reach a common judgment. There is no possibility of reaching a common decision unless there are "meetings about business," and it is no contradiction to the principle of the direct leadership of the Spirit to set *times* and *places* for such gatherings. Conscious of the existence of the extreme anarchists, who claimed to be so spiritual that they were shocked at the very idea of an announced gathering, Barclay answered with robust common sense, "As to place, it is with our bodies we must meet, as well as with our spirits; and so of necessity we must convey our bodies unto one place, that we may speak and act in those things we meet for: and that must be in some *certain place,* where all must know where to find it; having herein a regard to the conveniences and occasions of such as meet."[6]

[4] *Ibid.,* p. 264 [X, iii].
[5] *Truth Triumphant,* p. 203.
[6] *Ibid.,* pp. 204, 205.

In like manner, the author declared, it is no contradiction to set *times* to meet. How else, being human, could we gather at all? He saw that excessive spirituality, far from being an asset, would be ultimately destructive of the Christian life. The Christian knows very well that he has a body as well as a spirit, and, in fact, the Spirit leads us to guide our bodies. "God hath led us by his spirit, both to appoint places and times, where we may see the faces one of another; and to care one for another, provoking one another to love and good works." There may be times when a Christian ought to be alone, but the value of gathering together is amply demonstrated by "the good fruits and effects, which we daily reap thereby." These fruits, says the Christian empiricist, are "as a seal and confirmation, that God is well-pleased therewith, and approveth us in it."

What should the Church do when it is gathered for the conduct of its business? The first task is that which first called for some order in the early Church, "The care of the poor; of widows and orphans." "Who," Barclay asks, "will be so un-Christian as to reprove this good order and government, and to say, it is needless?" Barclay was following in the footsteps of George Fox when he stressed the work of compassion which is intrinsic to the nature of any Christian society. Already in 1673, just after his return from America, Fox had expressed his hope that "all the family of God, women, as well as men, might know, possess, perform and discharge their offices and services in the house of God, whereby the poor might be better taken care of and looked after, and the younger sort instructed, informed and taught in the way of God; the loose and disorderly reproved and admonished in the fear of the Lord."[7]

Since members of the Church are human, and therefore fallible, it is only reasonable to expect disputes between them. Foreseeing this, Barclay held that the Church must provide adjudication and conciliation among its members. It is a sign of failure, he thought, "to go out to others for equity and justice, because we cannot find it among ourselves."[8] For Christians to air their controversies in the world is to bring a reproach on the truth. In like manner, we are told, it is highly inappropriate for Christians to fail to submit to the judgment of the fellowship in questions of marriage. Marriage being "of the greatest

[7] *Journal* (1952), p. 668.
[8] *Truth Triumphant,* p. 207.

importance, a man or a woman can perform in this world," must be carried out as a religious undertaking and "therefore it doth very fitly among other things, when it occurs, come to be considered by the people of God, when met." The health of the fellowship is of such great importance that it must be valued by the Christian, even above his private feelings of romance. "Therefore no true tender heart will prefer his private love to the good and interest of the whole body."[9] This will seem shocking to the modern reader, but it at least provides a measure of the value which Barclay attached to the gathered Christian community.

Being a realist, Barclay was quick to admit that there might be evil persons within the apparent fellowship of the Church. What then? Though he was adamant against the use of the temporal power in handling Church disputes, he admitted that action must sometimes be taken by the Church itself. He knew that absolute toleration would soon amount to anarchy, in which case nothing could be accomplished. Therefore, he continued from the passage just quoted,

> . . . we are far from judging that in the Church of God there should not be censures exercised against such as fall into error, as well as such as commit open evils; and therefore we believe it may be very lawful for a Christian Church, if she find any of her members fall into any error, after due admonitions and instructions according to gospel order, if she find them pertinacious to cut them off from her fellowship by the sword of the Spirit, and deprive them of those privileges which they had as fellow-members; but not to cut them off from the world by the temporal sword, or rob them of their common privileges as men.

The criterion, so far as government was concerned, was carefully outlined. The state ought to interfere with the Church, when it engages in an act "destructive to human society," but it dare not concern itself with heresy "within the sphere of those duties of doctrine or worship which stand betwixt a man and God." Such purely spiritual matters in "no ways come under the magistrate's power." Thus the extremes of both anarchy and tyranny are avoided. In this, as in so many other matters, Barclay understood clearly that the Christian must avoid errors on both the right and the left.

Because Barclay was conscious of the many conflicting ideas about

[9] *Ibid.*, p. 211.

Church government, and because he thought that he saw flaws in the systems of both Romanists and Protestants, it was incumbent upon him to present a plan which seemed to him to be truly Christian. He thought that the general mistake of others was that of selecting only a few to make decisions, whether in synods or papal advisory boards. His hope, by contrast, lay in a meeting of Christians where there was no limitation to "persons particularly chosen; but that all, that in a true sense may be reckoned of the Church, as being sober and weighty, may be present, and give their judgment."[10] The proposal was that of a radical democracy, though not one in which a vote would ever be taken. The solution of a problem "may prove the judgment of the plurality; yet not to be decided thereby, as if the infallibility were placed there, excluding the fewer." The basic conviction was that, with real openness to the Spirit, the group would finally and lovingly be led to a common decision, very different from that reached by counting heads. While we may doubt Barclay's conclusion in saying that the judgment could be "infallible," we must be careful not to miss his central point, which is that the Church must aim at a standard higher than that of secular gatherings, in which voting so often leads to bitter divisiveness between victor and vanquished. The Church, Barclay thought, must be of a radically different order, in which the members seek to learn, not how to outwit their opponents, but how to learn reverently what God's will truly is. Christian decision, like worship, is always based on holy obedience.

The middle ground between papal authoritarianism and libertinism, Barclay held, is simply the authority of the reverent *group*. Christians should come together, not to assert their own wills, and not to listen to *one man* but rather to seek God's will *together*. They should test their own individual leadings by the leadings of their fellow members and submit lovingly to correction by the fellowship. Those who really become members one of another may "receive help, whether by counsel or supply, according to their respective needs." Since this involves the testing of each one's own leading by the leadings of his reverent fellows, it "doth not at all contradict the principle of being led inwardly and immediately by the Spirit."[11] Though the Spirit is infallible, men are not. The truth will be found, not by counting votes, as

[10] *Ibid.*, p. 234.
[11] *Ibid.*, p. 204.

in a worldly debate, but by dependence upon the Living God until He finally makes His will known to the entire gathered company.

We owe to Dr. Maurice Creasey the amusing yet significant observation that Robert Barclay was a "High-Church Quaker." The value of this observation lies in the fact that it calls attention to the way in which the Apologist elevated the conception of what the Church ought to be and, indeed, might be. "No one," says Dr. Creasey, "could exalt more highly and more sincerely than he does the dignity and high calling of the Christian Church as the body of Christ."[12] The more we study the words of Barclay, the more we see that this judgment is both true and important. He cared about separated individuals, but he was deeply conscious that Christ is revealed to men, primarily, when they are *together*.

Whether Barclay was a High-Churchman or not, it is obvious that his ideal of Church life has the merit of undoubted nobility. Far from expecting the gathered Church to be merely an audience listening to a speaker or observers of a ceremony, he saw the Christian community as one in which the members have unlimited liability for one another. The Church, in short, is meant to be a new kind of "family." Barclay was well aware of the fact that the early Church soon departed from the intensity of the fellowship described in the New Testament epistles. The disgrace was that what was intended by Christ as something truly holy later "became a means of preferment." Then "there was none so vile, none so wicked, none so profane who became not a member of the Church. And the teachers and pastors thereof, becoming the companions of princes, and so being enriched by their benevolence, and getting vast treasures and estates, became puffed up, and as it were drunken with the vain pomp and glory of this world."[13] The more Barclay observed the dead image or carcass of Christianity, the more he saw, by contrast, what the true Church would need to be. The dead Church, he claimed, was really no Church at all.

Barclay's final conviction was that the outward form of the Church was worth absolutely nothing. Apostolic succession is utterly irrelevant, because it has no necessary relationship to life and power. The only criterion is inner and spiritual. Thinking along this line, Barclay rose to heights of genuine eloquence, especially in the following:

[12] Creasey, Dissertation, *op. cit.,* p. 180.
[13] *Apology,* p. 266 [X, v].

It is the life of Christianity, taking place in the heart, that makes a Christian: and so it is a number of such, being alive, joined together in the life of Christianity, that makes a church of Christ; and it is all those that are thus alive and quickened, considered together, that make the Catholic Church of Christ: therefore when this life ceaseth in one, then that one ceaseth to be a Christian; and all power, virtue, and authority, which he had as a Christian, ceaseth with it.[14]

With a remarkable boldness, Barclay argued that the Living Church is really the *only* Church. After the life is gone it is easy to keep up ceremonies, titles, liturgies, and buildings, but these mean no more than does a dead body from which the life has departed. This is why he was not at all impressed by bishops who were obviously unconcerned with the life of Christ in men, and yet kept up the power and prestige involved in appointment to an office. Such a travesty on Christianity was, he thought, a return to pre-Christian conceptions which Jesus had found it necessary to attack in His life on earth. Having had close association with Roman Catholicism in his youth in France, he did not hesitate to affirm that the Church of Rome was apostate. It was apostate, he claimed, not primarily because of heretical doctrines, but because "Rome has introduced no fewer ceremonies and superstitions into the Christian profession, than were either among Jews or heathen; and that there is and hath been as much, yea, and more pride, covetousness, uncleanness, luxury, fornication, profaneness and atheism than ever was among any sort of people, none need doubt."[15] Barclay did not limit his attack to Roman abuses, but showed that Protestants were, in many places, equally concerned with pride and power rather than with the life of Christ in the human heart. To David Van den Enden he wrote from Aberdeen prison, March 17, 1677, "The Protestant Churches needs a reformation in the main not much less than the Roman did at what time Luther appeared."[16]

It was not his purpose, said Barclay, to enter into the arguments which produced controversies between Roman Catholics and Protestants. He desired, instead, to dig down to a far deeper level and to deal with fundamentals. He saw no better place to begin than with

[14] *Ibid.*, p. 275 [X, x].
[15] *Ibid.*, p. 267 [X, v].
[16] *Reliquiae Barclaianae*, p. 25.

the very idea of *ecclesia*. This, he explained, referred to the "called out." Accordingly he limited the Church to "the society, gathering or company of such as God hath called out of the world, and worldly spirit, to walk in his Light and Life."[17] If a man insisted on flattering titles it was obvious that he was not really in the Church, since Christ had given the example of one who rejected all struggles for prestige and power over other men. "Prince of the Church" and "Christian" were mutually contradictory conceptions.

Barclay was strengthened in his high conception of the nature of the Church by the frequently expressed New Testament idea that the true Church is made up of those called to be saints. The genuine marks of the Church member, then, are "sanctification and holiness." In *The Anarchy of the Ranters,* Barclay did not hesitate to declare that "the Church is such as are sanctified in Christ Jesus."[18] Though he was careful not to claim that men must be perfect *in order to be accepted,* he did say that a changed life will appear as evidence of "the formation of Christ in us." As early as 1672, in his *William Mitchell Unmasked,* he referred to the purpose of the ministry as expressed in Ephesians 4:13, "for the perfection of the saints," and added, characteristically, "it is folly to press after this, if there be no hopes of attaining it."[19] Barclay's purpose, like that of George Fox, was to avoid the temptation to achieve consistency by lowering men's standards to accord with their practices. This, he thought, was too easy a way out of the tension between ideals and deeds. Like Fox, Barclay refused to "plead for sin," by holding that sin was inevitable. That Fox was struggling with this difficult problem as early as 1647 is shown in his *Journal* entry when he says, "the professors were in a rage, all pleading for sin and imperfection, and could not endure to hear talk of perfection, and of holy and sinless life. But the Lord's power was over all; though they were chained under darkness and sin, which they pleaded for and quenched the tender thing in them."[20]

Of all points of controversy between Fox and Barclay, on one side, and conventional churchmen on the other, there was no idea

[17] *Apology,* p. 262 [X, ii].
[18] *Truth Triumphant,* p. 203.
[19] *Ibid.,* p. 91.
[20] *Journal* (1952), p. 18.

which aroused more antagonism than the Quakers' claim that the Church, in order to be the Church, had to be marked by a genuinely new life. The opponents could not bear, said Fox, "to hear that any should come, whilst upon earth, into the same power and Spirit that the prophets and apostles were in."[21] The chief difference between the Quaker founder and the Apologist was that the latter was more careful in his statement, because he was more aware of the dangers. He was well acquainted with the conflicting statements in Scripture concerning perfection and was somewhat worried by the petition in the pattern prayer, "Forgive us our sins."

While Barclay did not wholly solve the problem of perfection, he did perform a genuine service by maintaining that there is no real Church where there is not a serious expectation of a moral difference. He was not willing to settle for a merely forensic doctrine of justification. He granted that good works cannot be the "formal cause of justification," but held, nevertheless, that they ought to be the effect of it. He made a profound distinction concerning good works when he wrote, "For though properly we be not justified for them, yet we are justified in them."[22]

The problem which Barclay faced, when he tried to define the Church in terms of its fruits, was one which, as he well knew, was central to Reformation theology. Reinhold Niebuhr is referring to this issue when he asks whether the peace which the member of the Church finds in Christ is merely the peace of the forgiven man or the peace of the changed man. He sees some truth in both positions, the latter of which is Barclay's.

> There must be, and there is, moral content in it, a fact which Reformation theology tends to deny and which Catholic and sectarian theology emphasizes. But there is never such perfect moral content in it that any man could find perfect peace through his moral achievements, not even the achievements which he attributes to grace rather than the power of his own will.[23]

The importance of the problem which Barclay was facing was

[21] *Ibid.*, p. 33.

[22] *Apology*, p. 201 [VII, iii].

[23] Reinhold Niebuhr, *Christianity and Power Politics* (New York: Charles Scribner's Sons, 1940), p. 18 f.

emphasized by John Baillie, who confessed that his mind was torn on the question, as was Dr. Niebuhr's.

> What measure of holiness may I hope to attain? And is *some* measure of holiness a necessary ingredient of *any* truly Christian state of soul, in addition to the knowledge that one's lack of holiness has been forgiven? These are perhaps as searching questions as it is possible to put to ourselves, and it is in the answers they have given to them that the different Christian communions have differed most widely from one another.[24]

Baillie went on to say that it was the great contribution of the Protestant Reformers to insist, as Roman Catholics had not done previously, on the priority of justification over sanctification. Baillie said it was Martin Luther who made him see that he was, at the same time, both a saved man and a sinner. This, indeed, is the reason no man can save himself, and it was a reason Barclay gladly accepted. But is Luther's emphasis sufficient alone?

Professor Baillie was really arguing for the balanced view of Barclay. "But perhaps," he said, "Luther himself and certainly some of his followers have sometimes developed this true teaching in too one-sided a way. In their zeal for the recognition of justification, they have laid too little stress on the necessity of sanctification." This is Barclay's point exactly. Justification, indeed, comes first, and its only condition is willing obedience, but "there is something that must follow if salvation is to be complete." How else can we understand the words of Christ when He says, "You will know them by their fruits" (Matt. 7:16), and "By this all men will know that you are my disciples, if you have love for one another" (John 13:35)? In short, "justification which does not issue in sanctification is no true justification at all." What Barclay did, as a theologian, was to help his thoughtful readers to be keenly aware of a danger, "the danger of resting so complacently in the assurance of forgiveness that we cease to be sufficiently troubled about our lack of progress in holiness."[25]

It has been a matter of surprise to some readers of Quaker history to discover that there has been, among Quakers, a strong holiness or perfectionist movement. This is not a surprise, however, to anyone

[24] Baillie, *Invitation to Pilgrimage, op. cit.,* p. 82.
[25] *Ibid.,* p. 83.

who has taken seriously either the *Journal* of George Fox or the *Apology* of Robert Barclay. Indeed, one entire chapter of Barclay's major work was devoted to the subject of "Perfection." It does no harm today to admit that a great part of this particular chapter (Proposition VIII) is unprofitable, in that it is largely argument about opposing passages of Scripture. Its major strength lies, however, in the assertion that we are guilty of dogmatism when we arbitrarily set a limit to what the grace of God can do. Barclay's faith was so great that he really believed that, to God, "all things are possible." He considered it a very wicked thing for a finite human being to set any limit to the "power of God's grace."

Barclay was specific in his statement about his own life. Though he saw no reason to assert that a man cannot come into such a state that he is not able to sin, he did not claim this for himself. "Others," he wrote, "may speak more certainly of this state, if they have arrived at it. With respect to myself, I speak modestly, because I ingenuously confess that I have not yet attained it; but I cannot deny that there is such a state."[26] Here the author is on very firm ground in his double humility, both concerning his own achievement and his refusal to accept a negative universal proposition. When he makes his own statement of faith, he does not stand alone, but depends upon the conviction of the whole Quaker fellowship. Using the plural, he says, "we do believe that to those in whom Christ comes to be formed, and the new man brought forth, and born of the incorruptible seed, as that birth, and man in union therewith, naturally doth the will of God, it is possible so far to keep to it, as not to be found daily transgressors of the law of God."[27]

Having thus made his basic statement of faith, Barclay was careful to point out that the Christian hope of perfection does not rest at all on man's abilities, but wholly on the limitless power of God's Spirit. There is no similarity between Barclay's position and the secular perfectionism later espoused by Herbert Spencer. Spencer held that "the ultimate development of the ideal man is logically certain—as certain as any conclusion in which we place the most implicit faith; . . . so surely must the things we call evil and immorality disappear; so

[26] *Apology*, p. 235 [VIII, ii].
[27] *Ibid.*, p. 234 [VIII, i].

surely must man become perfect."[28] We smile at Spencer's naïve optimism, but we do not smile at Robert Barclay, for he shared no illusions about the human predicament. His point was, rather, that the power of God is not something to which a wise man will set a limit.

The probability is that part of Barclay's careful rejection of any imputation of perfection to himself, as a member of Christ's Church, arose from his familiarity with the warning of John Calvin, whose work was always his model. "I confess," said Calvin, "that in urging men to perfection, we ought to labour with unremiting ardour and diligence; but to inspire their minds with a persuasion that they have already attained it, while they are yet in the pursuit of it, I maintain to be a diabolical invention."[29]

Barclay exemplified a similar judiciousness by adding that such perfection as Quakers claimed to be possible was not such that it did not admit of daily growth or even such as a man could not lose, once he had it. Depending again upon experience, he said it was a fact that, even among the saints, there may be "divers ebbings and flowings." As we follow the argument, we can sense the tension in the man's mind. He wanted to state, with as much elevation as possible, what a truly Christian Church would be, but at the same time his honesty produced a mood of modesty, both about himself and about others who were called to be saints. The final answer was necessarily couched in paradox.

Superficially it seems strange that, when Barclay undertook to write his major work, he did not plan a separate chapter on the Church. Almost all that he wrote directly on the subject was preliminary to the discussion of the ministry. Why was this? The probable answer is that, though Barclay believed deeply in the Church as the body of Christ, he sought, in the *Apology,* to play down the Church as an institution. Because he was trying to reach seekers of all persuasions, he wanted to minimize Quaker organization. He gave a hint of this in his final letter to Princess Elizabeth when he wrote, "I pretend to be no sect-master and disgust all such, my labour is only as an Ambassadour to Instruct all to be reconciled to God."[30] In short, though he believed in the worth and necessity of the Church,

[28] *Social Statics* (New York, D. Appleton and Company, 1865), p. 79.
[29] *Institutes,* IV, I, 20.
[30] *Reliquiae Barclaianae,* p. 35.

he saw it essentially as a fellowship of evangelists, after the fashion of the Church of the first century. The clearest statement of this was made when he wrote, "So our care and Travel is and hath been towards those that are without, that we may bring them into the Fellowship of the Saints of Light." The primary purpose of the fellowship is thus evangelistic, though a secondary purpose is that of nurture of those already gathered, in order to prevent their being "drawn aside, either to the left hand or to the right."[31] The best thing Christians can do for other people is to bring them into the redemptive and strengthening fellowship of the Living Christ. It is never enough to became a separate little body, satisfied with sectarian enjoyments and privileges. The Church is really the Church only when it is continually drawing outsiders into the incendiary circle, where they are themselves so ignited that they consequently reach out to ignite others. This helps to explain why Barclay, when he wrote the *Apology,* decided to put the topics of Church and ministry together.

Barclay came to the conclusion that the isolated individual and the stereotyped institution are not the only possibilities in men's lives. There is, he believed, a third possibility, and he tried to tell what it was. The very best statement of this third possibility was that in which Barclay explained the overwhelming joy which true fellowship can produce. Each person is in some sense alone, and each must follow his inner leading courageously, but when we find that our particular insights are matched by those of others, a new quality is added. This occurs whether we find the matching in the Scriptures or in the testimony of other men in the post-Biblical times and today. The consequent mark of the Church of Christ is *joy!* The mutual corroboration comes, frequently, as a glad surprise. Those, then, who are responsible to the Spirit "do naturally love and are wonderfully cherished by that which proceedeth from the same Spirit in another; because such mutual emanations of the heavenly life tend to quicken the mind when at any time it is overtaken with heaviness."[32] Herein is an understanding of the Church which, because it is too good to be limited to any one group, ought to be given the widest possible dissemination. The Church is many things, but, above all, it is the "Fellowship of Corroboration."

[31] *Truth Triumphant,* p. 203.
[32] *Apology,* p. 87 [III, v].

CHAPTER XI

A REVOLUTIONARY MINISTRY

The hungry sheep look up and are not fed.
—John Milton

THE FARTHER Robert Barclay progressed in his constructive thinking, the more he adhered to "experiential reality." In trying to tell the truth about the Christian ministry, which he saw as absolutely essential, he sought to base his conclusions, not on scholastic argument, but upon what he had observed and, even more, on what he had personally experienced. Is a living ministry confined to a sacerdotal system or not? Very well, he replies, Look and see! This first-hand approach to an important subject led to the production of one of the inspired autobiographical sections which help to make Barclay's theological writing radically different from what is usually encountered in this kind of literature. Writing strictly in terms of experience he said,

And if in any age, since the apostles' days, God hath purposed to show his power by weak instruments, for the battering down of that carnal and heathenish wisdom, and restoring again the ancient simplicity of truth, this is it. For in our day, God hath raised up witnesses for himself, as he did fishermen of old; many, yea, most of whom, are labouring and mechanic men, who, altogether without that learning, have, by the power and Spirit of God, struck at the very root and ground of Babylon; and in the strength and might of this power, have gathered thousands, by reaching their consciences, into the same power and life, who, as to the outward part, have been far more knowing than they, yet not able to resist the virtue that proceeded from them.[1]

Here, indeed, is a remarkable testimony to a remarkable phenomenon. The ministry referred to in this passage was truly incendiary. "It was," says Hayes, "the nature of early Quakerism that every new member became, as it were, a fiery particle, capable of starting a conflagration of enormous proportions."[2] The most revealing feature of this highly quotable passage of Chapter X of the *Apology* is, however, not the reference to the power of the Quaker ministry of the seventeenth century in affecting others, but its power in affecting the author himself. Moved as he was by the "silent assemblies," Barclay was even more moved by the vocal ministry of simple men, for whom the ministry was not a *trade,* but a *calling.* "Of which I myself," he says, "am a true witness; and can declare from certain experience, because my heart hath been often greatly broken and tendered by that virtuous life that proceeded from the powerful ministry of illiterate men: so that by their very countenance, as well as words, I have felt the evil in me often chained down, and the good reached to and raised."[3]

By any reasonable standard, this is very impressive firsthand reporting. The new ministry that reached the young scholar when he was only eighteen years old, and continued to reach him in subsequent years, was powerful because it was *authentic.* It came from the lips of men who said, not what they had been taught to say, and not what was expedient to say, but what they knew in their own lives. In Penn's famous words, "They were changed men themselves before they went about to change others." But the authenticity came at a great price, the price of a radical revolution in ideas concerning what the ministry is or may become.

All that Barclay thought and said about the Christian ministry was set against the background of the professional ministry as ordinarily understood in the Christian world, whether Roman or Protestant. Much of it was open to criticism, not merely in details, but in its basic conception. The radical failure which Barclay observed

1 *Apology,* p. 303 [X, xxiii].
2 Hayes, Dissertation, *op. cit.,* p. 39.
3 *Apology,* p. 303 [X, xxiii].

was involved in the acceptance of the ministry as an institution which held out to men the promise of self-advancement.

Parents, seeing both the honour and profit that attends the clergy [he wrote], allot their children sometimes from their infancy to it, and so breed them up on purpose. And others, come to age upon the same account betake them to the same trade, and having these natural and acquired parts that are judged the necessary qualifications of a minister, are thereby admitted, and so are bred up in idleness and pleasure, thinking it a disgrace for them to work with their hands; and so just study a little out of their books, to make a discourse once or twice a week during the running of an hour-glass.[4]

The entire institution of the professional ministry seemed to Barclay to be debased because, in radical contrast to the sacrifice and danger of the ministry of the early Church, it had become a business. He saw that men prized their ecclesiastical positions in so far as they brought (a) money, (b) idleness, (c) prestige. He likewise saw that all this was in direct opposition to what Christ clearly outlined when He began the fellowship which was to be in contrast to the standards of the world. What had begun as a protest to worldliness had succumbed to that which it opposed! Far from providing an antidote to self-seeking, ministers were illustrating it.

Barclay was forthright in describing the way in which the clergy were drawn by the lure of money. He mentioned the "vast revenues that had been superstitiously bestowed upon the church," and said that these revenues often came to men who were called ministers. By this means there was "a bait hid for covetousness," so that "many, being led by the desire of filthy lucre, do apply themselves to be ministers, that they might get a livelihood by it." The consequence was, he said, "that a fat benefice hath always many expectants; and then what bribing, what courting, what industry, and shameful actions are used to acquire these things, is too openly known, and needs not to be proved." All this appeared to our author to be a well-known scandal, so well known, indeed, that there was a proverb to the effect that "the kirk is always greedy."[5]

If the desire for wealth was a scandal, it was not the only one. Barclay spoke of

[4] *Apology,* p. 311 [X, xxvii].
[5] *Ibid.,* p. 322 [X, xxxii].

that luxury and idleness that most of the clergy live in, even among Protestants as well as Papists, to the great scandal of Christianity. For not having lawful trades to work with their hands, and being so superfluously and sumptuously provided for, they live in idleness and luxury; and there doth more pride, vanity, and worldly glory appear in their wives and children than in most others, which is open and evident to all.[6]

Forgetting the Biblical admonition to give freely what has been freely received, these clergymen "preach for hire, and divine for money, and look for their gain from their quarter, and prepare war against such as put not into their mouths, etc." In what may be a reference to Milton's attack on the clergy in "Lycidas," he used even stronger language by speaking of "shepherds who feed themselves, and not the flock."

The struggle for power and prestige seemed to Barclay to be as radically opposed to Christianity as was the struggle for money. He said that "the ministers our adversaries plead for, are such as strive and contend for superiority, and claim precedency over one another; affecting and ambitiously seeking after the afore-mentioned things."[7] Nothing seemed to demonstrate the motivation of pride more than the sharp division into "manifold orders and degrees; not without innumerable contests and altercations who should have the precedency."[8] The conflict between "the bishop of Rome and the bishop of Constantinople" was a disgusting example of this strife for superiority of status. Where, in Scripture, Barclay asks, are we to find any evidence of the use of flattering titles in the primitive Church?

The Christians speak to the apostles without any such denomination, neither saying, If it please Your Grace, Your Holiness, Your Lordship, nor Your Worship; they are neither called My Lord Peter, nor My Lord Paul; nor yet Master Peter, nor Master Paul; nor Doctor Peter, not Doctor Paul; but singly Peter and Paul and that not only in the scripture, but for some hundreds of years after.[9]

It seemed obvious to Barclay that the later decline from apostolic simplicity of address was instituted by clergymen themselves, "to

[6] *Ibid.*, p. 323 [X, xxxii].
[7] *Ibid.*, p. 326 [X, xxxiii].
[8] *Ibid.*, p. 266 [X, v].
[9] *Ibid.*, p. 492 [XV, iii].

satisfy their ambitious and ostentatious minds, which is a manifest token of their hypocrisy."

Barclay had no doubt whatever of the need of the ministry in the Christian movement, but he was equally clear that the ordinary professional ministry required a radical revolution in its basic concepts. A little change would not suffice. There was no subject more congenial to the mind of Robert Barclay, since he felt, in his discussion of it, that he was on very firm ground. He recognized, first, that there could not be any genuine Christianity without a ministry, and second, that the idea of the ministry had been lamentably debased in theory as well as practice. The only logical procedure, therefore, was to give his best thought to its reconstruction. There is no point at which it is more clear that early Quakerism sought to be a movement dedicated to Christian reconstruction on the grand scale than this one. Something of crucial value having been lost, the obvious task was that of renewal.

It has been perplexing to some readers to note that Barclay dealt with the ministry before he discussed worship. This is because many now envisage ministry as confined to the experience of worship, but Barclay had thought the matter through and saw, consequently, that ministry has a logical priority. Worship is only one phase of the religious life, while ministry covers all. Ministry is not confined to preaching, though it includes preaching, and does so in Barclay's judgment unapologetically. Though the word "preacher" has fallen into a certain disrepute in the twentieth century, it was not so when Fox and his closest associates were operating with such a flair. Indeed, Quakers seemed, in the beginning, to be a band of "wandering preachers" more than anything else. The outsider could not observe any Quaker buildings or public institutions, because there were none; neither could he observe a liturgy, since none existed; he was not likely to see the small gatherings of Friends, for they often met in private homes; but he *could* hear the Quaker preachers on a variety of occasions. Certainly this is how the Quaker image first appeared in Scotland. In the earliest history of Quakerism in Scotland we read of Richard Rae, who was by trade a shoemaker, and "one of the first in Scotland that became a 'Quaker preacher,' being also the individual who, earlier than any other of that people tasted imprisonment at Aberdeen, whither he had come in the love of the gospel to visit his brethren."[10]

It was of this man, who may be looked upon as representative of the new kind of ministry which Quakers gave to the world, that Barclay was evidently writing in the *Apology* when he said:

> Yea, I know myself a poor shoemaker, that cannot read a word, who being assaulted with a false citation of scripture, from a public professor of divinity, before the magistrate of a city, when he had been taken up for preaching to some few that came to hear him; I say, I know such a one, and he is yet alive, who, though the professor, who also is esteemed a learned man, constantly asserted his saying to be a scripture sentence, yet affirmed, not through any certain letter-knowledge he had of it, but from the most certain evidence of the Spirit in himself, that the professor was mistaken; and that the Spirit of God never said any such thing as the other affirmed: and the Bible being brought, it was found as the poor shoemaker had said.[11]

In recounting a story of this character, Barclay was simply reporting that, in his experience, the best ministry arose from something deeper than learning. Being enough of a scholar to realize that there is something finer than scholarship, Barclay was willing to defend the proposition that the only true Christian ministry is that of those who are "able to speak, from a living experience." Insofar as the spoken ministry is concerned, the basic element is *witness*. A man is more likely to "reach the hearts of his hearers," if he speaks, not speculatively, but of that of which "he himself is a witness."[12] This is consistent with Barclay's fundamental philosophy of radical empiricism. If the primary element in knowledge is experience, then the most important thing which one man can do for another is to give his personal testimony of how God has reached him, in his inmost heart. This is why a person who is "a poor shepherd, or a fisherman, and ignorant of all that learning, and of all those questions and notions; yet speaking from the Spirit, his ministry will have more influence towards the converting of a sinner unto God, than all of them who are learned after the flesh."[13]

[10] John Barclay, *Memoirs* of Scottish Quakers, *op. cit.*, p. 381.
[11] *Apology*, pp. 297, 298 [X, xix].
[12] *Ibid.*, p. 269 [X, vii].
[13] *Ibid.*, p. 303 [X, xxii].

Barclay asked specifically, "What maketh or how cometh a man to be a minister, pastor, or teacher in the church of Christ?" Though his own answer was the clear one just suggested, he recognized that this was not the answer offered by most alleged followers of Christ. The conventional answer, of both Roman Catholics and Protestants, was to the effect that the ministry was a matter of "succession." The idea was that Christ had given a call to apostles and disciples, who, in turn, conveyed this to their successors, providing thereby an unbroken chain of authority for ordination. If any happen not to belong to this chain of ordination, said Barclay, they "are to be accounted but intruders." He held up this idea for pitiless examination and concluded that all who accepted it as satisfactory were thereby declaring their ignorance, not merely of the ministry, but "of the nature of Christianity."

The conventional conception of the necessity of succession Barclay held to be inconsistent with the basic teachings of Christ. Christ, he reminded his readers, recognized that "this was the great error of the Jews, to think they were the church and people of God, because they could derive their outward succession from Abraham." He told them "that God is able of the stones to raise children unto Abraham." Christ's whole teaching, as Barclay understood it, was that of the necessity of getting away from the outward form of religion to the inward reality. How ridiculous, then, to call a man a minister if he has never known Christ inwardly or has ceased to know Him! As nothing can make a man a Christian except "the life of Christianity ruling in his heart," so nothing else can make a man a minister. In this clear stand, Barclay was following precisely in the footsteps of his revered mentor, George Fox, who had never received any official ordination, yet nevertheless conveyed the life of Christ to others in a most authentic fashion. Fox, as a young man of twenty-two, had experienced three fundamental insights which set the whole tone of his life, though they went directly against the general assumptions of his neighbors. These were really answers to three important questions: What is a Christian? What is a minister? What is a Church? The answer Fox gave to his first question was that none were Christians except those who passed "from death to life." In short, reality was everything and ceremony nothing. His answer to the second question was stated originally in a negative form, which Fox reported by saying, "the Lord opened unto me that being bred at Oxford or Cambridge was not enough to fit and qualify men to be ministers of Christ."[14]

The credentials of either scholarship or succession can belong to men of evident wickedness who, in Barclay's words, are "altogether destitute" of Christian vitality. A man may receive a degree in theological education and yet not care in the least for the promotion of the gospel of Christ. Such a man, Barclay saw as a matter of self-evidence, is not really a minister, whatever his official title and status may be.

> So the authority, power and heirship are not annexed to persons, as they bear the mere names, or retain a form holding the mere shell or shadow of Christianity; but the promise is to Christ, and to the seed, in whom the authority is inherent, and in as many as are one with him, and united unto him by purity and holiness, and by the inward renovation and regeneration of their minds.[15]

What is at stake, Barclay believed, is the whole validity of Christianity. If Christianity is merely another religious system, with a privileged priesthood and some necessary outward ceremonials, it is not really unique. The danger is always that of reversion to what Christ came to abolish. The Christian ministry accordingly, in Barclay's view, is meant to be unique. It has no similarity to a privileged priesthood or to the institution of a class of officials, such as those who operated in the Temple of Jerusalem and to whom Christ paid practically no attention. In sharp contrast to these, the Christian minister is a "servant," rejecting entirely the notion of personal pride in his position.

> The ministers we plead for, are such as, being holy and humble, contend not for precedency and priority, but rather strive to prefer one another, and serve one another in love; neither desire to be distinguished from the rest by their garments and large phylacteries, nor seek the greetings in the market-places, nor uppermost rooms at feasts, nor the chief seats in the synagogues; nor yet to be called of men master.[16]

The essential inspiration for such a conception of the ministry, in

[14] *Journal* (1952), p. 7.
[15] *Apology*, p. 278 [X, x].
[16] *Ibid.*, p. 326 [X, xxxiii].

contrast to the conventional one of clergyman, was derived from the recorded words of Christ, especially those in the twenty-third chapter of Matthew, and from the practice of the early Church. Barclay's ideal was that of the "ministry of the apostles and primitive church," before corruption had become standardized. In addition, there was also a profound admiration for the prophetic ideal in the life of Israel. The prophet was seen as one who rejects the whole priestly system of prestige and status, speaking boldly to all, whether high or low. The minister is a person, of any secular occupation, who has been so touched by the Living Christ that he is constrained to extend this experience to as many others as possible. Thus he is ambassador or evangelist as well as prophet, but he is also pastor and teacher, drawing out the powers of others in an equipping ministry.

The familiar passage (Ephesians 4:11) which provides the basis for what we now call the "equipping ministry" was valued by Barclay and employed more than once. But he warned his readers against the mistake of supposing that the Biblical reference to "apostles," "prophets," "evangelists," "pastors and teachers," indicated the acceptance of a hierarchy of status. His conviction was that, in so far as the Christian ministry is concerned, status was nothing and function was everything. It was a horrible mistake, he thought, to form these functions into orders "and so make several ranks and degrees to establish a carnal ministry of men's making, without the life, power and spirit of Christ."[17] The whole system, according to which some men are "reverend," while others are "most reverend" seemed to Barclay a complete perversion of what Christ obviously intended and therefore an archexample of self-contradiction. He spoke scornfully of the conception of a minister of Christ according to which a man insists that he "be distinguished from the rest by the colour of his clothes; for he must only wear black."

Since it was no part of this radical reformation of the ministry to reject ordination, the point was that it is God, not men, who can ordain. All that men can do, accordingly, is to watch and see who it is that God actually employs in His service. If He uses George Fox as a person by whom He stirs up new life, then George Fox is a minister, even though he has never attended theological lectures or

[17] *Ibid.*, p. 306 [X, xxiv].

had any ceremonial laying on of hands. The reality is everything; the externals are nothing! Once this principle is accepted, it follows that the ministry cannot rightly be monopolized by any group or class of men. The ordinary conception, according to which a few are clergy and so monopolize the public ministry, while the rest are held to be inferior, because they are laymen, is thus denied. Accordingly, any Christian may be called to minister, "whether rich or poor, servant or master, young or old, yea, male or female."

Perhaps the boldest part of Barclay's treatment of the subject of the Christian ministry is that in which he utterly rejects the generally accepted distinction between clergy and laity. The key sentence is, "That which we oppose, is the distinction of laity and clergy, which in the scripture is not to be found."[18] Barclay was well aware that the term minister, when it appears in the New Testament, refers not to a specially privileged or separated class, but may be applied to any Christian. He saw the conventional distinction between clergy and laity as one which does immense harm, the greatest harm being that it causes modest people to suppress the gift given to them. The shame is

> that good, honest, mechanic men, and others who have not learned the art and trade of preaching, and so are not licentiated according to these rules they prescribe unto themselves; such, I say, being possessed with a false opinion that it is not lawful for them to meddle with the ministry, nor that they are any ways fit for it, because of the defect of that literature, do thereby neglect the gift in themselves, and quench many times the pure breathings of the Spirit of God in their hearts.[19]

We are reminded, in this connection, that the "first preachers and propagators" of our Christian faith were themselves such men. If they had allowed their gifts to be suppressed or undeveloped, because of not being clergymen, the loss to mankind would have been incalculable.

The rejection of the distinction between clerical and lay Christians leads, inevitably, to the ministry of women, and Barclay is wholly willing to accept the logical implications of his position. "Seeing male and female," he says, "are one in Christ Jesus, and that he gives

[18] *Ibid.*, p. 311 [X, xxvi].
[19] *Ibid.*, pp. 312, 313 [X, xxvii].

his Spirit no less to one than to the other, when God moveth by his Spirit in a woman, we judge it no ways unlawful for her to preach in the assemblies of God's people."[20] Barclay was not intimidated by Paul's command that women keep silence (I Cor. 14:34), because Paul himself advised women on how to "behave themselves in their public preaching and praying" and spoke of those women who had labored with him in the gospel. The isolated text, Barclay thought, must always be balanced by the context. The greatest argument for the validity of the ministry of women, however, was, as has been noted in Chapter VIII, that women have been known to minister effectively in practice. This, for Barclay, was sufficient to put the problem "beyond all controversy."

One of Barclay's strongest attacks on the ordinary clerical system was that the ministry tended to become a trade which a man could take up as a means of livelihood or even of financial gain. Barclay had no objection to money and took good care of his own finances, but he was convinced that the Christian religion is inevitably debased if it is mixed up with the profit motive. Because Barclay's objection to a "paid ministry" may be easily misunderstood, it needs to be made doubly clear. It is very doubtful if his position could be seen as inconsistent with the modest subsistence of many contemporary servants of the Church, in which, because full time is given, outside earning is made impossible. What he objected to, primarily, was something well known in his generation, "the excessive revenues of the clergy." If a man entered the ministry, he thought, for the sake of the financial reward, he was false to his faith and therefore was no minister, but at the same time Barclay made it very clear that he favored the idea of financial support, providing it was not "superfluous maintenance." He referred specifically, in this connection, to "the vast revenues which the bishops and priests have, both Papists and Protestants." He thought it no hyperbole to state that some clerical individuals received more money in one year than Christ and the apostles "made use of in their whole lifetime."

So important did Barclay count this part of his philosophy of the ministry that he mentioned it even in the brief *Theses.* People who are called to the ministry, he said, are to give freely, "yet if God hath

[20] *Ibid.,* p. 313 [X, xxvii].

called any one from their employment or trades, by which they acquire their livelihood, it may be lawful for such . . . to receive such temporals . . . as are given them freely." Later, in developing this idea more fully, the author acknowledged "that there is an obligation upon such to whom God sends, or among whom he raiseth up a minister, that, if need be, they minister to his necessities."[21] If such support were denied, it is obvious that the ministry, particularly in its traveling form, would necessarily be limited to the well-to-do, and that would spoil the whole idea. There is every reason to suppose that Barclay wholly approved the practice, evidently followed by George Fox and other men and women not in easy financial circumstances, of accepting their living expenses from the donations of their fellow Christians. The idea was not that they were paid to minister, but that they were liberated, economically, in order to make their public ministry possible. If this seems like a distinction without a difference, Barclay replies that the evil of a "hireling" ministry is not in the use of money, but in the self-regarding motive of those who care more for the reward than for the service.

A serious problem was presented to the Apologist by the Continental theologian, Nicolaus Arnoldus, who honored Barclay with a critical rejoinder to his *Theses Theologicae,* before the *Apology* was completed.[22] As a theological professor, Arnoldus found serious fault with Barclay's use of the injunction, "Freely ye have received, freely give" (Matt. 10:8). The professor's rejoinder was, "We have not freely received, and therefore are not bound to give freely." The young theologian, the critic points out, spends a great deal of his own money in preparation for his work and in paying university fees. Is it unreasonable for him to expect to get a return on this expenditure? "As Arnoldus," says Barclay, "gets money for teaching his young students the art and trade of preaching, so he intends they should be repaid before they give it again to others." It is to Barclay's credit that he admitted that he found this position hard to refute. "The answer I confess is ingenuous and good; for if those that receive freely are to give freely, it would seem to follow by the rule of con-

[21] *Ibid.,* p. 314 [X, xxviii].

[22] Though several important manuscripts have turned up, the criticism sent by Dr. Arnold is not now known to exist. Our lack of knowledge about this man is unfortunate.

traries, that those that receive not freely ought not to give freely, and I shall grant it."[23] Barclay's only answer was to the effect that Arnoldus was justified, from a business standpoint, but that the life of the ministry is of another order. It will never thrive, he thought, if those who enter it are primarily concerned with gain.

Barclay was conscious that he had to be extremely careful if he were to do justice to the radical idea of the ministry which he sought to explain and to defend. Naturally he was misunderstood to mean that, in a true Christianity, there are no ministers, and this misunderstanding has carried over even into the twentieth century. Nothing, however, could be farther from the truth. It would be more nearly accurate to say that what Barclay rejected was the whole idea of the laity! He did not see how a person could be Christ's follower and not be involved in some kind of ministry. Barclay's reaction to the decay of the professional ministry was, therefore, very different from the anticlericalism which has appeared in so many generations. A poor ministry was bad, but no ministry, he thought, was worse. Therefore, the only solution lay in a reformed ministry. But in such a reformed ministry, would there be a doctrinaire egalitarianism? This is where Barclay had to be most careful in his thinking, as well as in his expression of a fresh idea.

The fundamental answer was that, though all Christians must be ministers, not all are, in fact, equal. All may speak; all have liberty to prophesy; all, if they have been touched by the central fire, are themselves enkindled; but some have a greater responsibility than others, because they have received particular calls. The formula then is, that there is both a general and a particular calling. All Christians have the former; a minority have the latter. All Christians must be ministers, but some must be ministers in a special way. This was Barclay's answer to those who objected that he made no distinction between minister and people. While he rejected the conventional distinction between clergy and laity, he accepted another, which he felt bound to make on the basis of experience. This is where unusual care is required on the part of his readers, because, since life is never simple, the adequate answer is inevitably complex.

Following his experiential method, Barclay could not deny that

[23] *Apology*, p. 316 [X, xxviii].

God uses some men as His messengers more than He uses others. This the young author had deeply impressed upon him when he attended London Yearly Meeting while his book was still being written. Though George Fox expected all Christians to be in the ministry, he was obviously in the ministry in a special sense. In any case he was what the New Testament calls a "pastor and teacher." Some twentieth-century Quakers, having been thrilled by the idea of the universal ministry, are shocked and puzzled when they first learn that Fox organized special meetings of "ministers" which did not include the rank and file of the members. It was Barclay's welcome task to explain why this was so. It was so, he said, because "we do believe and affirm that some are more particularly called to the work of the ministry, and therefore are fitted of the Lord for that purpose; whose work is more constantly and particularly to instruct, exhort, admonish, oversee, and watch over their brethren; and that . . . there is something more incumbent upon them in that respect than upon every common believer."[24]

The fact that the majority of Quakers in the modern world, including those of East Africa, have instituted some form of a pastoral system is a logical development of the careful distinctions in the Christian ministry which Barclay made. There are people, and Barclay clearly believed himself to be one of them, who are especially called to "constant labour in work and doctrine." That this was the case in the valuable ministry of George Fox, no one doubted. It seemed right to all that Fox should be liberated from secular pursuits in order that he might give full time to his ministry of stirring up the life in others. No one was surprised to find, therefore, that he and Penn spoke far more frequently and lengthily than did others. Henry J. Cadbury says that Fox apparently spoke in every meeting which he attended. "There is no mention I believe," he says, "of his having remained silent throughout."[25] Another relevant example is that of Isaac Penington. After Penington's release from imprisonment at Reading, he spent all of the remainder of his life (1670–1679) in the service of the Quaker Movement. Early Quakers had no men who were designated "pastors," but they had full-time min-

[24] *Ibid.*, p. 310 [X, xxvi].
[25] *Journal* (1952), p. 733.

isters, and sought, thereby, to demonstrate the New Testament pattern.

Barclay recognized that, within the general conception of the universal ministry, it was not illogical to expect more than one distinction. Thus he recognized the validity of the particular ministry of "elders." These might be people, he said, who seldom or never participate in the public vocal ministry of preaching, yet perform a very important ministerial service in counseling others. Apart from such loving counsel, some of the young might permit their particular gifts to lie undeveloped.

One of the most surprising, yet most reasonable, parts of Barclay's analysis is his assertion that, along with the factual distinctions within the general ministry, there could rightly be expected obedience and deference. If a man like Fox was so signally called to a special ministry of leadership, it was only reasonable that others should listen with especial care to what he might be led to declare. In a really Christian society one man's voice might have more weight than the judgments of a large number, not because of some office held, but because of the obvious way in which God uses him. Thereby the egalitarian idea, which some have supposed to be essential to democratic process, was rejected as a heresy. To claim that all gifts are equal or to deny that some are more truly pastors than others would, thought Barclay, amount to a denial of the truth of experience. Whatever else Barclay was, he was never a Leveller.

Because his own life had been changed by the ministry of illiterate men, Barclay tended to deny overmuch the worth of academic learning. He was careful, at one point, to say, "Though then we make not human learning necessary, yet we are far from excluding true learning; to wit, that learning which proceedeth from the inward teachings and instructions of the Spirit."[26] But after saying this, he went on for many pages, showing how valueless he considered training in divinity to be. Here he was attacking the scholastic system of study of which he had had a slight taste in Paris, and of which he knew by report in some other places. He evidently had a very poor opinion of what the Aberdeen students of divinity were supposed to be learning. There was a certain paradox in his attack on theological

[26] *Apology*, p. 295 [X, xviii].

disciplines, since it was theology that he was writing with such brilliance. Part of the oddity of the situation must have struck him, for, after dismissing the formal study of logic, he admitted that he was trying to be logical. "As to natural logic," he wrote, "we deny not the use of it; and I have sometimes used it in this treatise."[27] It is hard to read this without smiling when we note the great number of syllogisms in the *Apology*. Barclay had, we can agree, a point about the worthlessness of labyrinthian contentions, which are "far more fit to make a skeptic than a Christian," but he exaggerated this particular idea. As he himself demonstrated, though he was loath to admit it, the sharpened reason is needed, not in opposition to direct leading of the Spirit, but as a help in determining *which* leadings are authentic and which are not. This is what careful education in theology is for.

When we look at the treatment of the ministry as a whole, we can hardly fail to be thankful for the fresh insights which Barclay expressed. What is unfortunate is that he was apparently unable to handle the subject without excessive wordiness. He gave too many pages to items which seem obvious; he mustered too many Biblical texts; he criticized the professional clergy too harshly. Though the chapter on the ministry was very close to the author's heart, it would, nevertheless, have been much improved by revision, if later editions could have been arranged. Such a revision might have avoided much redundancy and also improved upon the order. An example of imperfect order is that of Article xxvii, in which he introduced the subject of the "maintenance of the gospel minister," but, before he dealt with it, discussed the preaching of women. Part of the difficulty, no doubt, arose from the speed with which the writing was done.

One of Barclay's mistakes which was mentioned by his critic, John Brown, so that he felt it necessary to reply in his *Apology Vindicated,* was his excessive emphasis on the leadership of the Spirit *at the time of gathering*. Brown pointed out that Paul advised Timothy to read, which indicated a kind of preparation. Barclay's reply was that he had never said "it is unlawful for men to read books."[28] What he missed, however, was an excellent chance to say that a man might be

[27] *Ibid.*, p. 299 [X, xx].
[28] *Truth Triumphant,* p. 848.

just as truly inspired in his study at home as in the meetinghouse. Why, we naturally ask Barclay, might not the Spirit reach a man as vividly on Tuesday as on Sunday? Barclay was not wholly fair to the professional ministers who, as Brown maintained, made adequate preparation in advance and then allowed their minds "to lie open to the influences of the Spirit . . . and so speak many things, which they had not once premeditated." In short, why should we conclude that preparation and continued openness to the leadings of the Spirit are incompatible? This question Barclay never wholly answered.

The influence of Barclay's treatment of the ministry was tremendous. He did a great deal, not only to support the idea that there could be no Quaker "laymen," but also to encourage the leadership of the more gifted. Friends showed very rapidly that they recognized the distinction in the ministry stressed by Barclay, between the general and the particular call, the best evidence being the setting up of the Second Day's Morning Meeting. This was a meeting of men ministers in London every Monday. Not only did those whose work, in Barclay's language, was "more constantly and particularly to instruct," examine and pass upon books for publication, but also they helped to plan the allocation of ministers at the London Sunday meetings. However much they believed in divine guidance, they also believed that some human thought and planning might be helpful. "Each week were recorded on a blank schedule, sometimes in autograph, the names of those who gave notice what meeting they expected to attend on the following Sunday."[29] One delightful practice was that according to which a seasoned Quaker minister would take with him, as he went to the gathering it had been decided that he would attend, a younger person who was only just beginning to come forward in the public ministry.[30] Though there was nothing comparable to "holy orders," the ministers, in Barclay's second sense, were officially "recognized" and all knew who they were. Many of these met together in London at eight o'clock on Sunday mornings for a devotional period and then dispersed according to plan. What Barclay did for this system was to provide it with a rational justification. It is no wonder that, when he died prematurely, these ministers

[29] *Journal* (1952) p. 733.
[30] See William Braithwaite, *Second Period of Quakerism, op. cit.*, p. 543.

did such a handsome job of preparing his literary works for publication. They had reason to be grateful.

One tangible result of the Quaker philosophy of the ministry, of which Barclay was the major exponent, was the widespread practice of "recording" a gift in the ministry in the effort to recognize the authenticity of a special call. This is still practiced in most of the Quaker Yearly Meetings of the world, though it was officially discontinued, so far as London Yearly Meeting is concerned, in 1924. The late T. Edmund Harvey, who was both a valued Quaker minister and a Member of Parliament, wrote, shortly before his death, of the value which such recognition had had for him. "I realized," he wrote, "that it came to me as a call to dedication, and it caused me sometimes, to put aside pieces of work which were good in themselves and which I should probably have undertaken otherwise, in order that I might have time to devote to concern for the work of the ministry."[31] Later he said, "We need for the service of the ministry the best thought and effort of which we are capable." Nothing could point more vividly than does this to the relevance of Barclay's thought for our generation.

[31] T. Edmund Harvey, "Our Quaker Ministry Since the Cessation of Recording," *Friends Quarterly Examiner*, No. 319 (July, 1946), p. 188.

CHAPTER XII

REALITY IN WORSHIP

Worship is the submission of all our nature to God.
—William Temple

BARCLAY'S TREATMENT OF worship has the longest literary history of his writings. Though we did not know it earlier, we now know, as a result of deciphering his shorthand, that as a very young man the Apologist was already jotting down some of the ideas on worship which were later offered to the reading public. Indeed, we can trace the development of some of his expressions in regard to worship more accurately than is possible in connection with any other subject. Partly because of time for development, and partly because he loved the topic, Barclay's chapter on worship is generally considered his best literary production. The one direct quotation from him which is better known than any other (it appears in Chapter II of this volume) is from the treatment of worship, which is Chapter XI of the *Apology*. Barclay's eloquence in this section is greater than in any other part of his work. One striking and timeless illustration of it is as follows:

When assembled, the great work of one and all ought to be to wait upon God; and returning out of their own thoughts and imaginations, to feel the Lord's presence, and know a gathering into his name indeed, where he is in the midst, according to his promise. And as every one is thus gathered, and so met together inwardly in their spirits, as well as outwardly in their persons, there the secret power and virtue of life is known to refresh the soul, and the pure motions and breathings of God's Spirit are felt to arise; from which, as words of declaration, prayers or praises arise, the acceptable worship is known, which edifies the church, and is well-pleasing to God.[1]

What is perhaps most remarkable about these beautiful words is that they are not at all sectarian. They could be employed as the ideal expression of what is intended in genuine worship in any assembly. But this is no accident. As Barclay advanced, he was more and more concerned to outline the standard for any Christian group which might take its calling seriously. He was providing an ideal which might be difficult to achieve in practice, but by which failure could be accurately measured. He intended to write for all who would listen, rather than merely for the few who were called Quakers.

Since the author accepted a task of such breadth and nobility, it was incumbent upon him to try to think clearly about the entire nature and purpose of religious worship. He saw at once that it could not be made into something small. "It is not limited to places, times nor persons."[2] Worship, then, must be deeper than words; more profound than ceremonies; more pervasive than celebration of particular holy days or seasons. Barclay, of course, did not deny that days are holy, any more than he denied the ministry. Following his usual practice of rejecting a limitation, he asserted "that all days are alike holy in the sight of God."[3] The answer is not less but more. Worship in one sense, therefore, ought to be and may be continuous, because it centers in prayer and prayer need never end. It can be experienced in the midst of business, though without audible words, from morning until night and on any day of the week. The largeness of this concept is expressed when Barclay says, "As then inward prayer is necessary at all times, so, so long as the day of every man's visitation lasteth, he never wants some influence more or less, for the practice of it; because he no sooner retires his mind, and considers himself in God's presence, but he finds himself in the practice of it."[4]

While asserting the possibility of worship at all times and in all

[1] *Apology,* pp. 335, 336 [XI, vi].
[2] This is in the original Thesis XI.
[3] *Apology,* p. 333 [XI, iii].
[4] *Ibid.,* p. 374 [XI, xxi].

places, Barclay was nevertheless enough of a realist to admit that, in our finitude, we need the help of one another. The reason for setting up particular occasions for worship is not that men *cannot* worship alone, but that they are more likely to be truly reached in worship if they are participants in the life of a loving and reverent company of their fellow seekers.

> To meet together [he wrote] we think necessary for the people of God; because, so long as we are clothed with this outward tabernacle, there is a necessity to the entertaining of a joint and visible fellowship, and bearing of an outward testimony for God, and seeing of the faces of one another, that we concur, with our persons as well as spirits; to be accompanied with that inward love and unity of spirit, doth greatly tend to encourage and refresh the saints.[5]

The setting up of a time and place is not really a part of worship, but simply a rational arrangement to enable people to be together and to see one another. It is, in Barclay's pungent phrase, "a preparatory accommodation of our outward man." Since God has given His children bodies as well as spirits, there is no point in neglecting them. It is "when we hear and see one another" that God reaches us in a special way. The inward life, though not a matter of the outward senses, may be encouraged by the senses. This important idea, so much in contrast to all mere individualism, was, in Barclay's philosophy, the primary reason for gathering. He had neither intellectual nor moral respect for a man who proudly claimed that he did not need the gathered experience of his fellows.

In developing the crucial importance of the fellowship in worship, the Apologist employed two attractive figures of speech. In the first place, he said, following Proverbs 27:17, when humble worshipers gather diligently to wait upon God, the result is like that of "iron sharpening iron." Human beings may be able to worship in solitude, but there is ordinarily far more reality in their worship when they are not alone. The irons may be of poor metal, but the truth is that they do sharpen each other. It is easy to imagine what Barclay's answer would be to a twentieth-century person who claims that he worships just as adequately while sitting in his own room, listening to a radio sermon. The second major figure of speech concerning worship is that of the many candles:

[5] *Ibid.*, p. 332 [XI, iii].

And as many candles lighted, and put in one place, do greatly augment the light, and make it more to shine forth, so when many are gathered together into the same life, there is more of the glory of God, and his power appears, to the refreshment of each individual; for that he partakes not only of the light and life raised in himself, but in all the rest. And therefore Christ hath particularly promised a blessing to such as assemble together in his name, seeing he will be in the midst of them (Matt. 18:20).[6]

Once Barclay had clarified so persuasively the reason for group worship he was ready to ask what the manner of a truly Christian worship would be. He was quick to see that the New Testament, in spite of the wide variety of its contents, does not include even one prescribed order of worship. It is striking, the author thinks, that though Christ emphasized worship, He limited Himself to saying that it must be in spirit and in truth and commanded "no set form of worship." Barclay was, of course, well aware that set forms had developed in sixteen centuries of Christian history, but he was eager to make his readers see that all of these, whatever their beauty, were human productions. He agreed that the New Testament commended praying, preaching, and singing, "but what order or method should be kept in so doing . . . there is not one word to be found."[7]

It is evident that some of the worship which has been set up by men is far from the Spirit of Christ. This is particularly true when it ministers to human pride and pomp. The Apologist was appalled when he saw how much of supposedly Christian worship had been corrupted by both superstition and idolatry. He was deeply disgusted by "the adoration of saints and angels, the veneration of relics, the visitation of sepulchres, and all those other superstitious ceremonies . . . and endless pilgrimages."[8] What had these, Barclay asked himself, to do with the life of Jesus Christ, who spoke out directly against ostentation? The only honest answer was that there was no lasting connection at all! It was possible, therefore, for a religion to become so corrupted that nothing of the original vitality was left.

Barclay was impressed with how easy it is for a man to go through the motions of praying or singing and yet not mean a thing. This seemed to him to be nothing less than a blasphemous offense. Any-

[6] *Ibid.*, pp. 364, 365 [XI, xvii].
[7] *Ibid.*, p. 348 [XI, x].
[8] *Ibid.*, p. 330 [XI, i].

body can learn to repeat a set form of words in a liturgy, regardless of his sincerity and general character. The strongest condemnation, then, lies in this, that purely external worship "may be truly performed, both as to the matter and manner, by the wickedest of men."[9] Indeed what is to keep a man who is personally an atheist from conducting worship as well as anyone, providing worship is a matter of set phrases and responses? The atheist might have a good voice and an attractive manner, but the entire operation would be a denial of reality. Barclay's deep conviction was that all outward form was valueless unless it was accompanied by sincerity of heart and moral regeneration. As a young man just finding his way, he wrote in shorthand, "Challenge the papists of the gross evil of several of their popes in whoredoms, adulteries, sodomy, bestiality, witchcraft, atheism; they will treat that nothing to the point."[10] The conviction grew on the young scholar that if there was to be Christian integrity there could be no separation between life and worship. The simplest prayer of the unschooled man was more genuine in worship than was that of the atheist bishop whose worship was like play-acting in which there might be polish and skill. Prayer, in a man's own power and without the help of the Spirit, was, he thought, entirely unprofitable.

One of the most interesting ideas developed by Barclay in his early youth was that style of worship may be fruitfully classified by the ease with which it can be disrupted. The more external it is, the easier it is to stop it, by taking away its props. Barclay stated this first in shorthand, and eight years later he presented it in a more complete form in the *Apology*. The important passage, as printed, is the following.

> Do but take away the mass-book, the chalice, the host, or the priest's garments, yea, do but spill the water, or the wine, or blow out the candles, a thing quickly done, and the whole business is marred, and no sacrifice can be offered. Take from the Lutherans or Episcopalians their Liturgy or Common-Prayer-Book, and no service can be said. Remove from the Calvinists, Arminians, Socinians, Independents, or Anabaptists, the pulpit, the Bible, and the hour-glass, or make but such a noise as the voice of the preacher cannot be heard, or disturb him but so before he come, or strip him of his Bible or his books, and he must be dumb: for they

[9] *Ibid.*, p. 388 [XI, xxviii].
[10] Shorthand Notebook, p. 18.

all think it an heresy to wait to speak as the Spirit of God giveth utterances; and thus easily their whole worship may be marred.[11]

It will interest the reader to turn to Appendix C where some of the shorthand is presented in English. Only the details were changed, when publication was contemplated. The obvious similarity is one of the best evidences of the authenticity of the Notebook. The controlling idea is that a mark of reality in worship is its invulnerability to interruption. This Barclay and his fellow prisoners illustrated brilliantly in the Aberdeen Tolbooth. They had no props, but they needed none. Though they were imprisoned for engaging in unlawful worship, the officers could not keep them from going on with it, behind the bars. It was to this glorious and surprising possibility that the author could point as a firsthand witness. In carrying out his purpose to describe the worship that does not depend upon things which enemies can take away, he wrote: "But when people meet together, and their worship consisteth not in such outward acts, and they depend not upon any one's speaking, but merely sit down to wait upon God, and to be gathered out of all visibles, and to feel the Lord in Spirit, none of these things can hinder them."[12]

Barclay was never unmindful of the constant background of actual or potential persecution. What he wanted to tell the world was that there is a reality in worship so great that it can demonstrate itself impervious even to human cruelty. He was not only a witness of this, but also an active participant and an object of attack. "It would be almost incredible to declare," he said, "and indeed a shame, that among men pretending to be Christians, it should be mentioned, what things of this kind men's eyes have seen, and I myself, with others, have shared in the suffering." He then gave some of the details of this testing experience. He said that the intruders "have often beaten us, and cast water and dirt upon us; there they have danced, leaped, sung, and spoken all manner of profane and ungodly words; offered violence and shameful behaviour to grave women and virgins; jeered, mocked and scoffed, asking us if the Spirit was not yet come."[13] The amazing result was not merely that such outrages failed to put an end to the worship of God, but that it increased

[11] *Apology*, p. 355 [XI, xviii].
[12] *Ibid.*, p. 355 [XI, xiii].
[13] *Ibid.*, p. 356 [XI, xiii]. Some of those who shared in such shocking behavior were students preparing themselves for the ministry.

the intensity of the worship. In contrast to what the intruders expected, the Lord, reports Barclay, "hath caused his power and glory more to abound among us, and hath mightily refreshed us by the sense of his love, which hath filled our souls." Even more amazing, some of the tormentors were personally reached.

Yea, sometimes in the midst of the tumult and opposition, God would powerfully move some or other of us by his Spirit, both to testify of that joy, which not withstanding their malice we enjoyed, and powerfully to declare, in the evidence and demonstration of the Spirit, against their folly and wickedness; so as the power of truth hath brought them to some measure of quietness and stillness, and stopped the impetuous streams of their fury and madness.

Thus worship in the face of violence was actually evangelistic in that some of the attackers were converted. Barclay's firsthand report was "that sometimes upon such occasions several of our opposers and interrupters have hereby been convinced of the truth, and gathered from being persecutors to be sufferers with us."[14]

Part of the reason why Barclay's chapter on worship has long been a favorite among sensitive readers is the fact that it is so clearly the record of his own experience. What he writes is far removed from the style of the scholastic theologian, who is discussing a subject in detachment. Barclay was powerful on the subject of worship because he was involved; he was himself a worshiping man, and he hesitated to say anything unless he had known it by direct acquaintance. This is what gives power to the following paragraph.

Yet many and great are the advantages, which my soul, with many others, hath tasted of hereby, and which could be found of all such as would seriously apply themselves hereunto: for, when people are gathered thus together, not merely to hear men, nor depend upon them, but all are inwardly taught to stay their minds upon the Lord, and wait for his appearance in their hearts; thereby the forward working of the spirit of man is stayed and hindered from mixing itself with the worship of God; and the form of this worship is so naked and void of all outward and worldly splendor, that all occasion for man's wisdom to be exercised in that superstition and idolatry hath no lodging here; and so there being also an inward quietness and retiredness of mind, the witness of God ariseth in the heart, and the light of Christ shineth, whereby the

[14] *Ibid.*, pp. 356, 357 [XI, xiii].

soul cometh to see its own condition. And there being many joined together in this same work, there is an inward travail and wrestling; and also, as the measure of grace is abode in, an overcoming of the power and spirit of darkness; and thus we are often greatly strengthened and renewed in the spirits of our minds without a word.[15]

A characteristic sentence is, "I shall insist a little upon this subject, as one that can speak from a certain experience, and not by mere hearsay."[16] He did not expect to attend worship, go through a performance, and leave unchanged. Every time of worship, he thought, should be approached with wonder and with expectancy. After all, worship means engaging in the boldest and noblest enterprise of which a poor finite man is capable, that of coming into direct and meaningful contact with God, who is "Lord of heaven and earth." A person who would face this as a dull routine matter would merely demonstrate thereby that he did not know what it was that he was trying to do. The rational expectation ought to be that, as people gather in the presence of the Lord,

they come to find the good arise over the evil, and the pure over the impure, in which God reveals himself and draweth near to every individual, and so he is in the midst in the general, whereby each not only partakes of the particular refreshment and strength which comes from the good in himself, but is a sharer in the whole body, as being a living member of the body, having a joint fellowship and communion with all.

This is a high standard of expectation, but low expectation seemed to Barclay to be a sin.

The Apologist's high expectations of what any true worship ought to mean to any true worshiper arose from what he had actually observed and felt. He saw no reason why emerging power should be exceptional. He reported that "the Lord often-times, when any turn towards him, and have true desires thus to wait upon him, and find great difficulty through the unstayedness of their minds, doth in condescension and compassion cause his power to break forth in a more strong and powerful manner." Thus he admitted both the difficulty which the finite individual may encounter, and the victory which may ensue, but he saw that victory comes only when the

[15] *Ibid.*, p. 338 [XI, vii].
[16] *Ibid.*, p. 336 [XI, vi].

conditions are met. "And when the mind sinks down and waits for the appearance of life, and that the power of darkness in the soul wrestles and works against it, then the good seed, as it ariseth, will be found to work as physic in the soul, especially if such a weak one be in the assembly of divers others in whom the life is arisen in greater dominion."[17] In short, the break-through of God's presence is more likely to occur if the individual will learn to wait and if, at the same time, he feels the support of the loving fellowship.

The reference to "waiting" leads naturally to Barclay's discussion of silence. There were several reasons why the author found it necessary to deal carefully with the subject of silence. One was that Quakers were already known for their use of silence, which seemed to most people so queer that it could hardly be comprehended. There were clearly twin dangers: first, that of not appreciating silence sufficiently, and second, that of valuing it too highly or fanatically. Barclay's close friend, George Keith, who tended to run to extremes in everything, illustrated the latter danger in an 18-page pamphlet called *The Benefit, Advantage and the Glory of Silent Meetings.* Barclay undoubtedly had this before him as he wrote his chapter on worship in the *Apology*. Indeed, there are some indications of direct indebtedness on the part of the younger scholar. An example of this is the use of the expression "from vessel to vessel."[18] Barclay wrote that "the seeing the faces one of another, when both are inwardly gathered unto the life, giveth occasion for the life secretly to rise, and pass from vessel to vessel." Keith's report was that, "in the silence or ceasing of all words they were drawn to meet often together, for that in the presence and company of one another, they were inwardly refreshed, comforted, quickened and strengthened, through that communion and communication of the spirit and life of God, from vessel to vessel, as from one upon all, and from all upon one."[19]

Though Barclay evidently learned from the dynamic Keith and even employed some of his expressions, his treatment of silence differed from that of his friend. Whereas Keith made silence the center

[17] *Ibid.*, p. 341 [XI, viii].

[18] Keith's essay was written in prison at Edinburgh and printed in London. 1670.

[19] *Ibid.*, p. 10.

of everything in worship, Barclay was careful not to be idolatrous about it. He saw clearly that mere silence might be mere nothingness. Consequently he said that silence was a preparatory discipline and nothing more. It was a means, not an end. Because reality in worship was what he believed to be possible and what he sought to encourage, he could not be satisfied to put the chief emphasis upon either silence or words. The reality lay, he thought, in the power of the Spirit for which silence might help people to be ready and of which spoken ministry might reasonably be a result. The key passage is the following, which, like so many of the best ones, belongs to the theology of witness rather than of speculation:

> Many are the blessed experiences which I could relate of this silence and manner of worship; yet I do not so much commend and speak of silence as if we had bound ourselves by any law to exclude praying or preaching, or tied ourselves thereunto; not at all: for as our worship consisteth not in words, so neither in silence, as silence; but in holy dependence of the mind upon God: from which dependence silence necessarily follows in the first place, until words can be brought forth, from God's Spirit. And God is not wanting to move in his children to bring forth words of exhortation or prayer, when it is needful; so that of the many gatherings and meetings, or such as are convinced of the truth, there is scarce any in whom God raiseth not up some or other to minister to his brethren; and there are few meetings that are altogether silent.[20]

By such a statement Barclay attempted to correct the popular caricature of absolute silence in worship. If people never had messages for one another, this would be an evidence, not of spiritual depth, but of vacuity. The normal expectation was, indeed, that there would be a great deal of praying and speaking, though without prearrangement. The reason for this was evident. "For when many are met together in this one life and name, it doth most naturally and frequently excite them to pray and to praise God, and stir up one another by mutual exhortation and instructions." Though a great deal of silence cannot therefore be expected, and will not, when the life is present, occur, "it is needful there be in the first place some time of silence, during which every one may be gathered inward to the word and gift of grace, from which he that ministereth

[20] *Apology*, p. 343 [XI, ix].

may receive strength to bring forth what he ministereth." The more we read passages like this, the more strange it seems that anyone would ever have thought of Robert Barclay as the chief architect of quietism in the Quaker Movement. In the subsequent quietistic period silence did sometimes become an idol, but it was never such for Barclay. He laid too much stress upon a powerful and heart-shaking ministry for that to be possible. He admitted that there could be a wonderful experience of group worship in which there would not be a single spoken word from start to finish, but this was the exception rather than the rule.

What we may call the modernity of Robert Barclay is indicated by the way in which his analysis of the basis of worship is reflected in contemporary Quaker thought. Though there was a time when Quakers divided in theory, as well as practice, some saying that true worship is on the "basis of silence" and others arguing that God's leadership may be known in advance, there is now a growing tendency to avoid such terms. On what basis do Christians gather for worship? Some, following Thomas Kelly, say the basis is that of "Holy Obedience," others speak of gathering on the basis of "expectancy," others say they meet on the basis of the Holy Spirit. What all of these expressions have in common is that, like Robert Barclay's, they express something more important than either words or absence of words, and something wholly affirmative, which silence is not. The happy phrase of the *Apology* leads us to speak of worship on the basis of "holy dependence."

The Quaker way of worship which Robert Barclay undertook to describe and to defend seemed to him to be the exact antithesis of something strange. How natural for honest reverent people to come together in order to allow God to speak to them jointly rather than singly; how natural for humble people to be still as they gather, thus waiting for God's guidance before speaking in their own power; how natural to be silent when there is nothing which we are led to say! It was not difficult for the author to cite numerous passages from the Bible which express the duty "to wait upon God, and to watch before him." One of the noblest of all prophetic passages is "They that wait upon the Lord shall renew their strength" (Isa. 40:31). Who can miss the relevance of "Be still and know"? (Ps. 46:10) "And though this worship," wrote Barclay, "be indeed very different from the divers Christians, and therefore may seem strange to many, yet hath it been testified of, commended and practised, by the most pious of all sorts, in all ages, as by many evident testimonies might be proved."[21]

It is important to understand that, in regard to worship as in regard to other items, Barclay sought to present Quakerism as non-sectarian. Not only was Quaker practice not strange; it was the closest approximation he could imagine to the gatherings of the earliest Christians. When people objected that worship on the basis of "holy dependence" was not found in Scripture, Barclay replied:

> I answer; We make not silence to be the sole matter of our worship; since, as I have said above, there are many meetings, which are seldom altogether silent; some or other are still moved either to preach, pray, or praise: and so in this our meetings cannot be but like the meetings of the primitive churches recorded in scripture, since our adversaries confess that they did preach and pray by the Spirit.[22]

Barclay did not doubt that what was said in gatherings based on the expectation of direct leading was far more like the messages of the early apostles than were the messages of professional clergymen, who had no counterpart in the early Church. He believed this the more, when he read that the apostles' speech and preaching was not "with enticing words of man's wisdom, but in demonstration of the Spirit and of power," that the faith of the hearers "should not stand in the wisdom of men, but in the power of God" (I Cor. 2:3-5). If Barclay had to choose, in the practice of worship and ministry, between congruence with the pattern of the established churches of his own day, or with the pattern of the Church of New Testament days, he unhesitatingly chose the latter.

Like every man who tries to be rational, Barclay had to fight on two fronts at once, and this was conspicuously true concerning worship. He saw equally the dangers of both the right and the left. The dangers on the left were represented by the exponents of spiritual anarchy who wanted no formality of any kind. Against these, he upheld sturdily the wisdom of meeting at an agreed time and place. The value of meeting on Sunday, he held, was not that Sunday is

[21] *Ibid.*, p. 361 [XI, xvi].
[22] *Ibid.*, pp. 365, 366 [XI, xvii].

more holy than are other days, and, since he recognized no binding command to keep the first day of the week more than any other, he was certainly not a Sabbatarian. The question was one of common sense and nothing else, with four reasons given.

> But first, forasmuch as it is necessary that there be some time set apart for the saints to meet together to wait upon God; and that secondly, it is fit at some times they be freed from their outward affairs; and that thirdly, reason and equity doth allow that servants and beasts have sometime allowed them to be eased from their continual labour; and that fourthly, it appears that the apostles and primitive Christians did use the first day of the week for these purposes; we find ourselves sufficiently moved for these causes to do so also, without superstitiously straining the scriptures for another reason.[23]

If the day had been Wednesday instead of Sunday that would have been all right. The point was to find *one* day, to insure a rhythm of the week. Assuredly the Sabbath was made for man and not man for the Sabbath.

How far Barclay was removed from the religious anarchists, who were a serious problem to early Quakers, is indicated by his defense of a reverent posture. "It becometh those who approach before God to pray, that they do it with bowed knees, and with their heads uncovered, which is our practice."[24] His common sense was further demonstrated by his frank admission that Quakers were, in fact, sometimes disobedient to the movements of the Spirit. In short, he recognized that Quaker practice did not always live up to the theory. Furthermore, he was honest enough to admit that the power of God's Spirit was sometimes evident, even in worship which was programed and prearranged. "That God sometimes condescends to them, we do not deny."[25]

Though the ideal of worship which Barclay described was undeniably a high one, it clearly involved problems. What, specifically, is the place of singing? Given the author's acceptance of the New Testament experience as his standard of comparison, he could not neglect singing. The injunction about psalms and hymns and spiritual songs was one which could not be avoided; nor was it one Barclay

[23] *Ibid.*, pp. 333, 334 [XI, iv].
[24] *Ibid.*, p. 370 [XI, xxiv].
[25] *Ibid.*, p. 381 [XI, xxiv].

wished to avoid. But the problem which occurs to all of us today is that good singing requires thoughtful preparation in advance. If it is to be well done, the notes must be available as well as words; and if there is an adequate choral production, there must be rehearsals. How can these conditions be met on the basis of direct and immediate spiritual leading at the time of the gathered assembly? There is no evidence that Barclay gave any serious thought to these questions.

His fundamental answer about singing was that it *occurred,* and that Quakers were far from rejecting it.

> We confess this to be part of God's worship [he says], and very sweet and refreshing, when it proceeds from a true sense of God's love in the heart, and arises from the divine influence of the Spirit, which leads souls to breathe forth either a sweet harmony, or words suitable to the present condition; whether they be words formerly used by the saints, and recorded in scripture, such as the Psalms of David.[26]

There was, apparently, more spontaneous singing in early Quaker meetings than has usually been recognized. In his first published book, *Truth Cleared of Calumnies,* Barclay denied the assertion that Quakers were opposed to singing, and, as he so often did in his later writing, added an autobiographical statement, though he was only twenty-one years old at the time. Singing, he asserted, "is a thing denied by no Quaker (so called) and is not unusual among them; whereof I have myself been a witness, and have felt of the sweetness and quickening virtue of the Spirit therein, and at such occasions ministered."[27] If an individual felt led to sing or if group singing should sweep through the company, Barclay wholly approved. What he did not approve was what he called "the formal customary way of singing." This he disapproved, not primarily because it had to be prepared in advance, but because it led, almost inevitably, to dishonesty. He thought that the abuses incident to singing were actually greater than those involved in formal praying and preaching, because the temptation to repeat what was not true was greater. A man, Barclay thought, might sing, "The Lord's praise is continually in my mouth," and not mean it at all, for the act of singing could cause

[26] *Ibid.*, p. 386 [XI, xxiv].
[27] *Truth Triumphant*, p. 30. See also p. 854.

him to be unaware of what he was claiming. The danger is, we are told, "that oftentimes great and horrid lies are said in the sight of God: for all manner of wicked profane people take upon themselves to personate the experiences and conditions of blessed David; which are not only false, as to them, but also as to some of more sobriety, who utter them forth."[28]

In this way, Barclay's theme of reality in worship caused him to reject what otherwise he would have been delighted to include. It was a hard decision. His refusal to depend upon anything external caused him, predictably, to reject the use of all musical instruments. These he dismissed quickly by saying, "But as to their artificial music, either by organs, or other instruments, or voice, we have neither example nor precept for it in the New Testament." It apparently did not occur to him that he used things every day which were not commanded in the New Testament, and that there is nothing wrong with the principle of development, providing people are loyal to really basic principles.

That Barclay's treatment of worship has in it an element of greatness is beyond dispute. His position does not represent the whole truth, though it does portray an important part of any sound philosophy of worship. We see the inadequacy of his position when we think of the religious experiences of undoubted value which the Barclay doctrine would necessarily eliminate. Consider, for example, the sense of nearness to God which comes to many as they listen to an oratorio, with orchestra, in a noble cathedral. If Barclay's view were universalized, as he hoped it might be, the stark truth is that there would be no cathedral, no oratorio, and no orchestra, at least none employed in the worship of Almighty God. With all of our respect for Barclay's integrity of mind and character, we are forced to say that such a world would involve a sad impoverishment, not only of culture in general, but of religion in particular. If Barclay's convictions had taken hold of Europe in his century, the world would have been deprived of the religious creations of J. S. Bach. Who, in all honesty, could wish this?

Another important negative criticism of Barclay's analysis of the meaning of worship is that he was too strict in refusing to participate

[28] *Apology*, p. 386 [XI, xxvi].

in acts of worship held in a manner other than that which he considered to be the right one. Because he was fearful of compromising his position, he refused to attend gatherings which he admitted might, on occasion, be the scenes of God's reaching out to men. That he felt keenly the necessity of defending the apparently ungenerous posture, is indicated by the following:

> Seeing then God hath called us to his spiritual worship, and to testify against the human and voluntary worships of the apostasy, if we did not this way stand immovable to the truth revealed, but should join with them, both our testimony for God would be weakened and lost, and it would be impossible steadily to propagate this worship in the world, whose progress we dare neither retard nor hinder by any act of ours.[29]

Here is a stance which very few in our day can admire. Certainly it would undermine the ecumenical movement, going expressly against the conception that there are several ways of worship which God can use acceptably, and that the different groups of worshipers have much to learn from one another. But perhaps this mood would be too much to ask of a people who were living a precarious existence, always liable to horrible persecution which was aided and abetted by the conventional religious leaders. Barclay had a special problem, that of how a vital minority, faced daily with ridicule and contempt, could even survive. He thought survival was not possible unless they learned to "stand immovable."

One of Barclay's contributions in his great essay on worship is his account of the origin of the nickname "Quaker." The value of his treatment is that it helps the modern reader to realize that the name, though meant to be abusive, was, in reality, deeply complimentary. The name, he said, "was first reproachfully cast upon us; which though it be none of our choosing, yet in this respect we are not ashamed of it, but have rather reason to rejoice therefore."[30] The record of what sometimes occurred during worship to give rise to the popular nickname is as follows:

> Sometimes the power of God will break forth into a whole meeting, and there will be such an inward travail, while each is seeking to over-

[29] *Apology*, pp. 382, 383 [XI, xxiv].

[30] *Ibid.*, p. 342 [XI, viii]. The same point is made, with a slight variation, in *Universal Love Considered*. See Chap. IV of this book.

come the evil in themselves, that by the strong contrary workings of these opposite powers, like the going of two contrary tides, every individual will be strongly exercised as in a day of battle, and thereby trembling and a motion of body will be upon most, if not upon all, which, as the power of truth prevails, will from pangs and groans end with a sweet sound of thanksgiving and praise.[31]

This seems to be a far cry from our contemporary experience, but it is by no means self-evident that the contrast is in our favor. Perhaps the most valid condemnation of the Religious Society of Friends in the last third of the twentieth century is that such a description seems unfamiliar. The sad truth is that the opprobrious nickname no longer fits; the worship is such that nobody trembles; *the Quakers have ceased to quake*. It is easy to keep the external marks of a way of worship and yet to depart radically from the spirit. The greatest departure is not that of those who have changed the form, but rather that of those who, making a form of their formlessness, have lost the breathless sense of expectancy. The measure of departure is the degree to which Barclay's description now seems alien to our experience.

[31] *Ibid.*, p. 342 [XI, viii].

CHAPTER XIII

THE MEANING OF SACRAMENTS

Our communion with Christ is and ought to be our greatest and chiefest work.

—Robert Barclay

OUTSIDERS who observed the vital new movement of Christian renewal which emerged in the latter half of the seventeenth century were always tempted to describe it in merely negative terms. It was easy to say that Quakers were odd people who had no clergy, no liturgy, no prayer book. Even more, there was a tendency to say that Quakers were distinguished from other Christians by the fact that they observed no sacraments. To many of their neighbors, these new people seemed to be unaccountably perverse. It was known that the explosive new group did not baptize with water, whether sprinkling or immersion, and that they also did not celebrate, in any outward form, the ritual of the Lord's Supper or Eucharist. How could this be? Even the friendly outsiders were puzzled, for the new practices seemed to them to constitute, not only a break with the entire Christian heritage of many centuries, but also an inexplicable disobedience to what had long been understood to be unequivocal commands of Christ. Clearly there was an urgent need for explanation, and to this task Barclay set himself in two chapters of the *Apology,* one of which dealt with baptism, and the other with Holy Communion.

As we analyze Barclay's thinking now, we can see that he was making a conscious effort to be affirmative in his testimony. He was setting his mind directly against the appearance of negativity in all phases of the Quaker way of life. Far from denying the ministry, he had already shown, in Chapter X of the *Apology,* that a true understanding of the gospel of Christ leads inevitably and necessarily to the ministry of every Christian man and woman. In a similar fashion, Barclay's clear purpose was to emphasize the reality of both baptism and Communion in the life of the committed Christian, liberating the conception, in each case, from dependence upon any external acts or ceremonies. In both, the basic principle was that, if a person has the reality, nothing else is required, and if he does not have the reality, nothing else will suffice. Here was a great idea, but it required both explanation and support. These Barclay was willing and able to provide. In doing so, he sometimes appeared verbose, but the careful reader soon discovered that the author provided genuine substance, including ideas which are still of contemporary significance, because they are dateless and owe very little to the thought forms which happened to be fashionable at the time of writing.

That it was not merely Barclay's contemporaries who required a careful explanation of Quaker practice in regard to the sacraments, is illustrated by Lord Macaulay, who professed himself shocked by the stand of George Fox. In a sarcastic vein, Macaulay wrote that Fox took literally commands of Christ which nearly all other Christians had taken figuratively, while he allegorized those which others interpreted literally. By the former he meant the love of enemies, while by the latter he meant the sacraments. Even those who have admired Quaker acts of mercy have been puzzled by the apparent inconsistency in trying so hard to be obedient to Christ in some areas of conduct and yet seeming to neglect His explicit commands in others.

As Barclay undertook his difficult assignment, he tried to make clear to his readers the radical nature of the religious revolution which Christ came to inaugurate. The temptation is to think that He came to purify an old order or to make new regulations, to take the place of old ones. But this, in Barclay's judgment, would be to misunderstand Him completely. The big change was not from one set of ceremonies to another, but from *all* ceremonies to an emphasis upon reality and on nothing else. No one doubts, says Barclay, that the religion of the Jews was one which involved sacerdotal acts, such as that of circumcision. It is a fact that ceremonial washing before meals was required, as well as obedience to carefully outlined dietary laws. None of this Barclay either denied or despised. The fact that such ordinances were once in effect does not, however, mean that they remain in effect, when needs and conditions are altered. "For the acts of God's compassion and indulgence at some times, and to some persons, upon singular extraordinary occasions, are not to be a rule of our actions."[1]

The important thing, thought Barclay, is to realize that Christ's coming has introduced a radically new conception of what true religion requires. We are too slow to recognize that we are in a new covenant, and, indeed, most of the mistakes of the long centuries of Christian apostasy have been produced by a failure to understand this fundamental idea. Christ, says Barclay, sought to bring us into a new order, which stands in sharp contrast to all religions of the world, since it "is neither limited to time, place nor person, but is performed in the Spirit and in truth."[2] As these words indicate, Christ's conversation with the woman at the well of Samaria had taken deep hold upon the Apologist's consciousness. The woman's mistake was not that of choosing *one* place of worship against another or *one form* of ceremonial in preference to others, but rather in her basic assumption that God's requirements had anything whatever to do with such matters. The reason why the woman's question could not be answered with a simple yes or no was that her presuppositions were wrong. Barclay was convinced that her presuppositions had lasted on in Christian history and that therefore what was demanded was a radical rather than a mild reformation. The point to which he returned, again and again, was that the commitment of the Christian is deeper than ritual; it, therefore, "is not acted according to set forms and prescriptions." Though the disciples did not wholly understand this, some of them left a record so good that it enables us to see beyond their confusion.

How little subsequent Churchmen have understood what they have been supposed to represent is shown by the interpretation of baptism

[1] *Apology*, p. 386 [XI, xxv].
[2] *Ibid.*, p. 405 [XII, vi].

as that which is efficacious *ex opere operato*. All who have held this are exposed to the charge that their religion has degenerated into magic. This seems like a harsh judgment, but it is very difficult to avoid any other conclusion when we see people working frantically to provide the ceremony of baptism to a sick child, who may be unconscious at the time. That such a view is held, implicitly if not explicitly by thousands today, helps us to see that the evil which Barclay proposed to attack was not at all an imaginary one. He was opposed to magic in all its forms, and he saw that it was by no means obsolete.

The constant danger of Christians, in Barclay's view, was that of falling back into pre-Christian positions which it was Christ's evident purpose to transcend. We know today that, apart from a ceremonial washing, the pagan convert to Judaism could not be qualified to have full status among the people of Israel, but why should anything like this be demanded of the followers of Christ? Christianity was meant to be something far more radical than a reformed judaism. Indeed, Christ apparently referred to ceremonial washing and rejected it by saying that what touches a man on the outside cannot make any real difference. Barclay did not hesitate to state bluntly that the critics of the Quakers who said that Quakers were not Christians because they were not physically sprinkled or immersed, were *Judaizers*. "But in this," he wrote, "our adversaries judaize, and renouncing the glorious and spiritual privileges of the new convenant, are sticking in and cleaving to the rudiments of the old."[3]

That there are many references to physical baptism in the New Testament, Barclay did not deny. What he did deny was that these references require any continuing ceremonial practice as something essential to the Christian life. What is required, he maintained, is moral and spiritual regeneration, and this interpretation of baptism he boldly accepted. If any one had asked Robert Barclay whether he were a baptized Christian his answer would undoubtedly have been affirmative. And he would not have been referring to the physical act of being baptized by water before he became a convinced Quaker. He believed with all his heart in the baptism of Christ, which, in sharp contrast to John's, was the baptism of the Spirit. "Such," he said, "is the baptism that we labour to be baptized withal, and contend for."[4]

[3] *Ibid.*, p. 405 [XII, vi].
[4] *Ibid.*, p. 406 [XII, vi].

Using this sense of the word, he did not hesitate to maintain that no one can be a Christian unless he is truly baptized, i.e. immersed in the love of Christ and brought thereby to newness of life. But this is obviously very different from a ceremony to which the insincere person may submit for reasons of expediency. Barclay is all for baptism, providing it is the real thing, and takes place within the heart.

Barclay's critics, and particularly the theologian Arnoldus, naturally brought up the point that Christians should submit to physical baptism today because we are supposed to follow Christ, and He is reported to have submitted Himself to John's baptism in the Jordan. Here was the perfect opportunity for the young logician to use his dialectical skill. Did the critic mean that we must do everything that Christ did? If so, then Christian males must be circumcized, for Christ was circumcized. If so, we must observe the Jewish feasts and rites, and keep the Passover. But these are requirements which neither Arnoldus nor any other modern Christian will suppose he must obey. Why, then, the manifest inconsistency? Must we be single because Christ was single? Must we speak Aramaic because He did? Here Barclay's position is really unassailable. Furthermore, he sees that emphasis on the work of John the Baptist, far from harming the Quaker case, provides it with one of its major supports. It was the Baptist who *contrasted* what he expected of converts with what his successor would expect, when he said, "I indeed baptize with water, but he who comes after me will baptize with the Holy Spirit and with fire" (Luke 3:13).[5] The more any thoughtful person ponders this, the less the Quaker emphasis on reality and nothing else will seem either inexplicable or perverse.

The idea of baptism by fire was exactly what Barclay needed to make his point about the metaphorical character of all baptism. Even the most extreme literalist does not insist on a literal interpretation of baptism by fire, it being evident to all that what is meant is a figurative entrance into an incendiary fellowship, in which one loving heart sets another on fire. But, if this is true of fire, why is it not likewise true of water? When our Lord says that He is the "door," no one is so perverse as to suppose that He means that He is made of wood. When we contemplate this we begin to see that the gospel language abounds in metaphors, such as those of "light," "leaven," "salt," and

[5] Other accounts, such as Acts 1:4, omit "fire."

many more. Barclay's conviction was that baptism is one of these. He considered it absurd to pick out one from the set and require a literal interpretation of it, though not of the others. If baptismal cleansing is metaphorical, Barclay is all for it. Baptism by water, then, means cleansing, while baptism by fire means enkindling. Thus, he concludes that being baptized with fire "is not to be understood of outward material fire, but rather 'by a metonomy.' " The only strange feature of this sophisticated treatment is that the author did not make use of the recorded statement of Christ's purpose when He said, "I came to cast fire upon the earth" (Luke 12:49).

It took a certain courage for Barclay to emphasize, as he did, the metaphorical language in which the gospel is necessarily expressed. He ran the risk of being accused of mere allegorizing. His purpose, however, was to analyze the language in order to discover the real, as against the fanciful, meaning. He understood, from John 2:21, that Christ spoke of His body when He said, "Destroy this temple and in three days I will raise it up." Barclay did not want to make the mistake of Nicodemus who, through his excessive literalism, misunderstood the new birth.

Another criticism of Barclay and his fellows, which some were quick to employ, was that, according to the gospel record, Christ commanded His followers to make disciples of all nations, "baptizing them in the name of the Father, the Son, and the Holy Spirit (Matt. 28:19). The Apologist's answer was that Quakers accepted this wholeheartedly. Who, indeed, was more evangelical in the effort to bring men everywhere to Christ? Who was more missionary-minded? The entire problem, however, centered on what it means to baptize. To baptize in the "name" said Barclay, means to introduce to the "power and virtue, and not a mere formal expression of words adjoined with water baptism."[6] What we are called to promote, then, is something that is truly life-changing, and this is what Christ evidently meant. "Baptizing with the Spirit is something further than teaching, or informing the understanding; for it imports a reaching to, and melting the heart, whereby it is turned, as well as the understanding informed."

By showing the deeper meaning of baptism, Barclay answered those

[6] *Ibid.*, p. 411 [XII, viii].

who asserted that Christ commanded it. They could not, he recognized, show that He commanded a *ceremonial*. But the case was strengthened by showing also that, whatever the disciples did or refrained from doing, Christ Himself did not engage in the ceremony of water baptism. "If water baptism," said Barclay, "had been to continue a perpetual ordinance of Christ in his church, he would either have practised it himself, or commanded his apostles so to do." But the striking fact is that we are specifically informed that He did not practise it (John 4:2). Undeniably the members of the early Church administered baptism as a rite, and may even have insisted upon its necessity for salvation, but they were not, in so doing, following the example of their Lord. Since the Gospels were not available until after many Christian practices were established, the early congregations were probably unaware of Christ's own practice. Perhaps this is why the author of the Fourth Gospel is so specific on the point, John 4:2 clarifying and correcting John 3:22.

In accepting the necessity of baptism, while interpreting the meaning of the sacrament in a radically different manner, Barclay was on firm ground, intellectually. He could find traces of this position in various parts of the New Testament. For example, he was deeply impressed by the fact that the Apostle Paul thanked God that he had baptized so few, "intimating that what he did therein he did not by virtue of his apostolic commission, but rather in condescension to their weakness, even as at another time he circumcized Timothy."[7] Paul's purpose, in Barclay's judgment, was to wean converts "from the former Jewish ceremonies and observations." The great insight came when he realized that neither circumcision nor uncircumcision avails anything, but only a new creation. Barclay believed that many alleged Christians were still operating on the circumcision level. Even those who held that some ritual was a requirement could not, he pointed out, agree on *which one*. The shame is that there has been so much "debate, contention, jangling and quarrelling" about the right method.[8] If there is "one baptism," what is it? Is it sprinkling or immersion? Clearly it is neither, since the argument here is about a triviality. The one true baptism is, as the original statement in *Theses Theologicae* said, "a pure and spiritual thing, to wit, the baptism of

[7] *Ibid.*, p. 406 [XII, vii].
[8] *Ibid.*, p. 390 [XII, i].

the Spirit and fire, by which we are buried with him, that being washed and purged from our sins, we may walk in newness of life."

On the occasion when Dr. Samuel Johnson saw a handsome new edition of Barclay's *Apology,* the great man seized the opportunity to argue with what he took to be the Apologist's position on one of the historic sacraments. According to Boswell, "Johnson remarked, 'He says there is neither precept nor practice for baptism; that is false.' Here he was the aggressor, by no means in a gentle manner; and the good Quakers had the advantage of him; for he had read negligently, and had not observed that Barclay speaks of infant baptism; which they calmly made him perceive."[9] Since all that Dr. Johnson was trying to quote was the brief statement in the Thesis, Boswell was correct. Barclay well knew that he was opposing the stand of much of the early Church about water baptism, so far as adults are concerned, but he had a right to claim that the early Christians were with him on infant baptism. Contemporary Baptists, in their insistence on "believers' baptism" are evidently correct in their claim that the earliest baptism was only that of adults. Barclay was very brief on this subject, alleging that the baptism of infants "is a mere human tradition." Since he had already rejected both the necessity and efficacy of adult baptism, the rejection of infant baptism logically followed. There is no justification of infant baptism, as ordinarily administered, except on the assumption of the objective efficacy of a rite, even when the individual is unconscious of it, and this Barclay was bound to deny as a magical perversion of the gospel. A service of dedication is, of course, another matter.

There is no doubt that Barclay made an important contribution to Christian thinking by his careful treatment of the meaning of baptism, even though he, naturally, did not persuade Doctor Johnson and many others like him. Schleiermacher was convinced that the rejection of water baptism on the part of Quakers had a certain justification, in that it rested on the desire to exalt the idea of regeneration and to minimize ceremony. He thought, however, that Quakers erred in not recognizing the influences of the fellowship on the development of the regeneration of the individual.[10] In view of Barclay's insistence on the place and function of the fellowship, we conclude that Schleiermacher

[9] Boswell, *op. cit.,* Vol. III, p. 298.
[10] *Der Christliche Glaube,* 2d. ed. pp. 136–38.

either had not read Barclay or had not understood him. The more we study Barclay the more we are convinced that he was very close to Augustine in the conception that true baptism means the ingrafting of the individual into the community which forms the body of Christ. This is what Barclay was arguing for, and it was the magnitude of this conception which made him unwilling to settle for anything less.

As a scholar, Robert Barclay was well acquainted with the contrasting positions on the sacraments which had led to bitter divisions at the time of the Reformation. The question whether there should be seven sacraments, as the Roman Catholics had reasserted at the Council of Trent, or only two, as the leading Reformers maintained, seemed to him to be beside the point because the question was wrongly formed. The arguments had often turned on *which* ceremonies Christ had actually instituted, baptism and Holy Communion being retained almost wholly on the ground that these alone could be proved to have been set up by Christ Himself. What Barclay, representing all Quakers, did was to break through this argument to a deeper basis of inquiry. It was idle to discuss *which* ceremonies Christ instituted if His manifest purpose was to take men beyond ceremonies to something more fundamental. If Christ was really introducing a "new covenant," the argument whether He meant His followers to be sprinkled or immersed became actually frivolous. The Apologist's deepest conviction was that Christ had come into the world to lead men and women into a genuine "reformation," which is of such a radical nature that it "puts an end to the shadows."[11]

We gravely misunderstand Barclay unless we realize how radical he thought the Christian revolution was meant to be. There is, in this, a measure of security. So long as we are resting on the basis of evidence for ceremonial institution, we are at the mercy of changing patterns of Biblical scholarship. Once it was universally supposed that Jesus had said "This do in remembrance of me," but this is true no longer. Growth in Biblical scholarship, however, far from harming Barclay's position, supports his primary insights, though he did not share the textual doubts of modern scholars. It is now agreed that the supposed words of the institution of the Eucharist do not appear in any of the four canonical Gospels. The words "Do this," which were once thought to be in Luke 22:19, are not found in the oldest manuscripts

[11] *Apology*, p. 403 [XII, vi].

and are therefore omitted both from the Revised Standard Version and the New English Bible except in the margin. The words of a famous and reverent Oxford scholar, C. C. J. Webb, state the new situation clearly:

> Few scholars would now be prepared to regard Matt. 28:19 and I Cor. 11:23 seq. as putting it beyond doubt that the historical Jesus actually prescribed the permanent observance of these rites by his followers. Thus the old question as to the number of sacraments cannot be argued on the old grounds.[12]

What is striking about Barclay's treatment is that, almost three hundred years ago, he had already transcended the old grounds of argument. He recognized, of course, that members of the early Church participated in the external observance of the Lord's Supper, just as they abstained from eating strangled meat and practiced the anointing of the sick with oil. It was no part of his mood to write disrespectfully of any of these practices, and if they were helpful, he was the first to rejoice. His strong point, however, was that these ancient practices are not required forever, because, being "but shadows of better things, they cease in such as have obtained the substance."

In his emphasis upon the substance rather than the shadow, Barclay had no objection whatever to metaphors about the body and blood of Christ and, in fact, rejoiced in them. With Augustine, he dwelt on Christ's affirmation that He was the living bread, which came down from heaven. He knew that this was poetry, but how else is the deepest truth to be stated? When he read, "Except ye eat the flesh of the Son of Man, and drink his blood, ye have no life in you," he did not refer to "cannibalism," as the contemporary prosy literalist does, but saw these words as a reference to a profound inner experience. The literalist, who would think of a body that could be weighed and measured, would simply miss the point. "Now all Christians at present generally recognize that the outward body of Christ came not down from heaven."[13] Therefore, the more figurative the language, the more real the experience.

[12] This appears in Professor Webb's brilliant article on "Sacraments" in the *Encyclopedia Britannica*, 14th ed., Vol. 19, p. 798.

[13] *Apology*, p. 424 [XIII, ii].

It is the soul, not the body, that is to be nourished by this flesh and blood. Now outward flesh cannot nourish nor feed the soul; there is no proportion nor analogy betwixt them; neither is the communion of the saints with God by a conjunction and mutual participation of flesh, but of the Spirit. . . . For the flesh (I mean outward flesh, even such as was that wherein Christ lived and walked when upon earth; and not flesh, when transformed by a metaphor, to be understood spiritually) can only partake of flesh, as spirit of spirit: as the body cannot feed upon spirit, neither can the spirit feed upon flesh. And that the flesh here spoken of is spiritually to be understood, appears further, inasmuch as that which feedeth upon it shall never die; but the bodies of all men once die; yea, it was necessary that the body of Christ himself should die. That this body and spiritual flesh and blood of Christ, is to be understood of that divine and heavenly seed, before spoken of by us, appears both by the nature and fruits of it.[14]

In this key passage we catch the combination of poetic insight and robust common sense which marked the Apologist's life throughout its course. Any reader who supposes, for a moment even, that Robert Barclay rejected the experience of Holy Communion, has missed the point entirely. Communion was what he did most assuredly accept as the very center of his Christian experience! The only practical question for the Christian is not *whether,* but *how* this communion is to be effected. The author invited all who might read his words to make the experiment of communing with Christ directly, with no mediation whatever. One consequence of this interpretation is that some Friends in the twentieth century now speak of their meetings as "Communion after the manner of Friends." To those who were tired of the controversies occurring in the different sects, about whether the physical bread is the real or only the symbolical body of Christ, he addressed himself.

I say, if for all this thou findest thy soul yet barren, yea, hungry, and ready to starve, for want of something thou longest for; know that that light that discovers thy iniquity to thee, that shows thee thy barrenness, thy nakedness, thy emptiness, is that body which thou must partake of, and feed upon. . . . And as the outward birth cannot subsist without some outward body to feed upon, some outward flesh, some outward drink, so neither can this inward birth, unless it be fed by this inward

[14] *Ibid.*, p. 425 [XIII, ii].

flesh and blood of Christ, which answers to it after the same manner, by way of analogy.[15]

Such a paragraph makes us see that, though Barclay was a theologian, he was much more. He was also an unabashed evangelist, trying to give new hope to those who were frustrated by endless arguments and word-chopping. With this in mind, he called attention to the words of invitation put into the mouth of the Living Christ by the author of Revelation, "Behold I stand at the door and knock; if any man hear my voice, and open the door, I will come in to him, and will sup with him, and he with me" (Rev. 3:20). In this invitation there is at once both a denial of limited election and hope for the millions who do not have available any material bread and wine which has been blessed by a priest. Barclay rejected the ceremony, not because he had any objection to its symbolism, but because the experience of communion is potentially universal. His answer to his critics was, essentially, "Your communion is too small." His clearest positive statement is the following:

> So that the supper of the Lord, and the supping with the Lord, and partaking of his flesh and blood, is no ways limited to the ceremony of breaking bread and drinking wine at particular times, but is truly and really enjoyed, as often as the soul retires into the light of the Lord, and feels and partakes of that heavenly life by which the inward man is nourished; which may be and is often witnessed by the faithful at all times, though more particularly when they are assembled together to wait upon the Lord.[16]

Once the author had made his affirmative emphasis, he was ready to meet specific difficulties which lead to perplexity in the minds of sincere seekers.[17] In the first place, he dealt tenderly with any who were really perplexed by Christ's reported words, at the Last Supper, "This is my body." Christ was using, says Barclay, a vivid metaphor, much as He employed one concerning water, with the woman at the well in Samaria. How can understanding occur without the use of figures of speech? By the use of a figure, Christ tried to make His followers see that, as the bread and wine before them, though ap-

[15] *Ibid.*, p. 428 [XIII, iii].
[16] *Ibid.*, p. 429 [XIII, iii].
[17] *Ibid.*, p. 434 [XIII, v].

parently lost, were really effective in preserving their lives, "so was he also to give his body and shed his blood for the salvation of their souls."[18] The key is an intelligent understanding of the word "is," which need not mean identity.

The second difficulty, which many felt and which Barclay recognized, concerned the Apostle Paul's advice (I Cor. 11). That, as a matter of fact, the congregation at Corinth practiced a ceremony, Barclay freely admitted, but he thought it was a strange leap of logic to conclude, on that account, that it ought to be similarly practiced in other congregations and other generations.

> I answer, That this infers no more necessary relation than any other religious act, and amounts to no more than this, That since the Corinthians were in the use of this ceremony, and so performed it as a religious act, they ought to do it worthily, or else they should bring condemnation upon themselves.[19]

Why, asks Barclay, should a particular practice in ancient Greece make any thoughtful person conclude that it is "a necessary religious act obligatory upon others?"

The third difficulty which the author found it necessary to face, was that of the supposed institution, "Do this in remembrance of me." Barclay pointed out, naturally, the absence of these words from the accounts in Matthew and Mark. Since he could not have known what modern scholarship has revealed, viz. that even the apparent institution in Luke (22:19) is doubtful, he dealt with the words straightforwardly. Of the expression, "Do this in remembrance of me," he said, "It will amount to no more than this, that being the last time that Christ did eat with his disciples, he desired them, that in their eating and drinking they might have regard to him, and by the remembering of that opportunity, be the more stirred up to follow him diligently through sufferings and death."[20]

One of the most attractive parts of the treatment of the sacraments which is found in the *Apology* is that concerning foot-washing. The author sensed, in this connection, the advantage which he had over his critics, and he did not hesitate to press it. He was quick to see

[18] *Ibid.*, p. 437 [XIII, v].
[19] *Ibid.*, p. 439 [XIII, v].
[20] *Ibid.*, p. 442 [XIII, vi].

that, in John's Gospel, there is only the barest reference to food at the Last Supper, all of the major stress being laid upon the acted parable of washing the feet of the disciples. Why, he asked, have conventional Christians been so insistent about the necessity of strict observance about eating bread and wine and so neglectful of this other symbolic action, the details of which are far more meticulously given? The breaking of the bread was a common occurrence, but "for the master to rise up, and wash the feet of his servants and disciples" was singular, indeed. If people are going to be literal, how can they honorably avoid making foot-washing into a sacrament? Barclay noted that Christ said positively and unequivocally that, as He had done to them, they ought to do to one another. Furthermore, the meaning is profound, representing the revolutionary nature of the new ethic which is being introduced. What kind of consistency is it which interprets one part of the Last Supper with rigid literalism, yet either interprets another part figuratively or neglects it entirely? The direct challenge is as follows:

> I would willingly propose this seriously to men, who will be pleased to make use of that reason and understanding that God hath given them, and not be imposed upon, nor abused by the custom or tradition of others; Whether this ceremony, if we respect either the time that it was appointed in, or the circumstances wherewith it was performed, or the command enjoining the use of it, hath not as much to recommend it for a standing ordinance of the gospel, as either water baptism, or bread and wine?[21]

The oddity of this situation has no reasonable explanation. The Roman Catholics retort that the Pope washes the feet of some poor people once a year, but this is no adequate answer, since the Mass is performed every day. Why, in short, did the medieval Church not list eight sacraments instead of merely seven, since the proposed eighth one has a far more direct connection with Christ's words than any of the standard ones? If it be replied that the washing of feet is only a ceremony, no one can demonstrate that the breaking of the bread is any more. In this analysis, Barclay clearly enjoyed moving over from defense to attack, asking why consistency was so lightly valued. If one ceremony was only for a time, why not the other? The rational con-

[21] *Ibid.*, p. 444 [XIII, vi].

clusion is that, since "the washing of one another's feet, is justly laid aside, as not binding upon Christians: so also the other for the same reason."[22] It is necessary to understand that Barclay was not arguing for the reinstitution of foot-washing, as the Brethren have done; all that he was asking was intellectual integrity. It seemed to him indecent for men not to accept the implications of their own positions.

In the end, in spite of his tough-minded analysis, Barclay expressed great tenderness towards those who still felt that they needed the outward ceremonies and gave it as his judgment that Christ reached them, even though they were not fully liberated. "Nevertheless," he wrote, "I doubt not but many, whose understandings have been clouded with these ceremonies, have notwithstanding, by the mercy of God, had some secret sense of the mystery, which they could not clearly understand because it was veiled from them by their sticking to such outward things."[23] Indeed, the Apologist even had some kind words for his old antagonist, John Calvin, especially in reference to Calvin's humility in confessing that he "neither comprehends it, nor can express it in words; but yet by a feeling experience can say, The Lord is spiritually present." The author's conviction was that, at this point, Calvin was very close to a break-through which would have made him see that the shadows were nothing and the substance everything. In no part of all of Barclay's many writings was his tenderness to those who had not moved into what he thought was the new day more evident than in the conclusion of his study of Holy Communion.

> If any now at this day, from a true tenderness of spirit, and with real conscience towards God, did practice this ceremony in the same way, method, and manner as did the primitive Christians recorded in scripture, I should not doubt to affirm but they might be indulged in it, and the Lord might regard them, and for a reason appear to them in the use of these things, as many of us have known him to do to us in the time of our ignorance; providing always they did not seek to obtrude them upon others, nor judge such as found themselves delivered from them.[24]

To a remarkable degree, the preceding statement has come to be

[22] *Ibid.*, p. 445 [XXIII, vi].
[23] *Ibid.*, p. 458 [XIII, x].
[24] *Ibid.*, p. 459 [XIII, xi].

accepted by Quakers as a sound position.[25] Following Barclay, most Quakers today are ready to admit that ceremonies, though unnecessary, are not intrinsically evil. If Christ reaches people in them, as He evidently does, that is reason to rejoice. But if any try to claim that no one can be a Christian without physical baptism and without participation in a physical ceremony of the Eucharist, that is another matter entirely. Here is the point at which Barclay, like most Quakers after him, decided to stand and fight. The basic formula is: Neither ceremonies nor lack of ceremonies will suffice, but only a new creation. Mere absence of ceremony is no justification of any man's life. This Barclay understood perfectly.

The strongest contemporary criticism of the Quaker insistence on the substance, rather than the shadow, is that this represents an excessive spiritualism. It has been argued by brilliant Christian thinkers in the present century, particularly Bishop Charles Gore and Archbishop William Temple, that it is a manifest error to underrate the physical. Temple's famous aphorism to the effect that Christianity is the most materialist of the world religions led him to uphold the use of the physical sacraments as forms of witness to the wholeness of experience. That the commonest of Palestinian foods could have come to be used as outward signs of spiritual grace seemed to him one of the best features of the Christian faith. A chapter in his Gifford Lectures, *Nature, Man and God,* bears the striking title, "The Sacramental Universe." God, he believed, is using the material and the spiritual together both for His glory and for man's salvation. The Word, we are reminded, became *flesh*. Bishop Gore's interpretation of the sacramental idea was similar. This he saw, not merely in the Christian Church, but in the entire creation. "The principle that spiritual values and forces are mediated through material processes runs through nature as a whole."[26]

Though Robert Barclay never had an opportunity to encounter this particular philosophy of sacramentalism, there is every reason to believe that he would have appreciated it. He had himself attacked those who were so "spiritual" that they did not even want a place in

[25] In a Dublin publication of 1698, William Penn and others, referring to the sacraments, wrote, "We judge not those that conscientiously practice them."

[26] Charles Gore, *The Holy Spirit and the Church* (New York: Charles Scribner's Sons, 1924), p. 146.

which to meet. He and his fellow Quakers, far from being superior to bodies, cared greatly for bodies, particularly broken and imprisoned ones. This was the origin of the *"Meeting for Sufferings,"* which continues to this day. Barclay could easily see the sacramental aspect of sex and gloried in a splendid family life. The point raised was not the denial of the sacramental aspect of life, but its limitation to one or two ceremonial acts. The objection to the then celebrated sacraments was not that they were material, but rather that they were artificial. Therefore, Barclay's whole emphasis was upon the real. The great reality which he knew by experience was the new life in Christ and this he could not bear to think of as being channeled in a mere ritual. He could not accept as valid the notion that there are only a few sacred acts, which the entire history of sacramentalism implied, thus leaving all of the remainder of life to a less exalted sphere! Though he did not object to the material, he was deeply skeptical of the formal, because it implied a limitation. He believed in the Real Presence, as much as did any Roman Catholic, but he had no reason to suppose that this presence was limited to an altar, where a particular form of words had been said or particular bits of matter had been blessed by a priest.

Barclay ended his entire treatment of worship and sacraments on a note of elation, and it is easy to see why he did so. He had experienced the Risen Christ. "For we certainly know," he said, "that the day is dawned, in which God hath arisen, and hath dismissed all those ceremonies and rites." Since Christ has risen, He is "leading his children out of those rudiments, that they may walk with him in his light: to whom be glory forever. Amen."

CHAPTER XIV

THE MODERNITY OF BARCLAY

While Calvin's axioms and postulates are of the waning past, Barclay's are of the widening future.

—*Alexander Gordon*

THE REALLY important question about Robert Barclay is the question of his relevance for the day in which it is both our responsibility and opportunity to live. His short life was an interesting one; he was a superlatively good man; he contributed crucially to the survival of the Quaker Movement by giving it an intellectual structure. All this we know, but it is not enough. Only a few people are deeply interested in a career which has merely historical significance. What we want to know is what Barclay has to say to searching men and women today. What is his contemporary significance, not merely for the tiny minority who happen to be called Quakers, but for all who seek to be both honest and profound about the spiritual life?

When we try to evaluate Barclay's thinking in its entirety, we finally conclude that his contemporary significance is very great indeed. He cannot be lightly dismissed as one who merely reflected the thought forms of his day. In spite of his limitations, he appears, when carefully studied, as one of the least dated of men. The major problems which he faced are with us now in an exaggerated degree.

Barclay's chief significance for our time is his demonstration of the possibility of finding a "third way" when the obvious alternatives are unacceptable. Nearly all of his mature life was lived during the Restoration period, with its conscious revolt against Puritanism. He was only twelve years old when the Stuart monarchy, with its licentious tendencies, was restored, and he died only two years after it ended. This then was the setting of his mature life. In the widespread revolt against Puritan standards of conduct, there was, for many, a sharp separation between religion and morality. How could a man of Barclay's integrity operate successfully in such a setting? The one thing which he could not do was to settle for the separation and live his life in compartments. He never gave up his youthful idea that religion, if it is genuine, must penetrate the whole of life. It is not enough to have a lucid theology; there must also be a careful application of the faith to common life. That is why he could not complete his *magnum opus* without a final chapter devoted to what might be called applied Christianity. Even though the chapter is inadequate, the pattern is sound.

Barclay had tried to defend, with cogency, every item in his system, but he realized at the end that the ultimate verification was that of character. Speaking of those who had been convinced and, accordingly, had accepted the principles already enunciated, he added,

> It will not a little commend them, I suppose, in the judgment of sober and judicious men, that taking them generally, even by the confession of their adversaries, they are found to be free of those abominations which abound among other professors, such as are swearing, drunkenness, whoredom, riotousness, etc.; and that generally the very coming among this people doth naturally work such a change, so that many vicious and profane persons have been known, by coming to this truth, to become sober and virtuous; and many light, vain, and wanton ones to become grave and serious, as our adversaries dare not deny.[1]

Barclay was honest enough to admit that "among so many thousands there will be some chaff," but he thought it a highly significant fact that Quakers were "generally a pure and clean people."

Now the problem is how a pure and clean people are to live in a licentious time. Ethically, Barclay was a Puritan, but it was his destiny to live and work in a period when Puritan morality was ridiculed. There were two obvious paths for such a man to take. One of these involved retirement from the world in exemplification of the monastic spirit. He was rich enough so that he could have stayed at Ury,

[1] *Apology*, p. 485 [XV, i].

tended to his own business, and thus avoided the temptations of court life. By this choice he could have kept himself so unspotted from the world that it would not have been necessary for him to write a "Vindication." But, if he had followed this course, he would have accomplished little and the probability is that we should never even have heard his name. This horn of the dilemma Barclay deliberately rejected.

A second possibility, and, in the eyes of many, the only alternative, would have been full accommodation to worldly ways. He could have gone along with the fashion, entered into intrigue, taken his share of the loot, and thereby become one of the crowd. His popularity would undoubtedly have been increased if he had been willing to laugh at scruples. By following this obvious path he would have been relatively inconspicuous. Had he so decided, he could have joined the King in his revels.

Barclay's great insight, which has particular relevance today, was that the ways of monastic retirement from the world and conformity to the world are not the *only* ways. The third way, which he understood and demonstrated, was what might truly be called "unworldly worldliness." He was a sufficiently keen philosopher to realize that paradox is not the same as contradiction, and that the complexity of life is such that it is usually necessary to employ paradox in order to express the truth. His solution was that of a delicate and difficult balance in which he lived *in* the world while he was not *of* it. He entered deeply into the fields of politics, scholarship, and controversy. He mingled with royality and nobility, not because he was a snob, but for the deeper reason that he knew where the power of decision and influence was. He agreed with William Penn that true godliness does not "turn men out of the world, but enables them to live better in it, and excites their endeavours to mend it."[2] This has become the classic statement of Christian worldliness.

In spite of his acceptance of such involvement in affairs, Barclay determined not to lower, in the slightest, his own moral standard. When adultery was something of which fashionable men were not even ashamed, Barclay's fidelity to his marriage vows was unquestioned. With bribes all around him, he was able to live with no taint of corruption. He was meticulous in his financial transactions and did

[2] William Penn, *Works* (1726), Vol. I, p. 296.

not even claim for himself the land which went along with the governorship of East New Jersey. His rejection of theatrical entertainments arose from the fact that, "in their masquerades," there was "all manner of obscenity." If he seems to us to be overrestrictive, we are less inclined to criticize his stand when we understand the extremes to which the fashion in entertainment had gone. When he saw many about him who were "crowned in lust, sensuality, and worldly pleasures," he thought it necessary for Christians to be bold noncomformists.

It must not be supposed that Barclay favored no relaxation. "For that men should be always in the same intentiveness of mind, we do not plead, knowing how impossible it is, so long as we are clothed with this tabernacle of clay."[3] Relaxation, he thought, was a human necessity, and was good "provided these things be not such as are wholly superfluous, or in their proper nature and tendency lead the mind into lust, vanity and wantonness, as being chiefly contrived and framed for that end."

One striking part of Barclay's unworldly worldliness was his refusal to employ obsequious and flattering titles. It is clear that this was a matter of principle and that he adhered to it, even in the face of the danger of appearing to be rude. This was remarkable, in view of the fact that he lived in a period when integrity was not supposed to have any bearing on manners. But for Barclay the bearing was obvious. To call a man "Your Holiness" when he was known to be far from holy was, thought Barclay, simply a matter of lying. We ought to be charitable, said the Apologist, but that is no excuse for downright dishonesty. "Charity destroys not knowledge: I am not obliged by charity, either to believe or speak a lie."[4]

The modern reader, who has had the patience to stay with Barclay's treatment of courtly language, may finally realize that he was really dealing with the kind of treatment of other humans which is an extremely important feature of the present struggle for civil rights, particularly in connection with racial discrimination. Having made it clear that the use of the plural of the second person in European languages arose from the desire of kings to seem to be more than single individuals, Barclay noted that "men commonly use the singular number to beggars, and to their servants." But the aristo-

[3] *Apology*, p. 510 [XV, ix].
[4] *Ibid.*, p. 491 [XV, iii].

cratic master would have been incensed if his supposed inferior had used the same language, in addressing *him*. "Thus the superior will speak to his inferior, who yet will not bear that the inferior so speak to him."[5] This is why Barclay was extremely careful in his own practice, refusing conscientiously to employ a double standard of address. When he spoke to his sovereign he used the same pronoun which he used when addressing his gardener, and expected the gardener to use the same in addressing him.

Anyone who supposes that such insistence on a single standard of address is a trivial matter has not thought very deeply about its significance, especially in the contemporary struggle for racial justice. The modern Negro desires equality of opportunity; he desires decent housing for his family and excellent education for his children; but even more he desires for himself, and for his children, genuine respect. Contempt is what he finds it hardest to bear. Yet respect, especially in address, is the last thing the white supremacist is willing to share. Thus, even in places in which there are adequate housing and fair wages for the black minority, there are great numbers of the privileged classes who resist adamantly the practice of referring to a Negro woman as Mrs. The maid is "Nellie" or "Jane," rather than "Mrs. Jones." This may seem, to those who look at it from above, to be a minor feature of social justice, but it does not seem so to those who look at it from below. We cannot know how much of the violent hatred expressed by the Chinese race arises from the invidious practice of habitually calling a grown Chinese man "Boy," but we can be sure that it has been a contributing factor to what is now bringing pain to the whole world.

Another major evidence of Barclay's flair for a third way is shown in his theology. There were, it appeared, two and only two roads which men could travel. One of these was that of mere intellectualism, which, Barclay saw, is almost sure to end in a stultifying skepticism. Then, as now, it was fashionable for men with pride of intellect to so reduce their religious belief that nothing of importance remained. Even some who wanted to call themselves Christians prided themselves, as some do now, on how much of the faith they could discard. Barclay was quick to see that a faith of this kind is not really worth

[5] *Ibid.*, p. 499 [XV, v].

both of the conventional possibilities are unsatisfactory, and Barclay saw that such is the case.

Barclay's third way, which evidently came to him after agonizing effort, depended on the recognition that what is true for a separated society is not necessarily true for a government which represents a great mixture of peoples, problems, and convictions. The fact that he was called to a life of nonresistance did not mean, thought Barclay, that all other men were so called at this particular point of history. It was, therefore, not necessary for him to denounce every soldier any more than it was necessary for Christ to denounce the Roman centurion. To conclude that, because he, as a Quaker, renounced participation in war, the British Government should have no armed forces, Barclay saw as a *non sequitur* and an evidence of intellectual confusion. In the *Apology,* after showing the sinfulness of war, which was, he said, "an evil as opposite and contrary to the Spirit and doctrine of Christ as light to darkness,"[9] he went on to affirm that it was not necessary for Quakers to be judgmental.

As to what relates to the present magistrates of the Christian world, albeit we deny them not altogether the name of Christians, because of the public profession they make of Christ's name, yet we may boldly affirm, that they are far from the perfection of the Christian religion; because in the state in which they are (as in many places I have largely observed), they have not yet come to the pure dispensation of the gospel. And therefore, while they are in that condition, we shall not say, that war, undertaken upon a just occasion, is altogether unlawful to them. For even as circumcision and the other ceremonies were for a season permitted to the Jews, not because they were either necessary of themselves, or lawful at that time, after the resurrection of Christ, but because that Spirit was not yet raised up in them, whereby they could be delivered from such rudiments; so the present confessors of the Christian name, who are not yet fitted for this form of Christianity, and therefore cannot be undefending themselves until they attain that perfection. But for such whom Christ has brought hither, it is not lawful to defend themselves by arms, but they ought over all to trust to the Lord.[10]

[9] *Ibid.,* p. 526 [XV, xiii].
[10] *Ibid.,* pp. 536, 537 [XV, xv].

This is probably the best example, in all of Robert Barclay's thinking, of his combination of intellectual sophistication and tender-mindedness. He showed himself tender enough not to excommunicate the vast majority of sincere Christians, and also sufficiently sophisticated to make the necessary subtle distinctions. He held that some military encounters were justified, not because they were good, but because any practical alternative, under the circumstances, would be worse. It was as though he saw, in advance, the modern situation in which a man who hates war with all his heart cannot honestly say that he deplores the existence of an armed force, when he sees it liberate a concentration camp and thereby release innocent prisoners from torture. Often, during the Second World War, Barclay's careful analysis brought relief to minds torn by an intolerable moral problem and eager, above all, to be honest. An example of such relief was provided by the late Professor H. G. Wood, who in the most agonizing of periods wrote an essay "Pacifism and Politics."[11]

One evidence of the enduring character of Barclay's paradoxical solution of a serious moral problem is that, four years later, in *The Apology Vindicated* (1679), he granted "the lawfulness of fighting to the present magistrates and States of Christians."[12] If by a pacifist, we mean a person who thinks that, because he takes no part in military affairs, the state ought never to do so, Barclay was certainly not a pacifist. He, like the other major thinkers of original Quakerism, recognized the duty of the secular state to suppress dangerous men within its borders and to oppose outside attacks from aggressor nations. We must remember that Barclay's published writings were carefully examined on many occasions by the leading Quakers and were given unqualified approval. In one commonly accepted modern sense of the word the Quakers of the great period were not pacifists, even though they believed that they, personally, should not fight and that peacemaking was their vocation. How little Barclay was alone in his paradoxical solution is indicated by a letter from George Fox, addressed to Oliver Cromwell.

> O, Oliver, hadst thou been faithful and thundered down the deceit, the Hollander had been thy subject and tributary, Germany had given up

[11] *Friends Quarterly Examiner* (July, 1941), pp. 199–211.
[12] *Truth Triumphant*, p. 871.

to have done thy will, and the Spaniard had quivered like a dry leaf wanting the virtue of God, the King of France should have bowed his neck under thee, the Pope should have withered as in winter, the Turk in all his fatness should have smoked, thou shouldst not have stood trifling about small things but minded the work of the Lord as he began with thee at first.[13]

Neither Fox nor Barclay saw any inconsistency between Fox's letter to Cromwell and his refusal of a commission in the Protector's army because he lived in the virtue of that life and power which takes away the occasion of all wars. The "peace testimony" was such that it was seen to be wrong to try to force it upon those "in the mixture." Barclay's aristocratic and deeply spiritual friend, Isaac Penington, was even more explicit in developing both sides of the paradox. After stating the Christian ideal, the saintly Penington went on to say, "I speak not this against any magistrate's or people's defending themselves against foreign invasions." Barclay and Penington had behind them the strong support of the classic Quaker declaration made when Charles II came to the throne. At that time Friends were eager to make the new sovereign understand that they were not plotting the overthrow of the government, as the Fifth Monarchy Men were. At the heart of the document presented to the King on January 21, 1661, is this powerful sentence: "All bloody principles and practices we as to our own particular do utterly deny, with all outward wars and strife and fightings with outward weapons for any end or under any pretense whatsoever; and this is our testimony to the whole world."[14] The phrase "we as to our own particular" is crucial. The Quakers at the beginning of the Restoration period were not saying that Charles II ought not to have an army. They were merely saying that *they* had none and were determined never to have one. Quakers were not telling the King what he, as the leader of a people unprepared for sacrifice, ought to do.

Barclay's great service, in regard to the relationships between the Christian and the state, was primarily a service of clarification. In writing to the ambassadors at Nijmegen he found no inconsistency in

[13] William C. Braithwaite, *The Beginnings of Quakerism* (Cambridge, Eng.: The University Press, 1955), p. 440. The manuscript is available at Friends House Library, London.

[14] William C. Braithwaite, *Second Period of Quakerism, op. cit.*, p. 13.

urging them to make peace, but, at the same time, recognizing their governmental responsibilities. He loved peace, but he also loved order, because it is by order that innocent people are protected. He disassociated himself sharply from all those who "under the pretence of crying up King Jesus, and the Kingdom of Christ, either deny, or seek to overturn all civil government."[15]

It is particularly relevant to modern problems that Barclay provided, without condemnation of others, a viable defense of the position of the sincere conscientious objector to military service. The sincere conscientious objector is often put in a quandary when his critic assumes that, because he does not fight, he desires that all capacity to oppose militant aggression should be abandoned. Barclay provides the hard-pressed young man with a rational answer. His intellectual defense inheres in the recognition that it may be right for an individual or a prepared group to take a position for which the general public is not yet ready. The conscientious objector may thus be part of an ultimately effective remnant. In accepting nonresistance for himself, yet seeing that it would be wrong to try to legislate it for the unprepared, Barclay was upheld by the conviction that advance comes only when a few go on ahead. While admitting realistically that the majority "are not yet fitted for this form of Christianity," Barclay maintained, with equal realism, that there should be some in the world who seek to present a standard of Christian perfection, by going the whole way *now*. The purpose is to raise a standard to which all men may eventually be drawn. It is clearly right that some, without being censorious of those who come to different conclusions, and being genuinely humble as well as loving, should, in the course of their present lives, provide a modicum of the pattern "which nations are to expect and travel towards." Such, in any case, was the peace testimony of Robert Barclay. That it was by no means negative is demonstrated by his tireless effort to encourage the architects of national policy to engage in conciliation and to remove the occasions of war. The practical outcome of his third way was that he was a peacemaker. Furthermore, his vocation as a peacemaker continued long after his death. An excellent example of his continued effectiveness is the fact that, in September, 1748

[15] *Truth Triumphant*, p. 710.

Friends gave copies of the *Apology,* in many languages, to all of the plenipotentiaries at Aix-la-Chapelle, to encourage them to make a just and durable peace.[16] It was the rational balance of his peace testimony which made the gift a suitable and acceptable one.

The relevance of Barclay transcends the distinction between faith and practice, as it transcends the distinction between generations and denominations. When this gifted man decided upon his lifework he did, indeed, dedicate himself to the exposition and promulgation of principles, but they were not seen as the peculiar principles of a particular generation or a particular sect. Instead, he was devoted, as sincerely as was possible, to the presentation of objective and universal truth. His are noble words in any generation and they are as appealing now as when they were first composed. It is not strange, therefore, that a set of answers proposed in one time of severe conflict and storm can appeal to men and women in another stormy period of the world's history.

16 From the unpublished "Book of Cases," Vol. III, Friends House Library, pp. 42–55.

APPENDIX

A. *Chronological Note*

The following dates are provided to assist the reader with a ready reference. To avoid possible confusion, all dates are given "New Style." This is especially important when dealing with Scottish dates, since the New Style went into effect in Scotland in 1600. In England, however, the first year to begin January 1, rather than March 25, was 1752. Events in January and February are, in this volume, treated as belonging to the new year. Because the older Quaker practice of numbering months is sometimes confusing to the modern reader, I have substituted the names of the months.

1610—Birth of David Barclay, later Colonel Barclay.
1648—Purchase of Ury estate by David Barclay.
1648 (Dec. 23)—Birth of Robert Barclay.
1659—Robert Barclay sent to Paris to study with his uncle.
1663 (March)—Death of Robert Barclay's mother.
1663 (August?)—Return to Scotland.
1667—Robert Barclay became a Quaker.
1670 (February)—Marriage, in Aberdeen, of Robert Barclay and Christian Molleson.
1670—New house built at Ury.
1672 (March)—Barclay walked in sackcloth in the streets of Aberdeen.
1672 (June)—Barclay's dream or vision.
1672—Barclay's first brief imprisonment in Tolbooth of Montrose.
1673—Attendance at London Yearly Meeting for the first time.
1674 (October)—*The Anarchy of the Ranters* completed.
1674—Publication of *Theses Theologicae*.
1675—Completion of Latin edition of the *Apology*. (The address to King Charles II is dated November 25, 1675.)
1676—Publication of *Apology* in Latin.

1676—First visit to Princess Elizabeth at Herford.
1676 (Nov. 7)—Commitment to prison in Aberdeen.
1677 (Apr. 9)—Release from prison.
1677 (July 26)—Embarcation with others, on major ministerial tour of Holland and Germany.
1677 (August)—Second visit to Princess Elizabeth.
1678—Publication of English translation of *Apology*.
1679 (July 6)—In Rotterdam. Last letter to Princess Elizabeth.
1679 (Aug. 13)—Ury erected into a free barony, with civil and criminal jurisdiction.
1679 (Nov. 4)—Last imprisonment.
1682 (Sept.)—Became Governor of East New Jersey (for life).
1683 (August)—Attack by highwaymen north of London.
1686 (Oct. 12)—Death, at Ury, of Colonel David Barclay.
1688—Summer in London, often with King James II.
1690 (Oct. 3)—Death of Robert Barclay at Ury.
1692—Publication of collected works with title *Truth Triumphant*.
1724 (Feb. 14)—Death of Christian Barclay.

B. *Bibliographical Note*

In addition to the information on books provided in the footnotes, some extra listing may be helpful. Because the literature by and about Robert Barclay is of great variety, it is hoped that the following classifications will be useful.

1. *Primary Sources*

Reliquiae Barclaianae (letters from and to Colonel David Barclay and Robert Barclay, plus other letters and family documents up to 1742), a holograph edition, produced in London, 1870. Eight of the letters were written by the Princess Elizabeth.

A Genealogical Account of the Barclays of Urie, with *Memoirs of the Lives of Colonel David Barclay of Urie, etc.* This was published at Aberdeen in 1740. The copy of this valuable work in Friends House Library, London, is autographed by Robert Barclay, eldest son of the Apologist, with the date of 1st month, 25, 1741, "being the Day R. B. entered into the seventieth year of his age." The book consists of 61 pages, the first 17 pages of which are devoted to the family tree, and the remainder to a factual history supported by letters. If we had only the printed form we might conclude that the son of the Apologist was the only author, but the manuscript in the Bury Hill Collection indicates that the actual writing was done by the Apologist's grandson, also called Robert. In the text he frequently refers to the Apologist as his grandfather. It is apparent, however, that the younger man must have depended substantially on information provided by his father, the Apologist's son, who knew many of the events at first hand and lived with his mother for thirty-three years after the Apologist's death.

Letters, published and unpublished. Three important letters written by

Robert Barclay, one addressed to Stephen Crisp, 1676, one to Sarah Fell, 1678, and a third to George Fox, 1679, are published in *Letters of Early Friends* (London, 1841). This collection was edited by John Barclay and seen through the press, after his death, by his brother A. R. Barclay. One of Barclay's letters to Princess Elizabeth, identical with one in *Reliquiae Barclaianae* and dated 1677, is printed in *Letters of Isaac Penington* (London, 1796). Otherwise unpublished letters, as well as a copy of the first letter sent by Princess Elizabeth to the Apologist, appear in Maria Webb, *The Fells of Swarthmoor Hall* (Philadelphia, 1896). The letter from Robert Barclay to Sarah Fell, a photograph of which is one of the illustrations of this volume, is preserved in the Crosfield Collection in the strong room of Friends House, London. The major collection of original letters is that of Bury Hill, which I have seen.

William Penn's Journal of His Travels in Holland and Germany. This firsthand account of the journey in which Barclay shared has been reprinted many times. A convenient edition is that printed in London in 1835.

The Record Book of Friends of the Monethly Meeting att Urie. One of the most valuable of sources, the original being preserved in Friends House Library, London. A faithful transcript appears in the *Journal of the Friends Historical Society,* Volume VII, Number 3 (September, 1910), pp. 91–98.

Diary of Alexander Jaffray, with *Memoirs of the Rise, Progress, and Persecutions, of the People Called Quakers in the North of Scotland.* A valuable source of information, edited by John Barclay and first published in London (Harvey & Darton), 1833. Another edition, with different paging, was published at Aberdeen in 1856. The editor frankly called his work a "compilation." Fortunately, the original manuscript has been preserved and is in the Bury Hill Collection.

Robert Barclay's Answers to his uncle Charles Gordon is a manuscript of 346 pages copied in 1678 by Robert Gordon and preserved in the Bury Hill Collection. This includes the most careful statement of Barclay's theological position to be found outside his collected works. A portion of this was published in 1864 at Cockermouth, by Henry T. Wake, in a 32-page pamphlet which is rare.

The Concurrence and Unanimity of the People Called Quakers (London, 1694), is a set of fourteen sermons, most of which are followed by prayer, and all of which were taken down in shorthand. The first of these, which provides our best means of acquaintance with Barclay's speaking style, is by the Apologist. Barclay's sermon was delivered at Gracechurch Street Meetinghouse, May 16, 1688.

A Dutch version of Barclay's letter to the ambassadors, called *Een Brief Van Liefde* (Rotterdam, 1678), is in the Bevan-Naish Collection at Woodbrooke, Selly Oak, Birmingham.

2. *Secondary Accounts*

William Sewel, *The History of the Rise, Increase and Progress of the Christian People Called Quakers* (London, 1722), "revised, with some amendments." Sewel gives a full account of Barclay's correspondence with the Dutch ambassador, Adrian Paets, adding analyses of Barclay's argument, pp. 536–52.

Some Account of the Life and Writings of Robert Barclay. This small book became a standard biography of the Apologist in the early decades of the nineteenth century and appeared in several different formats. It has sometimes been attributed to David Barclay, the Apologist's grandson, because in 1801 he brought out an edition to which he prefixed a hortatory letter to "the Descendants of Robert Barclay." However, in 1802 there appeared an edition without this appeal, and with no authorship attributed. A copy of this was given to "Friends Library of London," signed in ink by David Barclay. The same material was used to introduce the three-volume edition of *Truth Triumphant,* published at Philadelphia by Benjamin C. Stanton in 1831. The work was actually written by a group of Quakers, of whom Joseph Gurney Bevan was the chief. Bevan's joint editorship is asserted by Smith (*Catalogue,* Vol. I, p. 188) and the manuscript book "Sketch of the Life of J. G. Bevan" in the Bevan-Naish Library, Woodbrooke, also says Bevan wrote the book (p. 286).

Wilson Armistead, *Memoir of Robert Barclay* (Manchester, 1850). This, which is really a large pamphlet of 22 pages of small print, is a careful statement of what was generally known at the time. For the life of Wilson Armistead (1819–1868) see the *Journal of the Friends Historical Society,* Volume 50, Number 3 (1963), pp. 158–63.

Alexander Gordon, "The Great Laird of Urie," *Theological Review,* Volume XI (1874), pp. 524–55. Also, "The Marrow of Barclay," *Theological Review,* Volume XII (1875), pp. 387–406. Gordon was a Scottish theologian whose discovery of Barclay aroused in him great intellectual excitement. Of the *Apology* he said, "Probably no piece of theological writing has a higher finish or a more perfect form."

Frances Anne Budge, *The Barclays of Ury and other Sketches of the early Friends* (London, 1881). The Barclay section occupies pages 3–31. It is popularly written with little detail concerning sources.

Benjamin Rhodes produced, in 1883, a lively booklet on *George Fox, the First of the Quakers.* This was followed at once by similar essays on Penn and Barclay, so that the three were bound together and published in London, in 1884, with the general title, *Three Apostles of Quakerism.* The third part, dealing with Barclay, has been translated into Danish. The author was an English clergyman. See Appendix C for further reference to his work.

Charles Evans, *Friends in the Seventeenth Century* (Philadelphia:

Friends Book Store, 304 Arch Street, 1876). This book by a Quaker physician, though not really scholarly, is accurate and fair. Sources are seldom given, but the section on Barclay is dependable.

M. Christabel Cadbury, *Robert Barclay, His Life and Work* (London: Headley Brothers, 1912). 132 pages. This short book, supplied with illustrations, including one depicting a cell in the Aberdeen Tolbooth, is a satisfactory biography, though very brief.

Sir Leslie Stephen's article on Robert Barclay in the *Dictionary of National Biography* is in the "lean, terse style" which Stephen preached and practiced. Sir Leslie was the brother of Caroline Stephen, author of *Quaker Strongholds.*

J. Philip Wragge, *The Faith of Robert Barclay* (London: Friends Home Service Committee, 1948). A book of 153 pages, the greater part of which is devoted to excerpts from Barclay's writings. This is preceded by a sketch of Barclay's life, a comparison between the ideas of the Apologist and George Keith, and an essay, "The Message of Barclay for Today." Especially valuable is the presentation of quotations from Keith and Barclay in parallel columns.

A History of the Barclay Family with pedigrees from 1067 to 1933. Compiled by Hubert F. Barclay and Alice Wilson-Fox (London: St. Catherine Press, 1934). Pages 1–97 of Vol. III are devoted to Colonel David Barclay, while pages 98–191 deal with the Apologist.

John E. Pomfret, *The New Jersey Proprietors and Their Lands* (Princeton, N. J.: D. Van Nostrand Company, 1964). A thorough account of Barclay's governorship appears in pages 37–51. The treatment in this book may be supplemented by the same author's long historical essay, "The Proprietors of the Province of East New Jersey, 1682–1702," *Pennsylvania Magazine of History and Biography,* Volume LXXVII, Number 3 (July, 1953), pp. 251–93. Though Pomfret's two accounts cover some of the same historical problems, they are not identical.

Joseph E. Illick, *William Penn the Politician* (Ithaca, N. Y.: Cornell University Press, 1965). Provides evidence of the close political contact between Barclay and Penn, when both were deeply involved in colonization.

William H. Marwick wrote, in 1948, as part of the tercentenary celebration of Robert Barclay's birth, *A Short History of Friends in Scotland.* This was published by the Scotland General Meeting of Friends. The book deals with the contributions of the Barclays as the most eminent of Scottish Quakers.

D. Elton Trueblood, "The Vocation of Barclay," *Friends Quarterly,* Volume II, Number 4 (October, 1948), pp. 195–204. This represents a chapter in an early form of the present volume and reflects some of what was said in the Barclay Tercentenary Lecture at Edinburgh in August, 1948.

Quaker Religious Thought, Volume III, Number 1 (Spring, 1965) is devoted wholly to Robert Barclay. The major article is that written by Francis B. Hall, "The Thought of Robert Barclay: An Evaluation." This is followed by critical comment from Maurice A. Creasey, James J. Flood, and D. Elton Trueblood. At the end is Francis Hall's response to comments. Francis Hall's B.D. thesis at Union Theological Seminary was devoted to Barclay's thinking and is reflected in the article.

3. *Dissertations*

George P. Hayes, "Robert Barclay: His Life, Works and Position in the History of Quaker Thought." An unpublished dissertation presented in 1927, in partial fulfillment of the requirements for the Doctor of Philosophy degree at Harvard University. Dr. Hayes makes a careful examination of the style and content of the *Apology,* in both the Latin and English versions.

Maurice A. Creasey, "The Theology of Robert Barclay with special reference to his *Apology*." Thesis presented for the degree of Bachelor of Divinity in the University of Leeds, 1951. A typescript copy is available at Friends House Library, London.

Gerardina L. Van Dalfsen, *Het Inwaartsch Licht Bij De Quakers.* A doctoral dissertation presented at the University of Leyden in 1940 and published that year. Though the book is in Dutch, there is an illuminating conclusion, first in English and then in German. The typescript of an English translation is available at Swarthmore College.

Leif Eeg-Olofsson, *The Conception of the Inner Light in Robert Barclay's Theology*. An inaugural dissertation, written in English for the degree of Doctor of Theology at the University of Lund, 1954. This is a mature work, written with the conscious presuppositions of a Swedish theologian.

4. *Barclay's Works*

Truth Triumphant, published as Barclay's collected works in 1692 in one volume, is now more easily available in three volumes. The long (38 folio pages) Preface is generally attributed to William Penn. Testimonies of Barclay's associates concerning his character also precede Barclay's works. *Truth Triumphant* includes everything of importance which Barclay wrote for general publication. The second edition, in three volumes octavo, was published in 1718.

The *Apology,* because it has been published many times, is easily available in secondhand copies, and in many languages. The original Latin version, published in Holland, is not found except in great libraries. A second Latin edition was published in octavo in 1729. The first English edition of 1678 was published in Holland. There is really no good edition of the *Apology* now in print, though the stereotype edition

(Philadelphia, 1908) provides a faithful text. The index of the latter is, unfortunately, so poor as to be almost worthless. Consequently, there is great need of a new scholarly edition. The most attractive edition of the *Apology* is the handsome volume printed by Baskerville in 1765. This is sometimes called the eighth edition, though the numbering of editions is unreliable and confusing. When *Truth Triumphant* has appeared in three volumes, the second of the three has been devoted entirely to the *Apology*.

Barclay in Brief, a condensation of the *Apology* by Eleanore Price Mather, with a preface by Howard Brinton (Wallingford, Pa.: Pendle Hill Historical Studies, 1942), is intended to provide the essence of Barclay's thought for the general reader in 90 pages. This is not the first abridgement of the *Apology*. One, produced by George Harrison and published in London in 1815, included parts of all fifteen propositions. Another, edited anonymously and published at Sunderland in 1817, included only eight propositions.

Barclay's Apology in Modern English, by Dean Freiday, is a wholly new approach. As Barclay translated from the Latin to English in 1678, Dean Freiday has translated from the English of 1678 into the English of 1967. The book is distributed by Friends Book Store, 302 Arch Street, Philadelphia.

C. *The Barclay Notebook*

The search for original Barclay manuscripts makes a fascinating story which has continued for almost a century and a half. In the autumn of 1826, John Barclay (1797–1838) made a fortunate visit to the old mansion at Ury, with opportunity to search the Apologist's study one hundred and thirty-five years after his death. Under date of 9th Month, 1826, he wrote, "I have this morning examined the library throughout, and found already several interesting things."[1] John Barclay's later report was that, "among other manuscripts to all appearance much neglected and which might have been ere long utterly lost sight of, lay the earlier portion of the present Diary in a corner of the Apologist's study." The diary here referred to is that of Alexander Jaffray, which John Barclay later edited for publication. He found detached fragments of another manuscript, "in a very tattered condition, in a loft of a farm-house not far from the old mansion; these were quickly recognized, among heaps of waste paper, as being in the same handwriting, and proved to be a counterpart of the other." What is most important for the student of the life of Robert Barclay is the light which the material was able to shed on the persecutions which he and his father suffered.

It is evident that John Barclay prized what he found and that he guarded it with care. This led to the formation of what is now known as the Bury Hill Collection. One of the most valuable of the treasures in the family collection is a notebook, attributed to the Apologist, mentioned in the Preface to this volume and quoted freely in the book. Nineteenth-century writers, if they referred to its existence, did not distinguish between it and the diaries.

There is good reason to believe that the Notebook was seen once or

[1] *A Selection from the Letters and Papers of the Late John Barclay* (London, 1841), p. 225.

twice in the nineteenth-century by persons who were not members of the Barclay family. The chief evidence is that we find references to Barclay's dream of 1672, which appears in the Notebook, and, so far as is known, nowhere else. In Benjamin Rhodes' *Three Apostles of Quakerism,* we are made suddenly aware that this non-Quaker author had means of knowing about the manuscript record. "On the 24th June, 1672," he says, "on awakening early in the morning, he seemed to see a great store of coined money that belonged to him lying upon his table."[2] This, of course, does not mean that Rhodes *saw* the Notebook, but it certainly means that he knew, with some accuracy, something that may be seen in it today in the handwriting of the Apologist. It is interesting to compare Rhodes' version with the original, which is: "The 20th day of the 4th Month 1672 I RB having awakened early in the morning and afterwards falne asleep had this visione which after followeth. Methought I had great store of coyned money lying upon a table which did truly belong unto me." The discrepancy of four days leads to the probable conclusion that Rhodes had not himself seen the book, but was depending upon the report of someone who had done so. His footnote says "From the Bury Hill MSS, quoted . . . by Alexander Gordon, M. A."

Whether or not Rhodes ever saw the Bury Hill manuscripts, there is good reason to believe that Alexander Gordon did. The two brilliant articles on Barclay which Gordon published in the *Theological Review,* in 1874 and 1875 indicate thorough research, part of which was his visit to Bury Hill to see the manuscript collection. In a footnote he wrote, "From the archives at Bury Hill, for access to which the writer cannot sufficiently thank the liberal owner."[3] Rhodes, then, was evidently quoting the Bury Hill manuscripts solely via Gordon, a conclusion strengthened by the fact that both men date the dream June 24, rather than June 20. Alexander Gordon, able writer though he was, did not exhibit sufficient care about the dating of episodes. For example, he said that the controversial act of walking the streets in sackcloth came *after* the dream, when in fact, as has been pointed out in Chapter II, it came three months *prior* to the dream. This we know by reference to Barclay's own dating, as found in *Truth Triumphant,* p. 107.

For our present purposes the most valuable result of Gordon's view of the manuscripts, about 1874, is his suggestion that the Notebook now under discussion is only *one* among others. He speaks of the "dream or vision, which he records in one of his manuscript notebooks."[4] Gordon's remark convinced me that further search was worthwhile.

The possessors of the manuscripts in the nineteenth century guarded them jealously. Rhodes evidently sought access to them, but was denied

[2] Benjamin Rhodes, *Three Apostles of Quakerism* (London, 1884), p. 93.
[3] Alexander Gordon, *Theological Review,* Vol. XI (1874), p. 539*n.*
[4] *Ibid.,* p. 551.

it, though it was not difficult for him to see *Reliquiae Barclaianae*. On a sheet formerly attached to the Flounders copy of *Reliquiae Barclaianae*, presented to the Flounders Trust by J. G. Barclay, there is the following letter, which indicates the delicacy of the situation:

28th July, 1884

DEAR FRIEND WM. S. LEAN

I do not see any objection to Rhodes being allowed to borrow the copy of Rel. Barclaianae which you have and making use of any information therein contained. But I do not wish the book quoted because I found that J. B. Braithwaite who was the real author of the work and had obtained leave of the Barclay of Bury Hill who possesses all the Ury manuscripts had not as it appeared obtained their consent to anything like a publishing the extracts and I do not think they quite liked my having done this to J.B.B.

However I presented them with several copies and nothing further was said at the time or since. I quite think that a good deal of interesting matter lies hid there still tho' my uncle John Barclay before he published Alex. Jaffray's diary had an opportunity as he states in that very interesting work of looking through the documents then to be found at Ury before the death of the owner, R. Barclay the well known walker of 1000 miles.

I am truly thine,
J. G. BARCLAY

The most confusing feature of the problem is that Rhodes wrote that he had access to "numerous unpublished letters in the keeping of a member of the Barclay family." What did he mean by this? Possibly only that he had seen *Reliquiae Barclaianae*. The problem is increased by the assertion of J. G. Barclay, in the letter already quoted, that J. Bevan Braithwaite was the "real author of the work." That Braithwaite was allowed to see the Ury manuscripts is easy to believe, since he was one of the most eminent Quakers of his time, but he may not have seen all.

The hypothesis that Rhodes did not have direct access to the Bury Hill MSS is supported by the fact that he wrote, p. 95, "He kept a diary, but it seems to have been lost," and added, in a footnote, the query, "Is this amongst the Bury Hill MSS? The extract quoted from the Theological Review looks like a passage from it." Apparently, then, he was primarily quoting Gordon.

The Notebook, as it appears today, is bound in leather, with the Ury arms and the words

Barclay of Ury
Old Note Book
Robert Barclay
The Apologist

on the cover. The binding is evidently nineteenth-century work. The pages are approximately 3½ inches wide and 5½ inches long, opening at the end, in shorthand style. The contents are approximately 114 pages, most of them with writing on both sides, but some blank. Inks of different colors were used, some brown and very faded and some black. Not all of the handwriting is identical, though some of it is in the same style as that of Barclay's known letters. The slight contrast may arise from the use of different pens. There are 28 pages of shorthand. On page 14 is a penciled note "Two leaves sent to Jos.h Tatham Leeds for interpretation John Barclay 1829." This date supports the conclusion that the Notebook was part of the treasure which John Barclay discovered in the Apologist's study at Ury. The two leaves sent to Leeds for deciphering might be valuable to us, but the strong probability is that they have been irretrievably lost. Joseph Tatham kept a boarding school at Leeds and was much admired by his students. As to dates, we know that he retired from teaching in 1838 and died in 1843.[5] The sending of the speciman pages to him does not mean, necessarily, that he was an expert in shorthand, but that, because of his high academic reputation, he was expected to know who the experts were. In any case there was no success!

It appears that members of the Barclay family attempted more than once to decode the material which they were unable to read. Inside the cover there is a loose portion of sheet with the following note, "There is a treatise on Cypher in the B. Museum date about 1640 to 1650 whose Characters are very similar to this." Then follow the initials R B/ R and the date of ninth month, 75. This, of course, was 1875, and the new effort at deciphering came about the time of the interest of Alexander Gordon, forty-six years after the known effort of 1829.

Now, after ninety-two more years, it is our good fortune that the shorthand can be read. We owe this happy outcome to Douglas Lister, who also has to his credit the deciphering of the shorthand of Edward Haistwell, the secretary who once accompanied George Fox. The alphabet Barclay used has been identified as that of John Willis (1620 and later). The writing follows the general principles laid down by Willis, but with some personal variations and the use of some forms and abbreviations used in other systems of the time. A particular difficulty has been that of the syllabic structure of Willis's system, with its peculiar order of writing, and the rather wide separation between parts of the same word. Proper names are hard to read, since even some of these are written in shorthand.

The part of the book which is in shorthand begins at the reverse opening and proceeds toward the front until it meets the part which is in ordinary writing. Though most of the longhand proceeds from the front, some of it must be read from the reverse, as the shorthand is. Both parts represent the growth of Barclay's ideas in his youth, the earliest

[5] See *Annual Monitor* (1844), pp. 95–97. See also Wilfred Allott, *Leeds Quaker Meeting—History* (1966).

part being dated prior to his public acknowledgment of himself as a Quaker. Why he used shorthand we do not know, but it may be that he did so in order to save both time and paper. The saving of paper is indicated by the rather surprising fact that one small page translates to more than 700 words.

Very early in the shorthand section we learn of the youth's visits to the area immediately south of the Scottish border, where he seems to have had his first introduction to Quaker ideas. Also in shorthand is a trial essay signed with the pseudonym Bernardus Adolphus, and letters to an imaginary correspondent. In association with this occurs an early expression of what became the very center of his philosophy: "Many more things did pass betwixt us in our discourse as of the principle of these people viz: as concerning the light which that people bear testimony to, mainly as to its operation in the soul of man and what validity it is of as to man's salvation."

The question of the authenticity of the Notebook, though it is bound to arise, is essentially settled by the fact that, in the shorthand section, we find early or crude statements of ideas which appeared in a more polished form in the *Apology,* about nine years later. Of particular importance as evidence of authenticity is an early form of a statement on worship which later appeared, with only minor changes, in the famous chapter on worship. The contemporary reader is enabled to compare the early and late forms of Barclay's claim that true worship is that which cannot be disturbed. As we watch the development of the young man's mind we are not surprised that his mature chapters on worship, prayer, and ministry were his most brilliant. It was about these that he had thought longest and most deeply.

The revealing part, in Lister's translation, is as follows:

> This day is declared another thing, a worship of another kind to be performed in the spirit expressed by Christ himself to the woman of Samaria, a worship spiritual and true, which the children of truth can perform in despite of all opposition, which the devil by all means external cannot hinder them from as they in their inward part keep stayed upon the Lord, which no pursue can stop, no violence can interrupt, no instrument without by throwing down of ever so many temples, and robbing any, and burning any book, and study to make ever so much confusion, can stop or hinder. But where is there a worship among the Christians that the devil cannot thus reach into, or that some storm of persecution cannot shatter and interrupt?
>
> Take from the papists their mass book and no mass can be said. Nay, none without lighted candles. Take away from the priest his laver and no sacrifice can be performed. Yea, remove but the altar stone and his work is stopped. Take from him his breviary and he is incapacitated to say that which by being ordained and a priest he is obliged to do. Take from a Lutheran or any English Episcopalian his service or

Common Prayer Book and no worship can be performed. Take from a Calvinist or Scottish Presbyterian his Bible and his commentaries and no worship can be done. Keep from any of them bread and wine, no communion or participating of the body and blood of Christ. Withhold from them water, and no baptizing or making them members of the Church of Christ.[6]

Though the comparison of passages found in the Notebook with those later developed and published provides excellent evidence of the authenticity of the former, there is an added and really crucial evidence which comes in connection with the dream or vision of 1672, part of which has already been quoted in Chapter II. The account of this important step in Barclay's career appears in the longhand part of the Notebook, far removed from the shorthand section. In spite of this, however, Barclay began the recounting of the dream in shorthand! Then he stopped abruptly and shifted to ordinary writing, duplicating a few lines. This duplication has been valuable in the task of decipherment, but it is even more valuable in connection with the problem of authenticity. The fortunate fact is that the longhand version is in Barclay's already known handwriting and the shorthand is identical in form with that at the other end of the Notebook. In the beginning we were naturally skeptical and entertained the possible hypothesis that the shorthand might have been written by someone other than Barclay. Now we know that it, like the longhand, is his own. The clinching argument is the presence, in the shorthand, of the distinctive cypher RB.

The Latin pages of the Notebook, which have been translated by Professor Hans Buchinger of Earlham College, are preliminary notes for the *Catechism and Confession of Faith* and may be dated 1672. The words of the long title appear, in almost identical form, in the Latin notes, while other pages provide what is clearly the first statement of something which was elaborated later. It is revealing that the author should have made his notes in Latin, when the developed book was written in English. The Notebook thus shows how truly bilingual the Apologist was.

The inequality of the notes is striking. We find mathematical jottings, the first five chapters of Matthew in legible Greek, and reports of discussions with the students of Aberdeen. We once contemplated a complete reproduction, but this now seems unwise, partly because the material is so unequal. The decision finally reached was that of using all of the relevant parts in connection with the subjects of this book, as has been done.

The Notebook, though it includes a few references to events, is not itself a diary, but a commonplace book. It is the intimate workbook of an ambitious young man. Since it is not a diary, it does not provide

[6] Compare quotations from the *Apology*, pp. 206, 207 of this book.

many dates, but there are enough to identify the period of production. The first precise date, the 28th of February, 1666, appears in the shorthand section. An unintended means of dating is the reference, on the nineteenth page of shorthand, to the death of a certain Major Weir, who is known by independent sources to have been burnt in April, 1670. Thus we know that part of the shorthand was written after this date. In the longhand section are notes for *William Mitchell Unmasked,* which appeared in 1672. One of the later insertions refers to the student debate which is known to have occurred as late as April, 1675. We conclude that the Notebook was filled in a period of about nine years.

One interesting part provides evidence of a projected history of Quakerism in Scotland, which sheds light upon the manuscript which John Barclay found at Ury in September, 1826. The first significant notes, after the report of the decisive dream, deal with the inadequacy of both Catholicism and Protestantism and the consequent need for a third way. Thus the Notebook provides us an insight into the first glimmerings of what came to be Barclay's most original and creative ideas.

D. *The Diaries*

The diaries are two small pocket books of about 150 pages each, bound in vellum. The first covers the period from 1678 to 1685, while the second starts in 1685 and runs to 1690, shortly before the author's death. Some, but not all of the formerly blank space in Diary II was used by the Apologist's eldest son after his death, the son's diary occupying 52 pages. At the beginning of the second volume Barclay wrote, "I ended my former pocquet book (which is the first I ever made use of that kind) with the death of K Charles the 2nd, being the beginning of the month called February, 168¾ and began this as K. Ja the 2nd begins his reign."

By this we know that there is no point in looking for any more. It seems curious that a man of Barclay's character never kept a diary until he was nearly thirty years of age, but we have his word for it.

There is a certain good fortune in the way in which the Notebook deals with ideas, in the scholarly period, and the diaries deal with financial transactions, travels, and events in the public period. Each is revealing in a different way.

The diaries are not a journal comparable to that of George Fox and other Quakers. They do not include ideas, as the Notebook does, and they do not describe religious experiences. We know that Barclay preached a sermon in London on May 16, 1688, because the sermon was printed, but Diary II does not mention it. We do, however, know from the diary the precise day on which he arrived in London that spring. The entry for April 13 says, simply, "Arrived at London." With rare restraint, he did not even mention in his diary his last meeting with King James at Whitehall, but he did write, under date of November 20, 1688, "Took journey post from London."

The record is uniformly brief and matter of fact, dealing largely with finances. The diaries, accordingly, make us understand, as we could not have understood otherwise, how extremely complicated Barclay's business affairs were. He was virtually a banker without a bank, for he was constantly giving and receiving notes or bonds. He borrowed a great deal and he loaned a great deal. Indeed, the diaries, at first glance, appear to be ledgers or account books, but on further scrutiny we find more than pounds, marks, and dollars. Without the diaries we could not know how numerous were the connections between the Apologist and the Dutch merchant, Arent Sonmans. Their business together increased greatly with the growth of East Jersey responsibilities. The death of Sonmans, as a result of being shot by the highwayman, was a bitter blow. The reader must not allow the brevity of Barclay's autobiographical reports to blind him to the depth of feeling. The unadorned entry for the particular period is

> Going from Huntington at Stonegate Hole we were robbed and Arent Sonmans wounded, came to Stilton where he died the 14.
>
> As this was the greatest outward cross ever I met with, so I hope through the mercy of God it shall be of greatest use to me.

Striking as these sentences are, in their simplicity and their restraint, the notation which came between them is even more striking. We discover that Barclay's immediate concern, in the shocking loss of one of his dearest friends, was for justice. Thus the same page which records robbery and death also includes a careful financial reckoning. Finding that he owed his friend £24 2*s.* 6*d.* he wrote that the "small account which standeth thus be given to his wife." We have long known how meticulous Robert Barclay was in dealing with ideas. We now know that he was equally meticulous in dealing with money. If he made a mistake it was always, Arent Sonmans had already told him, to his own hurt.

Index of Subjects

Index of Persons